Protecting the Arctic

Studies in Environmental Anthropology
Edited by Roy Ellen, University of Kent at Canterbury, UK

This series is a vehicle for publishing up-to-date monograph studies on par-ticular issues in particular places which are sensitive to both socio-cultural and ecological factors (i.e. sea level rise and rain forest depletion). Emphasis will be placed on the perception of the environment, indigenous knowledge and the ethnography of environmental issues. While basically anthropological, the series will consider works from authors working in adjacent fields.

Volume 1   *A Place Against Time*
            Land and Environment in Papua New Guinea
            Paul Sillitoe

Volume 2   *People, Land and Water*
            William Lancaster and Fidelity Lancaster

Volume 3   *Protecting the Arctic*
            Mark Nuttall

Volumes in Preparation

Volume 4   *Transforming the Indonesian Uplands*
            Tania Murray Li

Protecting the Arctic

INDIGENOUS PEOPLES AND CULTURAL SURVIVAL

Mark Nuttall

harwood academic publishers
Australia • Canada • China • France • Germany
India • Japan • Luxembourg • Malaysia
The Netherlands • Russia • Singapore • Switzerland

Copyright © 1998 OPA (Overseas Publishers Association) N.V. Published by
license under the Harwood Academic Publishers imprint, part of The Gordon
and Breach Publishing Group.

Amsteldijk 166
1st Floor
1079 LH Amsterdam
The Netherlands

British Library Cataloguing in Publication Data

Nuttall, Mark
    Protecting the Artic: indigenous peoples and cultural survival – (Studies in
    environmental anthropology; v. 3)
    1. Arctic peoples   2. Indigenous peoples – Arctic regions   3. Arctic
    peoples – Political activity   4. Natural resources – Arctic regions
    5. Arctic regions – Civilization
    I. Title
    306'.089'944

    ISBN 90-5702-354-7 (Hardcover)
    ISSN 1025-5869

Table of Contents

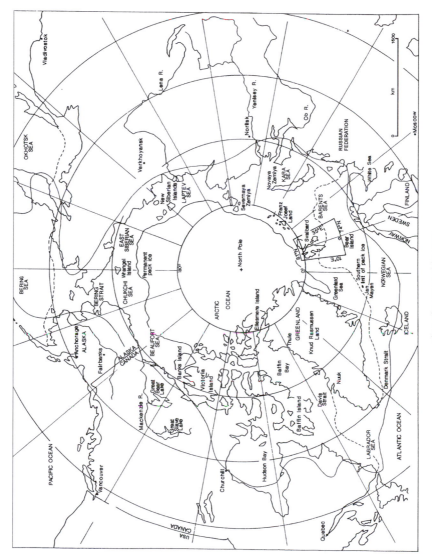

Physical Features of the Arctic

Chapter 1

INDIGENOUS PEOPLES AND THE ARCTIC ENVIRONMENT

In recent years concern over global warming, atmospheric pollution, ozone depletion, overfishing and uncontrolled resource extraction has focused international attention on the Arctic as a critical zone for global environmental change. The global quest for natural resources, the expansion of capitalist markets and the influence of transnational practices on the periphery has resulted in an internationalisation of the circumpolar north. The anthropogenic causes and consequences of environmental change and degradation demonstrates how regional environmental change in the Arctic cannot be viewed in isolation, but must be seen in relation to global change and global processes. Development and the threat of irreversible environmental damage has precipitated intense debate about the correct use of natural resources and proper ways forward for Arctic environmental protection. Indigenous peoples' organisations, environmentalists and, more recently, national governments, have stressed the need to implement appropriate resource management policies and environmental protection strategies. Yet science-based resource management systems designed to safeguard wildlife and the Arctic environment have, for the most part, ignored indigenous perspectives.

This book illustrates some of the ways indigenous peoples have mobilised themselves to take political action on Arctic environmental and sustainable development issues. While these issues are of urgent concern to indigenous peoples throughout the Arctic, this book discusses them with particular emphasis on Alaska and Greenland. These are two areas I have come to know through fieldwork and research and I draw on some of my ethnographic experiences and first-hand knowledge in the chapters that follow. While the geographical focus may be somewhat limited, the topics I discuss and the themes I explore are nonetheless generic. It would be difficult to go into detail about the particular situations of every indigenous group and to cover every region of the circumpolar north in a thorough and comparative way. My aim is to both stimulate debate and to lay the groundwork for future research and analysis. With specific reference to the Inuit this book illustrates how, in setting out to protect the Arctic environment, develop strategies for sustainable development and gain international recognition as resource conservationists, indigenous peoples make claims that their own forms of resource management not only have relevence in an Arctic regional context, but provide models for the inclusion of indigenous values and environmental knowledge in the design, negotiation and implementation of global environmental policy.

While they have environmental concerns, indigenous peoples nonetheless argue that resource development in the Arctic is not wholly incompatible with its protection. With few choices available on which to base the economic development of many circumpolar communities, indigenous peoples are increasingly involved with the extraction of non-renewable resources. To ensure a workable participatory approach to the sustainable management of resources indigenous knowledge is being incorporated into the design of environmental projects and the implementation of environmental policy. Indigenous groups have begun to outline and put into practice their own environmental strategies and policies to safeguard the future of resource harvesting, while indigenous peoples' organisations see themselves in the vanguard of indigenous human and environmental rights not only in the circumpolar north, but worldwide.

INDIGENOUS PEOPLES AND CULTURAL SURVIVAL

The Arctic and sub-Arctic regions are homelands for diverse groups of indigenous peoples, each having their own distinctive cultures and languages, histories and economies ranging from reindeer herding, subsistence seal hunting and sheep farming to more commercial pursuits such as industrial fishing, salmon canning, timber production, oil-related business or financial enterprise. In Alaska they are known as Inupiat and Yup'ik Eskimos, Alutiiq and Athabascans; in Greenland they are the Kalaallit and Inughuit; in northern Fennoscandia the Saami; and in the Russian North the 26 so-called 'Northern Minorities' include the Chukchi, Evens, Evenks, Nenets, Nivkhi, Saami, Sakhas and Khants. Often, in their own languages these names mean simply 'the people' and they are the original inhabitants of northern tundra, forest and coast. As they enter the 21st century the indigenous peoples of the circumpolar north will continue to rely on natural resources for their economic and cultural survival, but they are increasingly tied to global networks of production and exchange and subject to the consequences of globalisation and modernity. Technology, industrial development, environmental problems, social change, immigration and tourism all pose threats to traditional lands, livelihoods and cultures. In response indigenous groups have fought for and, in some cases, have achieved increasing political power and self-determination, as well as a degree of control over resource development and management.

Article 1 of the International Labour Organisation's 'Convention concerning Indigenous and Tribal Peoples in Independent Countries' (ILO No. 169) defines indigenous peoples as people who are regarded as indigenous on account of their descent from the populations which inhabited the country, or a geographical region to which the country belongs, at the time of conquest or colonisation or the establishment of present State boundaries and who, irrespective of their legal status, retain some or all of their own social, economic, cultural and political institutions.

Furthermore, the ILO Convention states that 'self-identification as indigenous or tribal shall be regarded as a fundamental criterion for determining the groups to which the provisions of this Convention apply'. In other words, being indigenous is what people can regard themselves as being (or not being). It is a socially constructed identity with reference to putative similarity or difference (Jenkins 1996, 1997). The flexibility of this definition of indigenous peoples allows for many different groups already identified in ethnic terms to claim the right to be recognised as indigenous populations, be they Palestinians or Scottish Highlanders (e.g. for a discussion of the Scottish case see Jedrej and Nuttall 1996). In such cases it is notable how politically potent being 'indigenous' can be, and why the assertion of 'indigenous-ness' matters, especially in situations where land rights and the legal, social and economic status of minority or ethnic groups remain controversial issues. As Plant (1994: 7) points out when minority groups cannot be easily seen to be indigenous peoples, 'they are now likely to seek to identify themselves as indigenous peoples, precisely because of the greater protection offered under emerging international law'.

In the Arctic political movements to achieve self-determination and land claims settlements have been fuelled and propelled by the construction and assertion of ethnic and cultural identity and notions of aboriginality and 'indigenous-ness'. To claim that one is a member of an indigenous, rather than a local or even a minority group, is to play on the rhetorical value of these notions in articulating, displaying and defending one's social identity and to claim that one belongs to a group or place. The use of such rhetoric has become essential for Arctic peoples as they argue that their demands for ownership of or title to lands and resources are based on two undisputable claims: that they have a unique and special relationship to the Arctic environment which is essential for social identity and cultural survival; and that they have never given up their rights over lands and resources in the first place— rather, land has been expropriated and resources exploited without due regard to indigenous peoples. Claims to lands and resources are thus based on cultural and historical rights: the Arctic environment not only sustains indigenous peoples in an economic sense, it nourishes them spiritually and provides a fundamental basis for the distinctive cultures and ways of life they are fighting to protect.

Whatever the differences in culture, language and economy, or whether they live in remote villages or large urban centres in Greenland, Siberia, Norway, Sweden, Finland, Canada or Alaska (Iceland has no indigenous population), indigenous peoples have remarkably similar histories in relation to their experiences of colonialism and culture contact. The indigenous peoples of the Arctic have suffered especially because the circumpolar north has been regarded as a wilderness or wasteland. At the same time the Arctic has been viewed as a vast storehouse of natural resources which have often been exploited with scant regard for the people who live there. The exploration and exploitation of the Arctic from the sixteenth century, but especially during the nineteenth, resulted in frequent and extended contact between indigenous peoples and outsiders. As well as economic and ideological influences, whalers, traders and adventurers brought diseases such as smallpox, influenza, typhoid and tuberculosis, which struck at and undermined the social and spiritual fabric of everyday life, as well as virtually wiping out the population of some areas.

Non-Native attitudes to the Arctic environment have been influenced by the idea of the circumpolar north as a frontier, an idea that has shaped both the course of economic development and the post-contact history of indigenous peoples. As an economic frontier, the circumpolar north has played a significant role in the development of those nation-states with Arctic and sub-Arctic territory, and social scientists have tended to analyse resource extraction, economic development and social change in terms of classic models of metropolitan/hinterland or core/periphery relations, while the concept of internal colonialism has been used to analyse and interpret socioeconomic and sociocultural development (see Young 1992: 37–55).

The colonisation and settlement of Arctic regions has often taken place primarily with resource extraction in mind. The development of Alaska, for example, has been made possible by the exploitation of sea otter furs, whales, gold and oil. In Canada, an expansion in mining activity, together with the development of hydrocarbon projects following the Second World War, reinforced a southern Canadian vision of the north of the country as a source of boundless wealth, and since the 1960s oil and gas exploitation has shaped the industrial frontier of the Canadian Arctic. Siberia played a similarly important role in the development of the Soviet Union, and while Denmark was a more benign colonial master with regard to Greenland, the indigenous Inuit were nonetheless implicated in a trade network based on sealskins and blubber.

As indigenous peoples have been brought within the economic and cultural mainstream of the nation-state, they have experienced disruption and cultural change, and have been drawn into situations of political subordination and cultural and economic dependency. Young (1992: 39) argues that while the sources of dependence can be traced to early contact with Europeans, some 'extreme cases of economic dependence are an outgrowth of social transformations taking place during the twentieth century'. Like many other scholars, Young identifies the beginnings of economic dependence with the onset of the fur trade, which involved indigenous peoples in international market economies. The introduction of a cash-economy has altered social and economic relationships, assimilationist policies have meant that nomadic groups have been settled into permanent communities and forced in some cases to abandon traditional activities, and the imposition of state education systems has conflicted with traditional ways of learning. While these changes have consequences for Native groups all over the circumpolar north, it is in Russia where some of the severest problems are to be found, and where the policies of a previously totalitarian state have led to an 'ethnic catastrophe' (Vakhtin 1994: 32). The transformations taking place thoughout Russia have prompted international concern both for the Arctic environment and for the one million or so indigenous peoples living in the country's northern regions.

While remote, the diverse regions which make up the circumpolar north are developed, modern populated areas, not frontiers or wilderness areas (Coates 1994). In some parts, especially in Russia, they are heavily industrialised. Arctic regions are also integral parts of complex nation-states and are influenced by and dependent upon dominant legal systems, economies and cultures. As such, they are characterised by what Coates calls a 'culture of opposition' resulting from the interaction between indigenous and incoming populations and the social, economic and political institutions the latter are seen to represent. Indigenous communities are also characterised by their mixed economies of informal (i.e. subsistence) and formal activities, but many have limited market opportunities and are heavily dependent on government transfers.

Indigenous peoples have become minorities (except in Greenland, where they constitute the majority population), dominated economically, politically and culturally by nation-states and by 'white settlers' and incomers who are often agents of those states. Sojourners and outsiders, who have long been part of the social and cultural landscape of the Arctic (whether as whalers, traders, colonial administrators, missionaries, police, doctors, nurses, wildlife biologists, anthropologists, or transient migrant workers), today make up an increasingly large percentage of the population of the Arctic regions, often outnumbering indigenous peoples in many places, particularly in urban centres.

Out of a total population of some ten million living north of 60° only about 1.5 million (or one sixth) are defined as indigenous peoples. As in the past, many migrants to the circumpolar north do not stay long. They move to the Arctic on short-term contracts, staying from anywhere between several weeks to several years, fully intending to leave once their work is completed, or their contracts expire. For example, many of the Russians and members of other ethnic groups who moved to the Russian North and Far East this century did so as a result of Soviet economic development plans. They were needed to provide the skills necessary for large-scale development, but while some Russians were volunteers, others were forced labour, sent to the far-flung reaches of the Soviet empire as a punishment (Armstrong *et al* 1978: 50). According to Vakhtin (*ibid.*: 50) between 1917 and 1926 'the incomer population of the North grew between 5 per cent and 8 per cent per annum but between 1926 and 1935 the growth was 15–20 per cent. In 1926 the Northern Minorities constituted 20 per cent of the total northern population, by 1937 their population was estimated at a mere 7 per cent'.

Increasing numbers of migrants either stay on, or move to the Arctic on a more permanent basis. For some, a move to the northern regions represents a lifestyle option attractive to those jaded by life in large cities, or to those excited by the prospect of challenge and adventure. These people likewise call the Arctic home and this gives them a claim in having a say in development and policy making. Today, for instance, the Native peoples of Alaska make up 15% (about 85,000 people) of the total population and the state is home to Americans from all over the United States. Some work in the oil industry, some are military personnel. Others are successful and wealthy lawyers, while still more are academics, environmentalists, national park wardens, storekeepers, trappers, fishermen, cannery workers or seasonal labourers. Like most states, Alaska is a microcosm of the cultural and ethnic mosaic that defines the United States. Anchorage, known by many Alaskans as 'Los Anchorage' (and, as a local saying goes, is only twenty minutes from Alaska) is a true American metropolitan area with a population of some 250,000, roughly half the population of the state. It is a city of migrants (Cuba 1987), with a growing population of not only white Americans, but also attractive to Koreans, Filipinos and other ethnic groups. Similarly, Alaska's other major urban centres, Fairbanks and Juneau, have their share of Asian minority communities, in addition to Alaska's own indigenous urban migrants (those who move or drift to the towns from rural villages).

This picture of ethnic diversity is a similar one in northern Canadian towns such as Whitehorse, Dawson and Yellowknife, and in the Russian North, in such places as Murmansk, Noril'sk and Yakutsk. Although Native peoples make up the majority in parts of Canada's Northwest Territories, northern Quebec and Labrador, in Yukon Territory the indigenous population comprises 25%. In Greenland, while the majority of non-ethnic Inuit residents are Danes, the traveller will also bump into itinerant Moroccans, Norwegian and Faroese doctors, Italian mechanics, Dutch geologists, Irish helicopter pilots, Thai hotel maids and many other people from different parts of the world who, for some reason or other, have ended up in the country.

The consequence of such changing demography is that indigenous peoples fear that not only are they outnumbered, but that their lands are constantly in danger of being expropriated. As a result, there is often conflict between indigenous and incoming residents. Some of this conflict is evident in the social and economic impact on small predominantly indigenous communities of short-term economic development such as mineral exploration and exploitation. Migrant labourers may be resident for short periods, and this is especially the case with the construction of oil and gas pipelines, roads and buildings. The lifestyles of newcomers to Arctic settlements contrast sharply with those of the indigenous population (e.g. Brody 1975, Paine 1977). They are often from different cultural backgrounds and speak a different language. They may disregard and have disdain for local culture, beliefs and rituals, and believe themselves to be culturally and morally superior to the locals, whom they dismiss as 'primitive'.

This sense of superiority is reinforced by the high wages and special status which incomers are afforded by governments and their employers. Greenland, for example, was long considered a 'hardship posting'. Although this is no longer the situation, Danes were given better housing than Greenlanders, good pay, free return travel home and other benefits, breeding resentment amongst the indigenous population. In Canada, the Inuit were regarded as wards of the state, which only made them seem more childlike in the eyes of the colonial administrators, teachers and health workers sent North to care for them and bring them into the modern world. And in Russia, a 1932 law divided the entire population of the Russian North into two categories: 'The first category comprised professionals...who received a 10 per cent yearly increase of salary, a 50 per cent reduction of taxes, privileges in allocation of apartments, university entrance and so on' (Vakhtin 1994: 51). There was also a relatively small number of indigenous people who fell into this category and who received the same benefits. The second category comprised the rest of the population. Vakhtin (*ibid.*) describes how this group

> could enjoy these privileges only if they came as workers to the North from other areas of the USSR, which automatically excluded the vast majority of the native population and created two categories of payment for the same work. For example, two carpenters, a Russian and a Chuckchee, who worked together in the same team, would receive different payments. This was the germ of the ugly situation

that still exists today throughout the North: the differences in wages for the same work can reach three times and more.

Indigenous peoples also face challenges to cultural survival from environmental problems originating from both within and outwith the circumpolar north. Threats to land, animals and people not only come from the impact of non-renewable resource extraction, such as hydrocarbon development, but from airborne and seaborne pollutants such as cesium isotopes, lead and mercury entering the Arctic biosphere from industrial areas far to the south. As the various chapters of this book show, in setting out to counteract such threats, indigenous peoples argue that environmental policy-making will only be successful if it includes local knowledge and recognises cultural values. However, as a background to later discussion of the policy responses of both indigenous peoples' organisations and state governments to environmental problems, it is necessary to give a brief overview of exactly what those environmental problems are and how they constitute a threat to the traditional homelands of Arctic peoples.

AN ENVIRONMENT AT RISK

The Arctic has the unenviable advantage of being a natural scientific laboratory for studying global environmental issues. Some of the most alarming illustrations in recent years that Arctic environmental problems are global rather than regional concerns include the contamination of lichen and reindeer (which eat the lichen) in northern Scandinavia in the aftermath of the Chernobyl disaster, the discovery of PCBs in the breast milk of Canadian Inuit women (which were found to be four times higher than those found in women living in southern Canada), and Arctic haze, which provides the best example of long-range transportation of atmospheric pollution. A photochemical smog which is most problematic during winter, Arctic haze contains pollutants which originate from industrial activity such as coal and oil combustion and steel manufacturing which are transported by air from Eurasia towards the north polar regions where, because the colder air is more stable, the haze particles persist (Shaw 1980). Sulphur particles are the most common component of Arctic haze and not only do they threaten low-level ozone, they disrupt atmospheric energy flows and contribute to acid rain (Kemp 1990: 111). Other pollutants include copper, lead, zinc and arsenic. They have been found in lichens and mosses in Alaska, Sweden, Norway and Finland, but also fall in some of the Arctic's prime fishing grounds.

It is difficult to travel far in the Arctic without encountering the workings and effects of the global capitalist industrial system, decades of socialist ideological excess, or reminders of how strategically important the region was during the Cold War. Vast oil producing complexes, such as Prudhoe Bay on Alaska's North Slope, are linked to metropolitan centres by an ever increasing network of gravel supply roads. Oil and gas pipelines, some of them rusting and leaking, snake across hundreds of miles of tundra and mountain ranges, while seismic trails and the scars of clear-cut logging are etched deep on boreal and tundra landscapes. Industrial activity is often accompanied by urban development, which creates new social structures and new forms of settlement that concentrates population rather than disperses it. This has especially been the case in the Russian Arctic. Yet the impact of urbanisation goes beyond the immediate area and has consequences for rural populations. Urban development has transformed and polluted wildlife habitat and has denied indigenous peoples access to traditional hunting, fishing and grazing lands (Pika and Prokhorov 1989). Pryde (1991: 173–74) cites a case in Siberia of how economic development can adversely affect wildlife migration routes:

> When major pipelines were built from distant natural gas fields into Norilsk, inadequate provisions were made for migratory reindeer to cross the lines. Confused, reindeer sometimes found themselves trapped between two parallel pipelines, with the result that whole herds of them were funneled into downtown Norilsk. There, they became the accidental victims of automobiles and the intentional vicitms of poachers.

Even in remote areas, far from any human habitation, unwelcome encounters with rubbish and industrial and military waste are reminders of the fragility, brittleness and vulnerability of the Arctic, and of the intrusive nature of human activity. In the northeast of Greenland, for example (an unpopulated area within a protected national park), plastic bags, fishing nets, barbed wire, fuel tanks and beer bottles are to be found washed up on shores seldom visited by humans. On Alaska's Seward Peninsula local people have discovered corroding aircraft batteries in rivers which provide drinking water for summer fishing camps, vehicles dumped by the United States military, and cannisters of mustard gas half-buried in the tundra. And in 1994 five years after the *Exxon Valdez* ran aground, spilling 11 million gallons of North Slope crude oil into Prince William Sound, it was possible to talk to fishermen from southern Alaska still trying to come to terms with the impact of the disaster on their livelihoods.

The *Exxon Valdez* incident in Alaska's Prince William Sound in 1989 illustrated the dangers of transporting oil by sea, and recent leaks from Russian oil pipelines have raised questions about their reliability and safety. Somewhere between 5–10% of Russian oil production is thought to be lost through leaks, oil-well blow outs, waste and theft. Minor discharges from marine vessels, such as tankers, freighters, fishing boats and coastal ferries, operating in northern waters are also a source of pollution and may not be readily monitored, but their impact on Arctic ecosystems may be significant nonetheless (Neff 1988). Polar bears, seals, sea otters and sea birds are already frequent casualties of oil contamination, while bowhead whale migration routes through oil and gas lease areas in the Chuckchi Sea could be seriously disrupted if development goes ahead. Stirling (1988) has described how the curiosity of polar bears leads them to readily investigate unfamilar objects and smells, including offshore drilling sites and oil cannisters in Arctic villages and Inuit hunting camps. They also risk death by ingesting oil directly, through licking oiled fur or through eating contaminated seals or birds (Derocher and Stirling 1991).

Oil persists for longer periods in the Arctic because low temperatures result in low rates of evaporation and relatively little light during most of the Arctic year reduces ultraviolet radiation necessary for decomposition. The impact of oil pollution on tundra environments may remain visible for several years with lichens, which constitute the main source of food for reindeer, and other plants especially vulnerable to contamination. On land snow and ice cover may stabilise the oil during winter, but spring melt only releases it (thus coinciding with the arrival of migrating birds), while in marine environments Arctic sea ice reduces wave action, which in more temperate regions would help to mitigate the effects of oil pollution. Oil fires also produce smoke clouds that are concentrated at very low atmospheric levels by Arctic air inversions. Not only do smoke clouds from oil fires reduce crucial levels of solar radiation, they contain pollutants harmful to both human health and to the productivity of marine and terrestrial environments.

Other threats to the Arctic environment and human populations are less visible, but no less real. UVB radiation has effects on human skin, eyes and the immune system. Atmospheric and marine pollution means organic contaminants enter the food chain at every level. Because these persistent organic pollutants break down more slowly in the Arctic than in warmer regions, they pose greater dangers to human and animal populations. For example, polychlorinated biphenyls (oily, man-made substances known more popularly as PCBs, and which evaporate from rubbish dumps and burning oil) have been found in the breast milk of Canadian Inuit women. PCBs cause cancer and damage the neurological and hormonal development of children. There is also high concentration of PCBs in some seal, walrus and polar bear populations which threatens their reproduction. High levels of mercury have also been found in the liver tissue of ringed and bearded seals—both species constitute the primary source of food for polar bears, as well as forming the basis for the subsistence hunting culture of many Inuit communities. In Greenland, one in six people have dangerous levels of mercury in their blood, while other toxic chemicals found among Inuit include toxaphene and chlordane. Tundra and marine ecosystems are also at risk from the dumping of nuclear waste and heavy metal contamination. Nuclear test explosions have been carried out near Novaya Zemlya in the Russian Arctic, while radioactivity affects the northern Atlantic and Barents Sea. The highest levels of radioactive pollution along the Norwegian coast, for example, have not originated in Russia, however, but from radiochemical plants in the United Kingdom and France.

Global warming caused by increased emissions of greenhouse gases also threatens to have a significant impact on the Arctic and on the livelihoods of indigenous peoples. Arctic ecosystems are extremely sensitive to climate change and a likely increase in average winter temperatures of between three to six times the global average is predicted. There is already evidence that winters in the Arctic and sub-Arctic regions are becoming warmer. While the average temperature of the earth's surface is predicted to increase by between 2°–5°C during the next fifty to one hundred years, the Arctic regions are expected to have greater temperature increases, of up to 10°C. Global warming could reduce the extent of sea ice, permafrost would thaw more quickly in spring but take longer to refreeze in autumn, fish stocks would fluctuate and the migration routes of animals such as caribou would be disrupted as forest, tundra and coastal habitats adapt to new environmental conditions. Climatic change is also likely to disrupt millions of migratory birds as they find less food at stop over points, wintering sites and breeding grounds. Hunting, trapping and fishing activities would be severely affected and the economies of small, remote communities, already vulnerable to changes in global economic conditions, would suffer drastically.

Arctic climatic processes influence global conditions, which in turn contribute to further change in the Arctic. In a summary of research on climatic change in northern latitudes, Lewis and Wood (1996) however are careful to point out that, while global temperature data sets seem to suggest that there has been a surface warming of between 0.3 and 0.6°C over the last one hundred years, regional studies do not confirm that there are any worldwide trends. Rather, atmospheric temperature trends in the Arctic are seasonally and spatially variable. Nonetheless, there is considerable alarm at the prospect of global warming, while affecting the Arctic, melting the polar ice caps and resulting in a rise in sea levels, thus threatening coastal towns and cities and low-lying countries such as Bangladesh and the Netherlands. The melting of Arctic permafrost will release huge amounts of methane which will contribute further to the greenhouse effect. Climatic warming may also result in greater cloud cover and higher levels of precipation as a result of more water vapour (another greenhouse gas) in the atmosphere. A hole in the ozone layer has been found over the Arctic (as well as over the Antarctic) and if the ozone layer thins or if the hole gets bigger, then scientists argue that there are a number of implications not only for the Arctic but for the planet as a whole. As ozone, a gas found between 20–50km up in the earth's atmosphere, helps to reduce or filter high-energy ultraviolet radiation from the sun, the thinning of the ozone layer means that more ultraviolet radiation will reach the earth's surface. Possible consequences include mutations in vegetation growth and an increased risk of skin cancer in humans and animals. Ozone depletion may also contribute to a gradual warming of the earth's surface. One of the main causes of ozone depletion is the emission of chloroflourocarbons (CFCs), human-made gases used in refrigerators and aerosols which are unreactive and, once released into the atmosphere, help to thin the ozone layer.

The most extensive industrial development north of the Arctic Circle is to be found in Russia, as is the largest human population in the entire circum-polar north (over eight million people). The region produces something like 92% of Russia's oil and some 75% of its gas, and accounts for 20% of the country's national income. Western Siberia, for example, is the major producer of oil and gas in Russia. It is also a major region for the chemical industry, for coal and iron ore mining, metallurgy and machine-construction. As a consequence of this heavy and advanced industrial base, the region has high levels of pollution. The effects are not only disastorous for the environment, but for human health. In western Siberia and other industrial regions of the Russian Arctic, billions of cubic metres of gas dissipate into the atmosphere each year as a result of inadequate mining practices and safety procedures, or because of ageing pipelines. Gas is also wasted and simply burned off because there is a lack of transporting and processing facilities.

Wolfson (1992), in a summary of environmental degradation in the former USSR, discusses such issues as how 'normal' ecosystems on the Kola Peninsula are hard to find, desertification in Central Asia, and the drying up of the Aral Sea and the consequences of salt storms for the Caucasus, the Pamirs and the Tien Shan mountains. A number of fish species in the Barents Sea and the Sea of Okhotsk have been overfished by commercial vessels, and discussing environmental issues in the Russian Arctic, Roginko (1992) reports how industrial development has destroyed over twenty million hectares of reindeer pasture since the early 1970s, including six million hectares in the Yamal-Nenets Autonomous District alone, and how lakes and rivers in the Magadan region have become seriously polluted. Agriculture suffers because soils are contaminated with heavy metals, deforestation is proceeding at a rapid rate (the Siberian cedar is almost extinct), river ecosysems are collapsing, reindeer pastures have diminished—the list of environmental catastrophes goes on.

Soviet industrial development rarely, if at all, underwent rigorous environmental impact assessment. Citing the example of the development of a fuel and energy complex between the Yenisey River and Lake Baikal in eastern Siberia, Pryde (1991) however discusses the impressive nature of the environmental impact investigations. But, he points out that environmental studies were not completed prior to construction and could not do anything to mitigate the effects of existing developments, such as air pollution. Environmental groups still express concern that Western oil and gas companies currently operating in Russia shortcut environmental legislation in an attempt to open up new industrial fontiers in the Russian Arctic. Although the World Conservation Union (IUCN) and the Oil Industry International Exploration and Production Forum published guidelines for oil and gas exploration and production in Arctic and sub-Arctic regions in 1993, the strengthening of environmental regulations for the energy industry will no doubt make Russia an attractive place for oil and gas companies which do not have regard for strict environmental standards.

The Kola Peninsula is the most industrially developed part of the Russian Arctic and is perhaps one of the best illustrations of the environmental impact of development in the circumpolar north generally. Covering $145,000km^2$, the Kola Peninsula has a population of well over one million and its regional capital of Murmansk is the largest city north of the Arctic Circle (Doiban *et al.* 1992). The exploitation of natural resources (such as mining of apatite-nepheline, iron ore, nickel and zinc), commercial fishing, timber production, and manufacturing underpins the economy. The Kola Peninsula has also been of great strategic importance, containing nuclear submarine and nuclear bomber bases. Development has resulted in a severe ecological crisis, especially in those areas affected by mining and smelting. Nickel smelters on the Kola Peninsula, in towns such as Monchegorsk and Zapolyarny, are possible contributors to Arctic haze and causes of acid rain leading to the destruction of Russian, Finnish and Norwegian forests. Satellite surveillance has revealed that about 100,000 hectares of the Kola Peninsula have almost no living plants as a result of industrial activity, while in other areas scientists have observed gradual defoliation of trees, structural changes in lichens, and a gradual southern shift of the boreal forest tree-line.

The environmental impact of oil spills is unlikely to be localised. In October 1994, oil spilled from a pipeline in the Komi Republic in the western

Russian Arctic and contaminated a large area of tundra and polluted the Kolva River. While Russian authorities in Moscow and Komi reported that 14,000 tons of oil had been spilt, American oil experts working in the region estimated that as much as 270,000 tons had poured into the area. The pipeline had been leaking since February 1994 and the oil had been contained within a specially-built dyke, which only burst following heavy rains. At the beginning of November a second spill from the pipeline was reported to be on fire and burning fiercely. With oil flowing into the Kolva River an entire ecosystem was a risk.

The Kolva is a tributary of another river, the Usa which in turn flows into one of the European Arctic's major rivers, the Pechora. The Pechora rises in the Ural Mountains and flows into the Pechorskoye Sea, at the southern limits of the Barents Sea, through a vast delta which lies to the east of the Nenetsky Nature Park. Conservation organisations were alarmed by the possible effects the oilspill would have on wildlife that breed and migrate through the wetlands of the Pechora Delta and the coasts of the Pechorskoye Sea. In some years, as much as 50% of the Western European population of Bewick's Swans use the Delta and nearby sites in the Gulf of Korovinskaia, while the Pechora Delta is also of vital importance for other migratory birds, such as whitefronted geese and common scoters, and breeding species such as pintails and rough-legged buzzards. Furthermore, about 4% of the entire Arctic and sub-Arctic beluga whale population (currently estimated to be about 50,000) is to be found in the Barents Sea, (with large numbers in the Pechorskoye Sea), the Pechora River is host to populations of migratory salmon and char, and on land large herds of both domestic and wild reindeer roam the tundra.

The oilspill in Komi illustrates the potential threat posed by oil pollution not only to the environment beyond the immediate locality, but also to the regional economy. The Pechora Delta has a large town, Nar'yan Mar, and a large number of its 20,000 people rely on salmon and char fishing as one of the main industries. In other parts of the Komi region, Nenets and Komi people depend on reindeer herding. Contamination of lichens through direct oil spillage or from chemicals and soot carried by smoke clouds would have a deleterious impact on the herding economy. Serious oil pollution in the Barents Sea would also pose a threat to commercial fisheries not only for Russia, but for Norway which depends on migratory fish stocks.

SELF-DETERMINATION

Despite the overwhelming nature of the social changes and the devastating environmental problems that have impacted upon the Arctic, many indigenous groups have maintained lifestyles based on hunting, herding and fishing. The land and its resources have sustained the peoples of the Arctic for thousands of years and cultural survival will continue to depend on this unique relationship between humans and environment. Indigenous peoples and their communities feel that many of the social, economic and environmental problems they experience can be overcome by achieving political autonomy and economic self-sufficiency. At the very least, they demand the right to be involved in the policy-making processes that affect their lives, lands and communities. Responding to external processes of culture change, expansions in resource development and the threat of environmental damage, Arctic peoples have demanded the right to self-determination and claimed self-government based on historical and cultural rights to the ownership of lands and resources. For indigenous peoples, self-determination is the right to live a particular way of life, to practise a specific culture and religion, to use their own languages, the ability to determine the course of future development and to be involved in the processes of Arctic policy making.

Whereas self-determination does not in itself mean that indigenous peoples have effective control over resources, self-government is about being able to practise autonomy. Indigenous peoples are often minorities within nation-states (although this is not the case in Greenland), but they distinguish themselves from other populations, and thus base their claims for having special legal status, by reference to their unique relationship to the environment and the importance of this relationship for cultural survival. Dahl (1993: 103) argues that the representation of the Arctic by outsiders as a frontier or wilderness and thus ignoring it as a homeland 'violates fundamental territorial and cultural rights and aspirations of indigenous peoples'. It is for this reason that land and resource rights are often at the very heart of indigenous discourses on self-determination and self-government. These discourses have been shaped in part by indigenous peoples' organisations, such as the Saami Council (the first international organisation of Arctic peoples, founded in 1952), the Inuit Circumpolar Conference (inaugurated in 1977), and the Association of Indigenous Minorities of the North, Siberia and the Far East of the Russian Federation (formed originally in 1990 as the Association of Northern Minorities and renamed in 1993). These organisations represent the rights and interests of the Arctic's indigenous peoples, focusing in particular on land rights, self-determination and sustainable development issues.

Most of the Arctic states have recognised the claims of indigenous peoples for self-government and a number of significant settlements have been negotiated and reached over the past three decades. Notable are the Alaska Native Claims Settlement Act of 1971, Greenland Home Rule (1979), the James Bay and Northern Quebec Agreement (1975–77), the Inuvialuit Final Agreement

(1984), and the Nunavut Agreement (1992). The concepts of self-government and self-determination mean different things to different indigenous groups, depending on the historical, social and political circumstances of each group. Land claims and self-government settlements are also situated within and shaped by mainsteam political and economic processes. Dahl (1993) argues that indigenous claims are also influenced and constrained by cultural differences between and within indigenous groups. Not all Greenlanders, Saami or Inuit, for example, have the same visions of the future or are agreed on the extent and nature of resource development. As we shall see, some indigenous peoples view land as an economic asset, while others stress the importance of land for cultural identity. As Patrick (1993: 13) points out, 'there is not only variation in the specific reasons for negotiating self-government, but also the arguments set forth to justify it'. Dahl (*ibid.*: 108) points out that, unlike some ethnic minorities struggling for political autonomy elsewhere in the world, the indigenous peoples of the Arctic are not demanding the creation of mono-ethnic states. Rather, acknowledging the limits of their influence on state systems, they are attempting 'to find a political niche within which they can survive'.

Dahl distinguishes between three types of indigenous autonomy: regional self-government, ethno-political self-government, and land claims agreements. Put simply, regional self-government is defined in geographical rather than ethnic terms, ethno-political self-government defines aboriginal rights in ethnic rather than geographical terms, and land claims agreements (while more limited than territorial self-government) refer to specific ethnic groups inhabiting specific territories and give these groups economic ownership of selected lands, without acknowledging political, cultural or social rights. Although it is beyond the scope of this book to assess the effectiveness of indigenous self-government and land claims settlements, or to examine their political, legal and cultural contexts, it is useful to briefly summarise some of the key agreements.

For those indigenous peoples of the circumpolar north fighting for self-determination and self-government, Greenland provides a model of regional self-government for which there is no precedent. A Danish colony between 1721–1952, Greenland achieved Home Rule in 1979. While Greenland remains a part of the Kingdom of Denmark, the Greenland Home Rule Authorities have assumed control over and responsibility for a number of public institutions, and have undertaken policies that aim to develop the country in terms of its own social and economic conditions and available natural resources. The Danes retain control over defence and, until recently, retained control over many public institutions. In the areas of health and education there are still very few well-qualified Greenlanders and large numbers of Danes still work as teachers and medical practitioners. Even at governmental level the Home Rule authorities rely on the political and economic expertise of Danish advisors. However, because of new educational establishments such as a university, more young Greenlanders are being trained to fill administrative positions previously held by Danes. Fishing, hunting and sheep farming are the main industries and provide the main means of employment for the majority of Greenlanders. Manufacturing depends on the fishing industry and much employment is provided in the fish and prawn processing plants found in every major town and settlement.

Despite continued dependency on Denmark, Greenland has achieved an impressive degree of political autonomy. Under the Home Rule Act, legislative and administrative powers in a large number of areas were to be transferred to the Home Rule authorities. By 1992 the Home Rule government had assumed control of health, taxation, industry, transportation, social services and education, making the process of transferring responsibilities to Greenland complete. Early on, production and export in the fishing industry had come under indigenous control. Fishing (for Atlantic cod, northern prawn and Greenland halibut) currently accounts for 80% of Greenland's total export earnings. On 1 January 1985 Greenland left the European Community but negotiated Overseas Countries and Territories Association status. This allows Greenland favourable access to European markets and a fishing agreement between Greenland and the EU is renegotiated every five years. Withdrawal from membership of the EC meant that the Home Rule authorities lost much-needed grants from the EU's development fund. However, the Home Rule authorities currently receive an annual payment of 37.7m ECUs per year for allowing EU member countries fishing rights in Greenlandic waters.

In Alaska, the discovery of oil at Prudhoe Bay in the 1960s led to demands for land claims by the Alaska Federation of Natives (AFN). In 1971 the United States Congress passed the Alaska Native Claims Settlement Act (ANCSA) which, while not recognising a Native claim to the whole of Alaska, nonetheless established twelve regional Native corporations, effectively giving them control over one ninth of the state. As a land claims agreeement, ANCSA extinguished claims to the rest of Alaska and gave Native peoples $962.5 million in compensation. As a settlement that only gave Alaska's Native peoples ownership rights to land (a total of 11% of the territory of Alaska) ANCSA gave no assurances for the recognition of aboriginal political, cultural and social rights. In addition to the regional corporations, some 200 village corporations were also established and given small amounts of cash. Regional and village coporations have surface rights, but only regional corporations have sub-surface rights. Despite ANCSA, indigenous rights in Alaska are not always recognised or guaranteed. For example, preferential rights of access to hunting and fishing were not given to Native peoples on all lands and subsistence issues divide Native and non-Native residents of the state. Furthermore, while ANCSA is a land claims agreement, the situation in rural Alaska is complicated in that village corporations exist side by side with tribal councils (a form of ethno-political self-government) and village councils (which do not discriminate along ethnic lines). These three structures may have conflicting interests

In the Canadian Arctic, although many indigenous land claims remain unresolved, some of the most successful settlements have been reached between the Canadian government and Inuit groups. Despite this, there is no one unified claim and different Inuit groups have advanced different claims based on their own historical, political and social circumstances. In response to oil and gas developments in the Mackenzie Delta, the Inuvialuit of the western Canadian Arctic formed the Committee of Original People's Entitlement (COPE) in 1969, and in 1971 the Inuit Tapirisat of Canada (ITC) was founded in Ottawa as a voice for Inuit throughout Canada's North. In 1984 the Inuvialuit became the first aboriginal people in the Northwest Territories to negotiate a comprehensive land claims settlement with the Canadian government. In the Inuvialuit Final Agreement (IFA), the Inuvialuit were granted surface ownership of 35,000 square miles, including gas, petroleum and mineral rights in 5,000 of those square miles. In 1975, the Inuit of northern Quebec signed a land claims agreement against the backdrop of controversy surrounding hydroelectric development in James Bay. In 1992 the Tungavik Federation of Nunavut and the Government of Canada signed an agreement which addressed Native land claims and harvesting rights and committed the federal government to establish the separate territory of Nunavut ('our land') in the Canadian Eastern Arctic. Nunavut will be created in 1999 and will comprise some 200 million hectares of northern Canada, including Crown lands on which Inuit are permitted to hunt and fish. While the majority population of Nunavut will be 80% Inuit, and although the government of Nunavut will effectively be Inuit led, the new settlement is not creating an ethnic state but is public government within the limits defined by the Canadian constitution (Creery 1994). Nonetheless, Nunavut will give Inuit a greater degree of autonomy and self-government than any other Native group in Canada. In co-operation with the Canadian government Inuit will co-manage terrestrial and marine resources, land-use planning and environmental protection, but the degree of autonomy granted under this form of regional self-government will not be as far-reaching as that given to Greenland under Home Rule.

In northern Fennoscandia, where expansion of agriculture, and the development of mining, tourism, forestry and hydrocarbon projects have all encroached upon Saami reindeer herding lands, the Saami have achieved a degree of ethno-political self-government. The governments of Finland, Sweden and Norway have established Saami parliaments which are, in effect, representative and consultative assemblies. The creation of these parliaments mark a turning point in how the Fennoscandian states view the Saami as an ethnic minority and a separate people. In Norway, for example, a policy of assimilation restricted the use of the Saami language during the first half of this century. In 1953 Saami from all three Fennoscandian countries met to discuss issues of common concern to Saami culture and livelihoods, and in 1956 the Nordic Saami Council was established to represent Saami interests. It was not until the 1960s that Saami rights to preserve and develop their own culture were officially recognised. In Norway, Sweden and Finland today the Saami are ethnic minorities and a separate people, although they remain citizens of those states. As democratically-elected ethnic bodies, the Saami parliaments deal with issues relating to Saami culture and economy. Land use and land ownership remain crucial issues for Saami in northern Fennoscandia and shape indigenous discourses on self-determination.

Some of the most complex and unresolved issues relating to the autonomy of indigenous peoples are to be found in Russia. Under the Soviets Northern minorities were given rights and privileges based on a recognition that these peoples were distinct. For example, the Komi and Yakut, who constitute the two largest indigenous groups were given their own autonomous republics (and thus a degree of sovereignty) in the 1920s and 1930s respectively. Yet, these rights have not always been recognised and all ethnic groups in the Russian North and Far East are now demanding forms of self-government and regional autonomy. Environmental problems and resource development place great strain on the indigenous peoples of the Russian Arctic. Reindeer pasture is under threat, lakes and rivers are polluted, land is expropriated by oil and gas companies, indigenous peoples suffer from a disturbing range of health problems, and local economies have collapsed. Dahl (1993) and Vakhtin (1994) provide summaries of the situation of the indigenous peoples of the Russian North, while Slezkine (1994) has written an excellent account of Russia's relationship and attitudes to its Northern minorities. Increasingly, these peoples are arguing for greater recognition of their political and cultural rights. But as they fight for regional autonomy and involvement in political decision-making, indigenous peoples not only come up against state interests, but against the rights and interests of non-indigenous peoples who not always accept that indigenous peoples have priority rights to land and subsistence (Dahl *ibid.*).

Against this background, in the rest of this book I discuss a number of issues of concern to indigenous peoples that continue to shape environmental discourse in the modern Arctic. Rather than take a broad sweep, I have chosen to focus on the involvement of indigenous peoples in international environmental policy-making; the claim and uses of indigenous knowledge; the issue of subsistence hunting and the involvement of indigenous peoples in the global economy; the involvement of indigenous peoples in the growing Arctic tourism industry; and the construction of an indigenous environmentalism.

Chapter 2 discusses the involvement of indigenous peoples' organisations in recent international Arctic environmental co-operation. With specific reference to the Inuit Circumpolar Conference, I show how indigenous peoples have influenced the Arctic environmental policy-making agenda by focusing on indigenous knowledge and sustainable development. In Chapter 3 I continue with this theme, showing how indigenous environmental knowledge has been institutionalised by the Arctic Environmental Protection Strategy and the recently-formed Arctic Council, and assess the potential for sustained cooperation on Arctic environmental issues in light of contested perspectives on sustainable development. Chapter 4 explores the claims made for incorporating indigenous knowledge in environmental management systems. Both anthropological and indigenous perspectives on indigenous knowledge are examined, and examples are provided of how attempts are being made to integrate indigenous world views with scientific knowledge. By looking at the issue of subsistence whaling, Chapter 5 considers how effective strategies of renewable resource management depend on the integration of indigenous knowledge and scientific knowledge. In particular the chapter discusses subsistence whaling in Greenland and shows how both environmentalist attitudes to Arctic whaling societies and the International Whaling Commission's category of aboriginal subsistence whaling restrict indigenous peoples from developing small-scale community initiatives based on their ideas of whaling as a sustainable activity. Chapter 6 illustrates how indigenous peoples, in attempting to meet the challenge of finding forms of sustainable development, are becoming involved in the growing Arctic tourism industry. Tourism is seen by many indigenous communities as a vitally important part of local diversified economies. Drawing on specific examples from Alaska, the chapter argues that indigenous peoples not only use tourism for economic benefit, but that they use it as a strategy to promote Native cultures and to renegotiate their perceived cultural identities. Finally,

Chapter 7 puts forward some critical reflections on the gathering of indigenous knowledge, assesses the argument that indigenous peoples are natural conservationists, and considers the political use of indigenous environmental knowledge. I show how representations of idealised human-environment relations are used for strategic gains, but also argue that there is a danger that this politicisation of indigenous environmental knowledge and the construction of an indigenous environmentalism decontextualises and reifies knowledge. Rather, this chapter argues that the strength of indigenous environmental knowledge lies in its localised nature.

BEYOND BOUNDARIES: A NOTE ON DEFINITIONS

If there is one thing that is sure about boundaries, it is that they are not fixed or unchanging. They are, however, contested. In their classic text *The Circumpolar North* (1978: 1), Armstrong, Rogers and Rowley point out that the 'circumpolar north is a convenient abbreviation for the Arctic and sub-Arctic'. Yet, there is considerable debate as to how the Arctic and sub-Arctic regions are to be defined, as anyone who reads textbooks and introductions to the circumpolar north will discover. Often the definition depends on the subject and the scientific discipline, and boundaries are most commonly drawn based on climate, mean monthly temperature, the extent of sea-ice, the amount of tundra, the southern extent of permafrost, the northernmost treeline, or the latitude beyond which the sun does not set during the summer solstice, or rise during the winter solstice (66° 33'N). Osherenko and Young (1989: 11) consider 'all the lands and seas lying to the north of 60° north latitude to be Arctic', but some scientists would disagree and argue that some lands included in this definition, such as southern Greenland and southern Alaska, are actually sub-Arctic. Similarly, when scientists use the 10° summer isotherm (where the mean monthly temperature is at or below 10°C) to define the Arctic, then western Alaska, the Aleutians and southern Iceland are excluded from this definition. However, when the treeline is taken as the southern boundary, then western Alaska, the Aleutians and southern Iceland are said to be Arctic, although vast forested areas of northern Russia (which may have mean monthly temperatures below 10°C) would be sub-Arctic. Such definitions are complicated further by attempts to draw geopolitical boundaries or to see the Arctic and sub-Arctic as defined by the limits of the imagination (Lopez 1986).

In this book I follow, with some deviation and flexibility, what most other social scientists would consider the circumpolar north as an area of study to be, that is all of Alaska (although some would exclude south east Alaska); northern Canada (Yukon Territory, the Northwest Territories, northern

Quebec, and Labrador); Greenland; Iceland; northern Fennoscandia (Norway, Sweden and Finland); and the Rusian North. I do not draw precise boundaries and admit that there may be some vagueness to what I term the 'Russian North', or 'northern Fennoscandia'. I also use the 'Arctic', 'sub-Arctic', 'circumpolar north', and 'the North' as interchangeable terms. I do the same with indigenous peoples and Native peoples. However, I am concerned more with processes and issues which have compelling similarities and structural parallels throughout the Arctic and which affect and impact upon the lives and lands of the indigenous peoples who live in this immense part of the globe.

Rather than draw any boundaries based on treelines, how cold it is in Greenland compared with Labrador, or whether the Inuit have a 'true' Arctic culture compared with other indigenous peoples, I am interested in the fact that what the regions and small communities of the circumpolar north have in common is that, by and large, they are remote. They are sparsely populated, peripheral and marginal, in the sense that they are geographically and economically distant from urban and industrial centres and markets. Small communities are predominantly indigenous in their demographic character, have mixed economies (incorporating both informal and formal sectors), limited education and employment opportunities, suffer from a range of social problems, and are struggling to escape from situations of dependency and underdevelopment by acquiring a degree of political autonomy and economic self-sufficiency.

Chapter 2

ENVIRONMENTAL PROTECTION AND SUSTAINABLE DEVELOPMENT

Identifying and understanding Arctic environmental problems attributed to the exploitation and mismanagement of natural resources and the globalisation of the economy only points to another problem: how to find solutions and how to design and implement workable environmental policies? Indigenous peoples' organisations have grown in strength over the last decade, gaining both visibility and credibility as they participate in policy dialogue and decision-making processes at regional, national and international levels. In this regard indigenous peoples' organisations play a pivotal role in agenda setting and political debate with respect to the Arctic environment and resource development, challenging the authority of the state and questioning both the processes and meanings of modernity and development (Wilmer 1993). Indigenous peoples have set themselves in the vanguard of environmental protection and have been the driving force behind many recent initiatives in Arctic environmental protection and sustainable development. This chapter discusses the involvement of indigenous peoples' organisations in the Arctic Environmental Protection Strategy, with specific reference to the Inuit Circumpolar Conference (ICC). Chapter 3 continues this theme with reference to the Arctic Council and assesses the potential for sustained co-operation on protection and development of Arctic resources.

The contested nature of knowledge is at the heart of critical debate on Arctic environmental protection, and while this is touched on briefly in this chapter, it is discussed in more detail in Chapter 4. Indigenous discourses on human-environment relationships question the legitimacy of orthodox scientific environmental management and stress that indigenous peoples offer a different and unique perspective on environmental protection and sustainability. Such discourses, on land, nature, animals, hunting, trapping, regulation and management, are also linked to wider contexts of 'whether or not traditional, pre-industrial human societies have something to tell us about how to live sustainably' (Hornborg 1996: 45). A category of indigenous 'experts' is constructed and enhanced by emphasising the crucial importance of traditional environmental knowledge which, in the words of Bauman (1992: 196), becomes a 'major resource, and experts the crucial brokers of self-assembly'. The Arctic Environmental Protection Strategy and the recent formation of the Arctic Council has institutionalised and given greater international recognition to indigenous knowledge and expertise.

Self-determination movements, the assertion of ethnic identity and demands for control over traditional lands are not only embedded within indigenous discourses about the protection of political, cultural and environmental interests and rights over resources, they often centre around access to the profits of resource development. Indigenous peoples' organisations such as the Inuit Circumpolar Conference have a clearly focused agenda: protecting indigenous homelands with environmental management programmes that integrate conventional scientific approaches with traditional or indigenous knowledge, yet arguing for the need to create the conditions necessary for a sustainable economic base in Northern communities. Indigenous peoples' organisations use environmental rhetoric related to human rights, social justice, equity and sustainable development in their attempt to achieve this.

POLICY RESPONSES TO ARCTIC ENVIRONMENTAL PROBLEMS

Just as security issues and militarisation dominated national and international interest in the Arctic during the Cold War, the easing of military threat between the superpowers in the mid-1980s coincided with increased concern over the Arctic's fragile ecology and greater awareness of how the Arctic is at risk from the intensification of development activity such as mining, oil and gas exploration and exploitation, commercial fishing, timber production, hydro-electric projects, pollution and urbanisation. As in any other part of the world the causes and consequences of Arctic environmental problems can only be understood by viewing them in relation to global processes. While many environmental problems are caused by activity within the Arctic, others are transboundary in nature, originating from areas geographically distant from the circumpolar north. Although global environmental change is not a late-twentieth century phenomenon (even if political, scientific and public interest in it gives the impression that it largely is), [1] current concern stems from both our awareness of its systemic and cumulative effects (for example, pollution may not originate at the local level but its effects are global), and concern about its level and extent (i.e. that it is truly global). As Beck (1992) points out, modern risks such as the environmental crisis are not restricted to place or time. Recent research in environmental history has sought to demonstrate the human role in ecological transformations in both prehistoric and historic times (Crumley 1994, Worster 1988), and this complements scientific studies that have focused specifically on past climatic changes in Arctic ecosystems (e.g. MacDonald *et al* 1993).

The critical analysis and evaluation of the capitalist economic system is central to many sociological and anthropological perspectives on global change and resource pressure on the environment. Of course, critiques of capitalism are not merely late twentieth century concerns, although theorists have focused on the social, political and economic aspects of capitalism, rather than its environmental impact. In the nineteenth century, for example, Marx laid much of the groundwork for the criticism of capitalism with his theory of historical materialism as an interpretation of social change. Marx was interested in how human beings relate to, rather than adapt to, the material world, and how they seek to master and subdue it. Marx argued that social change can only be understood by examining how people, as conscious agents who actively create history, dominate and control the material world for their own needs and purposes. They do this by creating and developing sophisticated and complex forms of technology and by expanding the forces of production. Wallerstein (1974) argued that capitalism has formed the basis for the modern world system, a complexity of economic and political connections spanning the globe and affecting every society. As the modern world capitalist system developed it was made up of a core of industrialised sates, such as Britain, France and Germany (but which now includes the United States and Japan), and which quickly began to organise and control world trade and the world economy in ways which would benefit them directly. Although European powers exploited natural resources they also created economies and societies based on cash crops such as sugar, coffee and tea grown primarily for export to overseas markets. According to world systems theorists the social, economic and environmental impact of the capitalist world system is felt particularly acutely in developing countries whose resources have been extracted for the benefit of other states. Capitalism has been criticised by dependency theorists as being responsible for exploitation, poverty and underdevelopment in many parts of the world. While not dealing explicitly with environmental concerns, dependency theorists point to the importance of understanding the linkages between developed and developing countries in terms of exploitative and dependent relations.

More recently, Giddens (1990) has analysed globalisation and the consequences of modernity, and his work has influenced theorists who see environmental change as one of those consequences. Giddens criticises world-system theory as offering only a partial account of globalisation and modernity because of its too narrow focus on economic systems and the nation-state. Giddens (*ibid.*: 64) defines globalisation as 'the intensification of worldwide social relations which link distant localities in such a way that local happenings are shaped by events occurring many miles away and vice versa', and defines modernity in terms of four basic institutions: capitalism, industrialism, surveillance capacities, and the control of the means of violence. Central to Giddens' theory of modernity is the notion of disembedding and distanciation. Giddens (*ibid*.: 21) defines disembedding as 'the "lifting out" of social relations from local contexts of interaction and their restructuring across indefinite spans of time-space', while distanciation refers to the separation of time and space. Giddens argues that in premodern cultures time was not always linked with space and the measurement of time was imprecise. Time has become standardised under conditions of modernity and localities are now penetrated and shaped by social influences distant from them. Distanciation is important for modernity because it makes the growth of rational institutions such as bureaucracy and the state possible and distances actions from their consequences. According to Giddens the institutions of modernity are truly globalising, and in terms of the global environment they do not restrict environmental degradation to space or time. Disembedding mechanisms also create a distinctive 'risk profile'. Because modern institutions have a global impact, identifying the origins of environmental damage and managing global environmental change becomes problematic. The separation of time and space also makes it difficult 'to allocate moral responsibility for environmental damage' (Milton 1996: 151). As Milton (*ibid*.) puts it, 'the involvement of a large number of actors in an industrial process makes it easier for each to abdicate responsibility for the outcome of that process; there is always someone else to blame'. This does not make the task of environmental policy-making any easier.

By drawing on these and other theories to understand the nature of the global economic system and further our understanding of the processes of globalisation, social sciences such as sociology and social anthropology have sought to make a contribution in recent years to understanding the human dimensions of global environmental change. Environmental sociologists in particular are concerned with examining both the anthropogenic causes of global environmental change (by focusing on processes connecting human activity and environmental change) and the human responses (in terms of policy solutions, public opinion, social movements, and environmental management systems). In attempting to understand human activity in relation to climate change, ozone depletion and loss of biodiversity, social scientists have pointed to population change, economic growth, technological change, politico-economic institutions and attitudes and beliefs as the main human dimensions driving global environmental change (Stern *et al.* 1992, Yearley 1991). Put simply, a growing population places more demand on resources, economic production has to keep up with demand, technological innovations change the ways resources are exploited and goods are produced, politico-economic institutions control production and markets, and attitudes and beliefs are important in the way they influence and shape relationships between culture and the environment.

Population growth is often singled out as the most significant threat to the global environment, but there is a contested debate about the level and extent of population pressure on the earth's resources. Harrison (1993) argues that population growth is a symptom rather than a cause of problems that the world currently faces. Population growth by itself does not threaten the global environment or create problems (although deforestation and loss of biodiversity is often the result of slash and burn cultivation by too many people competing for too few resources). Rather, economic, social and political factors which influence and shape the relationship between population, the environment and natural resources should also be considered. The thrust of Harrison's excellent book is that, while a growing population undeniably does require more resources to sustain it, we need to take into account a complexity of social, political and economic linkages and relationships. Harrison argues that it is difficult to link population growth directly with land degradation and environmental change. Instead, the opposite can be true: a growing world population can lead to environmental conservation. [2]

To claim that population growth results in environmental problems only ignores other factors such as economic policy, farming methods, climatic change, unequal distribution of resources and poverty. In many developing countries, poverty is often a root cause of population growth. But poverty is often induced as a result of the exploitation of developing countries by the developed world and by transnational corporations. Therefore the major issues which need to be addressed if global environmental change is to be tackled include social and economic inequalities, the expropriation of land for the production of cash crops, unequal access to and unequal distribution of resources, and how materialist values and global consumption patterns lead to environmental degradation. To understand Arctic environmental issues, we need a better understanding of the complex social, economic and political connections that span the globe and affect virtually every society and aspect of human existence. By pointing to these complex processes and how they affect the circumpolar north, social scientists often use the Arctic as an example when driving home the message that environmental problems are global rather than regional concerns.

Unlike the Antarctic,[3] the Arctic as a whole has not been subject to substantial multilateral international agreements until relatively recently, although there have been a number of unilateral, bilateral and multilateral agreements this century concerned with specific Arctic regions or the management of wildlife. Three of the most significant are the North Pacific Sealing

Convention of 1911, the Svalbard Treaty of 1920, and the Agreement on the Conservation of Polar Bears of 1973. The North Pacific Sealing Convention, was an agreement on the harvest of fur seals between the United States, Canada, Russia, and Japan (with Great Britain acting on Canada's behalf), which continued as a regulatory regime until the 1980s. It was confined to the northern Pacific Ocean 'and functionally limited to conservation and management of the fur seal stocks at the maximum sustainable yield' (Mirovitskaya *et al.* 1993). The Svalbard Treaty, which came into force in 1925, recognised Norway's sovereignty over the archipelago, while giving equal rights to the other signatory nations and allowing them access for resource development. It also ensured the protection of living resources and guaranteed that Svalbard should be a demilitarised zone (Singh and Saguirian 1993). The Agreement on the Conservation of Polar Bears was made between those five states with polar bear populations, i.e. Norway, the Soviet Union, Canada, the United States and Denmark/Greenland. While making provision for the protection of polar bears, the agreement also requires the member states to protect the ecosystems in which the bears live (Fikkan *et al.* 1993).

More recent attempts at environmental cooperation include a 1983 agreement between Greenland and Canada on Marine Environmental Cooperation, a 1987 agreement between Canada and the United States on the conservation of the Porcupine Caribou herd, and the North Atlantic Marine Mammal Commission (NAMMCO) established by Iceland, Norway, Greenland and the Faroe Islands (as a result of disagreement with the International Whaling Commission) for the management and utilisation of whales and other marine mammals. Although all these agreements are significant milestones for international environmental cooperation in the circumpolar regions, they deal only with certain parts of the Arctic or with particular species of animal.

Other international agreements, while not concerned directly with Arctic issues, involve Arctic states and other nations seeking to find solutions to transboundary environmental problems. These include the Convention for the Prevention of Marine Pollution by Dumping from Ships and Aircraft of 1972 (which covered the North East Atlantic up to the North Pole and was signed by thirteen west European maritime states), the United Nations Convention on Long-Range Transboundary Air Pollution of 1977 (signed by 34 nations in an attempt to deal with atmospheric pollution), the United Nations Convention on the Law of the Sea (UNCLOS) of 1982, the Montreal Protocol of 1987 (an agreement to cut emissions of CFCs and protect stratospheric ozone, which so far has had a fair measure of success), and the Convention on the Conservation of Migratory Species of Wild Animals (the

Bonn Convention or CMS). This convention has a proposed Agreement on the Conservation of Migratory African-Eurasian Waterbirds (AEWA) which would affect the Arctic from north-eastern Canada to Greenland, Svalbard and Western Siberia. And at the 1992 United Nations Conference on Environment and Development in Rio de Janeiro, a Global Warming Treaty was signed which called on industrial countries to reduce their emissions of greenhouse gases to 1990 levels by the year 2000.[4]

Ideas for multilateral cooperation on Arctic environmental issues were stimulated in 1970 when Canada passed its Arctic Waters Pollution Prevention Act. The Cold War and questions of unresolved sovereignty prevented intergovernmental activity, leaving the beginnings of circumpolar cooperation to indigenous peoples, who formed organisations such as the Inuit Circumpolar Conference (ICC). Formed in Alaska in 1977, in response to increased oil and gas exploration and development, the ICC represents the Inuit of Greenland, Canada, Alaska and Siberia. Since 1983 the organisation has had NGO status at the United Nations (Rosing 1985, Stenbaek 1985). As the ICC has claimed that '...most, if not all states do not possess a government representing indigenous peoples, and that indigenous peoples are often marginalized with respect to representation and the political life of states' (Sambo 1992: 31), it also sees itself as being in the vanguard of indigenous rights generally, especially with regard to self-determination. In December 1993, during the 'international year of indigenous peoples', the UN General Assembly passed a resolution to launch an International Decade of Indigenous Peoples beginning in 1995. Following on from this, at its meeting of the Executive Council in Anchorage in March 1994, the ICC resolved to continue to play an active role within the UN and to ensure that indigenous peoples are involved at all levels of UN decision making that affects indigenous peoples. This includes securing the participation of indigenous peoples in the establishment of the UN permanent forum on indigenous peoples.

In 1982 the UN set up a Working Group on Indigenous Peoples (WGIP) to draft a Universal Declaration on Human Rights and the ICC was involved in the discussion leading to the formulation of the text. From the beginning, the ICC's '...position on the right of self-determination remained the same: the Declaration must contain appropriate recognition of the fundamental right of self-determination, without discrimination or other limitation' (Sambo *ibid*: 30). Yet, when the Declaration was finally drafted in 1988, it included fourteen principles but did not mention the right of self-determination for indigenous peoples. At subsequent WGIP sessions the issue of self-determination was debated vociferously, along with social and cultural rights, and lands and resources. The ICC continued to lobby hard and finally, at the ninth session of the WGIP held in Geneva in July 1991, the right to self-determination, the protection of indigenous peoples' land and rights to surface and sub-surface resources were included in the text of the Draft Declaration (Simon 1992: 25). Each year, prior to the WGIP meetings, the ICC has participated at the Indigenous Peoples' Preparatory Meeting in Geneva with three other indigenous NGOs: the National Aboriginal and Islanders Legal Service, the National Indian Youth Council, and the Indian Law Resource Center.

As well as lobbying for human rights, the ICC has been active in attempting to reconcile the conflicting interests of environmental conservation and sustainable development in the Arctic. Challenging the policies of governments, the activities of multinational corporations, and the positions of environmental movements, the ICC argues that the protection of the Arctic and its resources should recognise indigenous rights and be in accordance with Inuit tradition and cultural values. The activities of the ICC illlustrate Beck's argument that while modernisation produces risks (in this case, to the environment), it also produces a reflexive process that enables those most likely to be threatened by those risks to reflect upon them and to question and criticise modernity. Thus, individuals, groups, or communities at risk begin to gather data and seek to understand the consequences of environmental risks. By gathering data and arguing for solutions, people become experts possessing knowledge of crucial relevance to policy-making (Beck 1992).

Since its formation the ICC has sought to establish its own Arctic policy, based on indigenous environmental knowledge and expertise, for an Inuit homeland that reflects Inuit concerns about the modernisation process and future development, together with ethical and practical guidelines for human activity in the Arctic (Stenbaek 1985). In 1985 the ICC set up its own Environmental Commission (ICCEC), to formulate an Inuit conservation strategy, worked out along the lines of the IUCN's world conservation strategy. The resulting Inuit Regional Conservation Strategy (IRCS) was not only the first indigenous strategy for conservation and protection of the Arctic environment, but also the world's first regional conservation strategy. The IRCS sketched out how best to design and implement sustainable resource management programmes that take into account the subsistence and cultural needs of local communities. Basically, the IRCS aims to secure for the Inuit the rights to continue to hunt and fish in traditional areas, to preserve and protect living resources, and so ensure the subsistence needs of future generations. These themes were fleshed out further in an ICC policy document, published in 1992, which set out a framework for a Comprehensive Arctic Policy. In setting out to counteract threats to the Arctic environment, the

Inuit have claimed the right for international recognition as resource conservationists and have begun to use indigenous knowledge as political action. The organisation has played an active role in both the Rovaniemi process (see below) and the United Nations Conference on Environment and Development (UNCED) held in Rio de Janeiro in 1992.

Since the late 1980s, there have been major developments in international Arctic cooperation which is indicative of the changing role of Arctic states and the emergence of the Arctic as an international political region (Griffiths 1988, Osherenko and Young 1989).[5] The turning point is seen by many to have come in 1987 when Mikhail Gorbachev, speaking in Murmansk in October, outlined proposals for how international cooperation in the Arctic could proceed. His speech was the most significant indication for many years of how the Soviet Union viewed Arctic policy, and among the most important points raised by Gorbachev was the need to establish the Arctic as a zone of peace, the utilisation of the resources of the Arctic, scientific activity and environmental protection. On the latter point, Gorbachev proposed

> joint work on a unified complex plan for protection of the environment of the north. The North European countries could set an example to others by agreement to set up a system of control of the state of the environment... It is necessary to hurry and safeguard the natural state of the tundra and forest tundra, of the northern *tagyar* regions.[6]

Gorbachev's speech, which must be seen within a context of wider concern about environmental degradation and environmental security in the Soviet Union during an era of *glasnost* and *perestroika*, led to a series of Soviet proposals for international cooperation in the Arctic, and since 1987 there have been a number of bilateral and multilateral scientific and environmental agreements. A Finnish initiative in 1989 led to the so-called Rovaniemi process between the eight Arctic states which resulted in the Arctic Environmental Protection Strategy (AEPS) of 1991. In 1990 the International Arctic Science Committee (IASC) was formed to identify, promote and coordinate international scientific research priorities. Global change and the Arctic was one of IASC's first scientific initiatives, and aims at an interdisciplinary programme integrating the natural and social sciences. In 1993 the foreign ministers of Norway, Sweden, Finland, Russia, and the EU Commission signed the Kirkenes Declaration which established the Barents Council and inaugurated the Barents Euro-Arctic Region (BEAR). The Kirkenes Declaration highlighted eight key areas of cooperation: environment, science and technology, economy, health, indigenous people, and culture and tourism. Other nations (the United Kingdom, France, Iceland, USA, Netherlands, Canada, Japan and Poland) participate in the Barents Council as observers. As an example of regional environmental cooperation, the work of the Barents Council is situated within and related to other Arctic initiatives, especially the Arctic Environmental Protection Strategy. 1991 also saw regional governments in the Arctic establish Northern Forum, which has a remit to focus on economic development, and the Canadian government announced plans to set up an Arctic Council which would draw its membership from the eight Arctic rim countries.

After much squabbling and disagreement over the text of the Arctic Council Declaration (mainly over sustainable development and indigenous participation), the Arctic Council was finally inaugurated in Ottawa on September 19, 1996. While the AEPS is underpinned by a specifically environmental agenda, the Arctic Council's mandate is to take cooperation on Arctic affairs beyond the environment. The Council is established to provide a high level forum for the Arctic states to address environmental protection (especially in areas of pollution), sustainable economic development, subsistence activities, health, community development, tourism, and transport and communications. Indigenous peoples organisations were also ensured permanent participation, although as we shall see below this is not without some controversy.

THE ARCTIC ENVIRONMENTAL PROTECTION STRATEGY (AEPS), INDIGENOUS PEOPLES AND NGOS

The Arctic Environmental Protection Strategy (AEPS) was initiated in Rovaniemi, Finland in June 1991 when environmental ministers from the eight Arctic countries signed the Declaration on the Protection of the Arctic Environment. Also referred to as the Rovaniemi process, the AEPS was intended to be a forum for Canada, Finland, the United States, Iceland, the Russian Federation, Denmark, Sweden and Norway to share information and to develop programmes and initiatives to deal with environmental problems such as Arctic pollution. The AEPS is a formally-negotiated environmental agreement, but nation-states have not been the only key-actors in the process. From the beginning a main objective of the AEPS has been to take notice of the concerns of indigenous peoples and to include indigenous perspectives on the Arctic environment.

In the original Declaration on the Protection of the Arctic Environment, the ministers emphasised not only 'our responsibility to protect and preserve the Arctic environment', but also the importance of 'recognizing the special relationship of the indigenous peoples and local populations of the Arctic and their unique contribution to the protection of the Arctic environment'. Just how vital indigenous participation in the AEPS is deemed to be was underscored in 1993, when the environmental ministers convened in Nuuk, Greenland for the second ministerial meeting and to review progress made since signing the original Declaration two years previously. This meeting resulted in the 'Nuuk Declaration', which established a programme with a secretariat to enable indigenous peoples' organisations to participate in future meetings and discussions of the AEPS. The Indigenous Peoples' International Secretariat opened officially in February 1995 and is located in the Greenland Home Rule Government's Danish office in Copenhagen. The Inuit Circumpolar Conference, the Saami Council and the Association of Indigenous Peoples of the Russian North were all granted observer status within the AEPS. The importance of indigenous participation and contribution to the AEPS was also explored in a seminar on indigenous knowledge, held in Reykjavik in 1994.

While indigenous peoples have organised themselves to take political action on Arctic environmental issues and are perhaps the main driving force behind much AEPS work, particularly with regard to sustainable development (with the ICC being by far the most active), other non-indigenous NGOs are either observers in the working groups or are active members of national delegations. NGOs involved in preparatory work of the Rovaniemi meeting included the World Wide Fund for Nature (WWF), the International Arctic Science Committee (IASC), the U.S. Arctic Network, the Canadian Arctic Resources Committee (CARC) and Kontaktutvalget for Nordområdene (KNO: Contact Committee for the Northern Areas). The involvement of all these organisations was very much in evidence at the third ministerial meeting held in Inuvik, Canada in 1996, where they lobbied to ensure the AEPS works to conserve and protect Arctic ecosystems. The World Wide Fund for Nature, in particular expressed disappointment that it had hoped to see more concrete results after five years of cooperation and was concerned that the AEPS had been distracted by discussions on the proposed Arctic Council.

Because of the involvement of both indigenous peoples' organisations and environmental NGOs in the AEPS and the Arctic Council, the Arctic provides an illustration of the transformation of power structures in world politics. Social responses to global economic and ecological interdependence are affecting and shaping world order (Lipschutz and Conca 1993) to the extent where the traditional state-centred world system now co-exists with a multicentred system dominated by NGOs and other transnational non-state actors, such as scientists and indigenous and non-indigenous social movements. In international relations, one of the basic arguments of interdependence theory has long been that greater economic interdependence and the influence of non-state actors would 'lead to the diminishing importance of states as institutional centres of supreme collective co-ordination and control' (List and Rittberger 1992: 87). Rosenau (1990, 1993) has argued that this involvement and influence of NGOs has resulted in a bifurcation of world politics. Existing alongside the traditional state-centred system of international relations, then, is another system which is multi-centred, comprising transnational non-state actors, what Beck (1992) calls a subpolitical system associated with the 'unbinding of politics'. This argument finds support in recent and 'emerging practices in global environmental politics' and while 'nation-states remain key actors...their interests, identity and power are rendered problematic by the growing importance of non-state actors' (Litfin *ibid*. 95–96). In this vein Waters (1995: 107) has claimed that 'the political leaders of nation-states have responded to the fears of their panicked constituencies by the only way possible, that is by reducing the sovereignty of the states relative to international arrangements'.

Rather than seeing this trend as signalling the end of the state, however, Litfin (1993: 94) claims that growing awareness of environmental problems and the need for international collaboration 'raises the question of the state anew', while List and Rittberger (*ibid*.) argue that the question is not what will replace the state, but 'how states can collectively manage global and regional interdependence'. The formation of international environmental regimes is one way of doing this, and Litfin argues that global environmental problems and policies formulated by governments to deal with them may ultimately result in the nation-state playing a newer and far greater role in the everyday lives of its citizens, because ultimately it is the state rather than non-state actors such as NGOs that has the political power and the financial means to deal with environmental isues at both national and international levels.

However, this is still not to deny the importance of indigenous peoples' organisations, such as the ICC, and NGOs, such as Greenpeace and the World Wide Fund for Nature, in Arctic environmental politics, or to assume that it is only governments that have taken the lead in efforts to solve Arctic environmental problems. While arguing that global environmental problems can only be solved if the state takes action, Litfin acknowledges that there are some important 'recent trends with respect to the actors involved in initiating, negotiating and implementing environmental regimes' (*ibid*. 96).

Increasingly, it is non-state actors that have persuaded governments to take action on the environment. Indeed, as the work of the ICC on environmental protection and sustainable development in the Arctic illustrates, NGOs and social movements are often able to take action themselves when state governments are constrained from acting or lack the political will to do so. According to Beck (1992), these groups and movements can be more reflexive and critical of modernity and its associated risks than central governments. In addition to the work of the ICC, the World Wide Fund for Nature, for instance, has been especially impressive in Arctic conservation by establishing new protected areas in Russia, supporting the gathering of indigenous knowledge and developing guidelines for Arctic tourism. And during the 1980s public protest in Russia aimed at the impact of development on the lands and peoples of Siberia and Central Asia (Arikayen 1991) was able, in some cases, to bring about the postponement of major projects such as gas development in the Yamal Peninsula (Sizy 1988, Vitebsky 1990).

Indigenous peoples' organisations and NGOs act as 'moral entrepreneurs' in environmental politics (Yearley 1991), by keeping Arctic environmental issues on the public and political agenda, and often by defining the environmental crisis as a globalising panic (O'Neill 1992). Yearley (1991: 50–51) argues that environmental groups characteristically develop concerns with aspects of society, politics or economics that they regard as problematic and then set about to persuade other people about the merits of their cause:

> The term 'entrepreneur' captures very successfully the kinds of activities in which they have to engage: they must find a market for their ideas and compete with other campaigning groups for resources such as press coverage and public attention.

Environmental groups then face an additional challenge of keeping the problem in the public eye, through the media and campaigns, exerting pressure needed for bringing about change and policy solutions. Indigenous peoples' organisations such as the ICC face the challenge of stressing the importance of the Arctic as a homeland for indigenous people, under threat from an industrial, urban world, while NGOs contribute to the global environmental panic by constantly constructing the Arctic environment as an environment at risk and by stressing the value of wilderness in the modern world (although, as we shall see in Chapter 6, indigenous peoples also represent the Arctic as a wilderness at risk). The globalisation of the economy has made environmentalists acutely aware of the pressure placed on the world's remaining areas of wilderness. In the Arctic, much environmentalist ideology and action rests on an argument that human activity results in the damage to, and loss of, wildlife and landscape, and therefore must be controlled.

Underpinning both indigenous and non-indigenous environmentalist discourse is a fundamental critique of industrialism and the global capitalist economy. Environmental groups working on Arctic issues (and whose members may or may not live in Arctic regions) share regional and and global concerns over resource depletion, such as over-fishing, timber felling and mining, environmental problems such as atmospheric and organic pollution, and oil, gas and hydrcarbon development projects. Examples include the environmental campaigns of organisations such as Greenpeace, the World Wide Fund for Nature (which has its own Arctic programme), the Sierra Club and the North Alaska Environmental Center. These organisations stress the need for conservation guidelines, the regulation of oil exploration and exploitation, the sustainable use of boreal forests, and the establishment and management of a network of circumpolar protected areas. Some groups are also concerned by the growth of tourism in the Arctic, fearing that large numbers of tourists will have an environmental impact and disturb vegetation and wildlife. As Chapter 6 discusses in more detail, the possibility of more development to cater for tourist demands is also a concern for indigenous communities.

The AEPS has allowed indigenous peoples' organisations and NGOs a greater international role in Arctic environmental politics and they have used the AEPS to position themselves to achieve international visibility with regard to environmental action. Indeed, indigenous peoples' organisations and environmental NGOs have formed alliances and working relationships that would have seemed unlikely a decade ago, when environmentalists and animal-rights groups would have been campaigning against hunting and trapping activities (although this is not to suggest that hunting and trapping has slid off the environmentalist agenda altogether). For example, WWF is developing a project for sustainable management of wild reindeer populations in Taimyr, northern Russia. Reindeer are an important resource for indigenous groups in the region, but are under pressure from hunting (both by indigenous and non-indigenous hunters) and from industrial activity in the region. There is also considerable cooperation between the Gwich'in people of northern Alaska and Yukon Territory and Alaskan environmentalist groups over support for protection of the Arctic National Wildlife Refuge (ANWR).

But there are also obvious clashes between indigenous peoples and environmentalists as to what constitutes wilderness and what is to be conserved. For indigenous peoples the Arctic is a homeland for which there is archaeological, historical and contemporary evidence of continued occupancy (e.g. Freeman 1976). For environmental groups, the Arctic is a pristine wilderness in need of protection. The Sierra Club's slogan 'One Earth, One Chance' typifies the message that environmental groups convey to their members, the public and to policy makers—"if we don't get it right this time, we lose what's vital and precious to us". Some environmental groups have specific local or regional concerns, while others are involved in Arctic-wide campaigns. The Sierra Club, for example, calls the Arctic 'a wild and unbounded place', although it is concerned primarily with Alaska. Like many other groups, the Sierra Club is concerned with the possible oil and gas development threatening the coastal plain of ANWR. The Club is also working to prevent the State of Alaska from selling land which transects three wildlife refuges and the Gates of the Arctic National Park and Preserve in the Brooks Range to developers and private owners.

As later chapters show, indigenous perspectives on human-environmental relations are ofen in conflict with these visions of Arctic environmental protection. While environmentalists, indigenous organisations and local communities all agree on the necessity of habitat protection and the conservation of ecosystems, all may not agree on the reasons. For indigenous peoples dependent on subsistence hunting and fishing, protection of breeding areas and closed seasons on hunting may be acceptable if an adequate and sustainable yield is maintained and made possible for future generations, without, to rephrase the accepted definition of sustainability, compromising the needs of present generations. However, for conservationists and environmentalists the absolute protection of certain species of wildlife, such as whales and polar bears, and of large areas of Arctic landscape, may be desirable.

Nonetheless indigenous communities and environmental groups share concern over environmental degradation and are agreed in their criticism of the global capitalist economy, modernity and the risks it generates. In contributing to discourses on global environmental issues, they point to the importance of understanding the linkages between developed and developing countries and the Arctic regions in terms of exploitative and dependent relations, arguing that Western capitalism has led to the systematic underdevelopment of Arctic communities, suppresses indigenous peoples and traditions in the process, depletes resources and degrades the environment.

TOWARDS AN AGENDA FOR SUSTAINABLE DEVELOPMENT

The objectives of the AEPS are to protect Arctic ecosystems (and here, humans are considered part of the ecosystem); to ensure the sustainable utilisation of renewable resources by local populations and indigenous peoples; to recognise and to incorporate the traditional and cultural needs, values and practises of indigenous peoples related to protection of the Arctic environment; to review regularly the state of the Arctic environment; to identify the causes and extent of pollution in the Arctic; and to reduce and eliminate pollution. The action of the AEPS takes place through five programmes set up to deal with environmental problems, such as oil pollution, the dumping of radioactive waste, contamination of the environment by heavy metals, acidification and Arctic haze. These programmes are: the Arctic Monitoring and Assessment Programme (AMAP), with its secretariat hosted by Norway; Protection of the Arctic Marine Environment (PAME), also led by Norway; Emergency Prevention, Preparedness and Response (EPPR), led by Sweden; Conservation of Arctic Flora and Fauna (CAFF); and Sustainable Development and Utilisation.

The Arctic Monitoring and Assessment Programme appears to have made the most progress of all the AEPS programmes. AMAP was established to monitor and assess the levels and effects of anthropogenic pollution on all components of the terrestrial and marine environments north of the Arctic Circle (together with the adjacent areas of permafrost to the south), and on human health, and given responsibility for producing reports on the state of the Arctic environment. In December 1991 the eight Arctic countries established an Arctic Monitoring and Assessment Task Force (AMATF), consisting of a board and permanent secretariat, to implement AMAP.[7] Non-Arctic countries, including the United Kingdom, Poland and Germany, international NGOs and indigenous peoples' organisations (ICC, Saami Council and the Russian Association of Small Peoples of the North) have been invited as observers to AMAP. In addition there are several observing and cooperating international organisations, such as the International Atomic Energy Agency, Northern Forum, World Wide Fund for Nature, the International Union for Circumpolar Health, the United Nations Environment Programme, and the World Meteorological Organisation. Funding for AMAP's monitoring projects has come from participating countries, but existing reports and research programmes currently underway outwith the auspices of AMAP have also been drawn on. For example, AMAP aims to link in with established research programmes on the causes and effects of global climate change, stratospheric ozone depletion and ultra-violet radiation. The involvement of indigenous peoples' organisations is reflected in the work of AMAP as much of its assessment work also aims to incorporate indigenous knowledge.

Much of AMAP's activities are geared towards seeking and gathering information on the health and lifestyles of indigenous populations. Representatives and research from indigenous peoples' organisations participate in gathering information on indigenous demography, settlement patterns, resource use and subsistence activities, consumption of subsistence foods, diet and nutrition. Some fifty programmes and projects are currently monitoring human health, the lifestyles of indigenous and non-indigenous residents, consumption levels of different types of food which may have been contaminated, and the socio-economic factors which influence health in Arctic communities. Some of the projects associated with AMAP's work include studies of air pollution and human health in the Norwegian-Russian border area, radioecological and human health assessment in the Russian Arctic, fetal exposure to heavy metals, human exposure to organochlorines in Greenland, and human contaminant trends in Arctic Canada. AMAP has not only produced and presented its State of the Arctic Environment reports to the Arctic ministers so that they can take action on Arctic environmental protection, but disseminates reports and results of AMAP's work to indigenous communities.[8]

The Protection of the Arctic Environment (PAME) working group was set up after the ministerial meeting in Nuuk with a mandate to evaluate existing legal regimes for dealing with pollution in the Arctic and identify the causes of land and sea-based pollution. PAME presented the findings of its first report at the Inuvik meeting. The working group's report showed that marine pollution in the Arctic is transboundary and has both land and sea-based sources, such as urban settlements, oil and gas exploration and production, mining and nuclear activities. Guidelines for offshore oil and gas development were presented to the Arctic ministers at the AEPS ministerial meeting in Alta, Norway in 1997. The Emergency Prevention, Preparedness and Response (EPPR) working group was the last AEPS working group to be established (before the Task Force on Sustainable Development was upgraded to a working group) and is concerned with how prepared the Arctic nations are and how they may be able to deal with oil spills, radioactive leaks or nuclear distaters in the region. EPPR has been busy drawing up plans and regional Arctic response strategies to coordinate response to such disasters, although the working group lacks an action plan.

CAFF held its inaugural meeting in Ottawa in 1992 and assumed responsibility for implementing the Biodiversity Convention throughout the Arctic. Its first Habitat Conservation Report, *The State of Protected Areas in the Circumpolar Arctic 1994* was the first concrete outcome of the entire AEPS process and provided a complete overview of nature reserves and protected ecosystems in the Arctic. CAFF's activities come under four broad areas— habitat conservation, species conservation, regional implementation of the Biodiversity Convention, integration of indigenous peoples and their knowledge. Indigenous peoples' organisations have been involved in CAFF since its inaugural meeting, with the ICC taking the lead in developing a programme on indigenous knowledge. CAFF sees indigenous peoples as playing an important role 'since they represent the repository of traditional ecological knowledge and skills of the Arctic' (CAFF Framework Document 1995, Appendix 2, p.3), and there are four main projects on the integration of indigenous peoples and their knowledge: the Beluga Whale Mapping Project; Indigenous Knowledge Data Directory; Indigenous Peoples and

Co-Management; and Ethical Principles for Research. Indigenous knowledge has become institutionalised within the AEPS process, with indigenous peoples regarded almost uncritically as experts on environmental conservation. This political aspect of indigenous knowledge is explored in Chapter 7. Despite the research programmes initiated under CAFF, the World Wide Fund for Nature argues that it lacks a long-term Arctic conservation and strategy plan (*WWW Arctic Bulletin* 1997: 3).

The ICC has criticised the AEPS for its initial narrow focus on conservation and emphasised a need to go beyond merely monitoring the state of the Arctic environment by including discussion of how to provide and maintain a sustainable economic base for Northern communities, which would move beyond the cycles of boom and bust that characterises much large-scale economic development. While the conservation of certain species such as whales and polar bears is important for indigenous peoples, science-based resource management systems often ignore indigenous perspectives and values. The designation of wildlife refuges and national parks to safeguard animals and the environment, for example, often restricts the rights of people to hunt, trap and fish in those areas, while international regulation has had an effect on subsistence whaling. The ICC position is that protection of the environment is a prerequisite for the sustainable development of Arctic resources (see Chapter 5).

The ICC has pushed the issue of sustainable development because the small, remote, predominantly indigenous communities of the circumpolar north are mostly characterised by their precarious mixed economies, combining the informal sector of customary and traditional subsistence activities, which provide the primary sources of food for many households, with the formal sector of wage-earning possibilities and transfer payments. The informal sector is not always easy to measure or analyse, combining as it does hunting, trapping and fishing based on long-term, consistent patterns of use and seasonal variation, non-accumulation of capital, sharing of wild foods, the generational transmission of knowledge, and non-monetary exchange based on kinship groups and other networks of close social association. Subsistence activities do not only provide the nutritional means for survival, hunting and fishing are important for cultural identity and embody notions of a specific relationship between humans and animals essential for the continuity of indigenous culture and livelihoods (Nuttall 1992, Wenzel 1991). Despite the cultural and economic importance of subsistence hunting, increasingly fewer residents of Arctic communities participate in or depend directly upon the harvesting of terrestrial and marine mammals. Furthermore, even if most wished to hunt or fish, subsistence activities cannot by themselves provide the basis for long-term sustainability in all Arctic regions. Instead, many Native people are involved in other types of economic activities, such as commercial fishing, the oil industry or mining.

Yet the informal and formal economies are, in many cases, interdependent making the boundaries between them blurred and not easily defined. Although a subsistence economy is usually differentiated from a capitalist economy in that the unit of production (in this case, the family) is also the unit of consumption, the subsistence economies of the Arctic are nonetheless dependent upon market forces and monetarisation. This has been the reality since Native peoples became involved with the fur trade. And as studies of commercial fisheries in remote Alaskan villages have shown, while people fish in order to sell rather than consume their catch, they nonetheless engage in activities which correspond to the spatial, seasonal, cultural and social organisational aspects of subsistence modes of production, such as resource diversification and the interdependence of households (Harris 1984, Langdon 1984). Similarly, in Labrador, the techniques and knowledge required for a commercial caribou hunt resemble aspects of harvesting caribou for subsistence purposes, except that the hunters are employed by a commercial enterprise and deliver the caribou to a processing plant. It is difficult to see the difference between a hunter who brings caribou meat home for his family, and the hunter who harvests the animal in exactly the same way but sells the meat to a processing plant in order to buy food for his family.

As the Labrador case illustrates, although some of the produce from hunting, herding, trapping and small-scale fishing may be consumed by the families of hunters, herders, trappers and fishers, some of it is traded, exchanged, or sold. While much of this happens in local and regional contexts, meat, fish, furs, and skins also find their way to distant markets, making informal economic activities dependent upon and closely interwoven with the global economy. Hunters, trappers and fishers and their families also depend on modern technology, such as outboard engines, snowmobiles, gasoline, rifles, and nets, which means a steady flow of cash is needed to support subsistence activities. Until the activities of anti-sealing and anti-trapping organisations virtually wiped out the markets for seal skins and furbearing animals such as beaver and muskrat, the principal source of cash for hunting families came from the sale of these commodities. In the north of Greenland, for example, the fall in the price of sealskins and even the loss of sealskin markets as a result of animal-rights activity in the 1980s meant that people in settlements dependent on hunting had to look elsewhere for a source of cash needed to supplement subsistence hunting. A modest fishery for Greenland halibut developed to meet this need (Nuttall 1992). Yet, overfishing has already resulted in a depletion of Greenland halibut stocks, as large-scale commercial fishing by boats from other parts of Greenland combine with local fishing to put pressure on the resource.

Generally, then, throughout the circumpolar north hunting families are characterised by pluriactivity in that cash is generated through full-time or part-time paid work, seasonal labour, craftmaking, commercial fishing or other pursuits that support or supplement subsistence activities. Although, ironically, full-time work restricts the time available for hunting and fishing, the casual, temporary or seasonal nature of many jobs does not allow for many households to be self-sufficient and independent of the formal economy. Subsistence activities may be something that individuals fall back on to supplement the paid work they have, or while they are looking for employment in the formal sector (Stabler 1989, 1990).

Some observers see informal economic activities as having great potential in forming the basis for economic diversification in indigenous communities. Ross and Usher (1986) stress the importance of the informal sector for small-scale community development, while Berman (1986) also argues that subsistence activities provide the best basis for self-sufficiency, in the sense that the local economy would be able to provide people with a real and regular income. The expansion of informal economic activities, such as the harvesting of terrestrial and marine mammal products on a more commercial basis, has been seen by some as the solution to reliance on non-renewable resource development. For example, in Greenland the Home Rule Authorities consider the production, distribution and exchange of food and products from hunting and fishing as vital to the development of local, small-scale sustainable community development (Greenland Home Rule Government 1995, Marquadt and Caulfield 1996). As Marquadt and Caulfield (*ibid.*:115) point out, the promotion of this system by the Home Rule government 'reduces the need for imports, promotes indigenous hunting practices, offsets the need for government subsidies to smaller settlements, and encourages consumption of nutritious and culturally valued foods'. As well as meeting demand from domestic and regional markets, indigenous business ventures are also looking to open up international markets. For example, Korean buyers regularly fly to Alaska's Seward peninsula and pay at least $50 for a pound of reindeer antler (which is then used as an aphrodisiac). In Labrador Inuit hunters kill around 1,000 caribou annually in a commercial hunt, while one Baffin Island community is meeting Japanese demand for the skins of ringed and harp seals.

But because of the interdependence between formal and informal economic sectors families and households are faced with the problem of ensuring a regular cash-flow. Opportunities for part-time work in small communities are limited and full-time jobs are even more scarce. The fur trade, the gold rush, and oil, gas and mining have all afforded employment opportunities to indigenous peoples, as well as impacted on indigenous ways of life, yet markets collapse, prices fall and jobs go. Recently, the growth of the tourism industry throughout the Arctic has allowed indigenous communities to capitalise on the desires of visitors to experience wilderness and Native culture, but the appearance of tourists is seasonal making it unlikely that tourism can form the basis for community development (see Chapter 6).

Indigenous communities and indigenous peoples' organisations are not against various forms of non-renewable resource development. Indeed, they wish to participate in, and profit from, development activities to ensure both economic and cultural survival. In the past, major industrial development rarely paid attention to the importance of the environment and its resources for indigenous peoples, or to the social and economic problems that often result from such development. As Young (1995) argues, the opportunities for dealing with the problems of indigenous economies can only arise if indigenous peoples have control over resource use and development, if the social and economic diversity of indigenous communities is recognised and maintained, and if indigenous skills and knowledge are enhanced. Furthermore, there are calls to take into account indigenous environmental knowledge in environmental impact assessment (Sallenave 1994).

In some respects, land claims settlements have allowed indigenous communities to make considerable progress, and some of the more significant developments have been the result of work by community cooperatives and Native-owned corporations. The latter have either entered into joint ventures with oil, gas and mining companies, or have developed initiatives of their own. For example the Northwest Alaska Native Association (NANA), the regional corporation for northwest Alaska, has supported and promoted Cominco's Red Dog lead/zinc mine, while the Arctic Slope Regional Corporation (ASRC) is the biggest Alaskan-owned corporation, successful because of its relationship to the North Slope Borough (Alaska's wealthiest regional government, partly because it taxes the oil fields) and the North Slope oil industry. ASRC has also invested heavily in business concerns elsewhere in the United States.

The Arctic ministers likewise take the view that environmental protection and sustainable development are not mutually exclusive. The programme on Sustainable Development and Utilisation originated as a Task Force on Sustainable Development (TFSD) set up following the Nuuk meeting mainly in response to pressure from the ICC to broaden the AEPS agenda. TFSD was upgraded to a working group at the Inuvik meeting. Its establishment indicated that the future direction of the AEPS would be concerned with broader issues of sustainable development, rather than with pollution and environmental damage. Initial emphasis on the harvesting of renewable resources and tourism seems to suggest that the working group was much more influenced by the input of indigenous peoples' organisations, and in particular by the ICC submission at the Nuuk meeting on how indigenous peoples could participate and how indigenous knowledge could be integrated within the AEPS process.

Sustainable development is also a priority area for the Arctic Council, which follows closely the 1987 Brundtland Commision definition as development which meets the needs of the present without compromising the ability of future generations to meet their needs. Canada, in its role as first chair of the Council, has defined sustainable development as 'development which seeks human well-being through an equitable and democratic utilisation of society's resources, while preserving cultural distinctiveness and the natural environment for future generations' (Graham 1997: 101). While the challenge facing the Arctic Council is to continue the environmental protection work begun by the AEPS, it recognises that it must link it more closely to sustainable development. Indeed, Oran Young (1996, 1997) has stressed that sustainable development should be the overarching framework for the Arctic Council as it sets out to chart new developments in international Arctic co-operation. Among other things, Young has recommended that subsistence preference, co-management, and the development of environmentally-appropriate technologies and practices should be some of the guiding principles for the Council's work on sustainable development.

In seeking to reconcile the diverse and contested perspectives of indigenous peoples, environmentalists, scientists and ministers, Canada argues that 'the Council's mandate, as well as its representative structures and processes..., can accommodate the concerns of all parties, under the rubric of *environmentally sustainable human development* (Graham *ibid.*: 51, emphasis in original). Mary Simon, Canada's Ambassador for Circumpolar Affairs, was reported as saying that the Arctic Council must not make the mistake of seeing environmental protection and sustainable development as distinct, as the AEPS had done, but that sustainable development must have strong environmental goals (Smith 1997). While the Arctic Council's view of sustainable development makes appropriate nods in the direction of the ICC position on sustainability, as development that allows social, cultural, spiritual and economic growth (ICC 1992), controversy over appropriate development strategies may come to dominate the initial progress of the Council. This is discussed in the next chapter.

1   One of the earliest works to emphasise the extent of the human transformation of the natural world was George Perkins Marsh's *Man and Nature, Or Physical Geography as Modified by Human Action*, published in 1874. Rather than view the modification of nature as some noble achievement of civilisation as it continues its inexorable path towards progress (as was the view of the Compte de Buffin in *Des epochs de la nature*, published in 1779), Marsh deplored the waste of natural resources and the destruction of the environment.

2   Neo-Malthusians such as Paul Erhlich, for example, argue that population growth is the main cause of global environmental problems. A growing population places greater stress on production because of increased consumer demand, which contributes to the depletion of natural resources (and to deforestation and desertification) and leads to scarcity and economic decline. Left unregulated, and under pressure from more people, natural resources will, as Hardin's original 'tragedy of the commons' thesis suggested, become overused and misused. This neo-malthusian view has been criticised by those who are optimistic about population growth and stress its associated benefits rather than problems. The American economist Julian Simon has argued that increased population leads to increased wealth in that it follows that more people means more markets, more ingenuity amd greater human inventiveness (in that more heads can be put together to solve problems). As a result resources will not become depleted, but will actually increase. According to Ester Boserup, for example, as population grows and more demand is made on the natural environment for food there is actually more investment in labour, agricultural productivity increases and in the process nurtures and improves the quality of land brought under production, rather than degrading it.

3   For a discussion of the Antarctic Treaty of 1959 and the organisation of national scientific activity in Antarctica, see Dey-Nuttall (1994), while Elliot (1992) is perhaps one of the best recent studies about the politics of environmental protection in Antarctica.

4   Both natural processes and human activities result in the emission of greenhouse gases. Carbon dioxide is released into the atmosphere, for example, from the burning of fossil fuels, but also as a result of deforestation and natural biomass decay. Atmospheric concentrations of carbon gases have increased by 25% since the mid-nineteenth century. In 1990 the United Nations Intergovernmental Panel on Climate Change (IPCC) endorsed scientific research which concluded that global warming was clearly happening as a result of human activity enhancing the greenhouse effect.

5   Griffiths (1988: 3) has defined an international political region as 'a system of interaction that serves to allocate assets and operating conditions among states in a part of the world that has distinct physical characteristics and whose politics form a subsystem of the global system of international relations'.

6   See T.E. Armstrong (1988) for a translation of the version of Gorbachev's speech printed in *Pravda* 2 October 1987.

7   Much of this information on AMAP comes from *State of the Arctic Environment*, Draft proposal for AMAP, prepared by the State Pollution Control Authority, Norway, December 1990, and *The Monitoring Programme for AMAP*, AMAP Report 93: 3, July 1993, AMAP, Norway.

8   AMAP presented its state of the Arctic environment report *Arctic Pollution Issues* at an international symposium on Environmental Pollution in the Arctic in Tromsø on 2 June 1997. The scientific documentation was published as *The AMAP Assessment Report: Arctic Pollution Issues* in autumn 1997. Among the findings detailed in the report are that high levels of mercury, pesticides and PCBs are found in the food of indigenous peoples and are transferred during pregnancy. As a result, newborn babies have levels of persistent organic pollutants between 2–10 times higher than in southern regions.

Chapter 3

SUSTAINING ENVIRONMENTAL CO-OPERATION

The idea for an Arctic Council linking the eight Arctic states was originally proposed by the Canadian Prime Minister Brian Mulroney on a visit to northern Russia in 1989. In 1991 a more substantial framework was put forward by the Canadians, suggesting that the Council would provide a forum for the governments of the Arctic states to collaborate with indigenous peoples' organisations to seek solutions for problems facing the Arctic. Initial interest was expressed by the Nordic countries, but not by the United States. In the mid-1990s, however, the Clinton administration reviewed US Arctic priorities and announced a new Arctic policy with greater emphasis on Arctic environmental protection. During a visit to Ottawa in early 1995, President Clinton endorsed the formation of the Arctic Council. The appointment of Mary Simon, a former president of the ICC, as Canada's Ambassador for Circumpolar Affairs gave greater impetus to the creation of the Council. Finally, after several years of meetings, negotiations and setbacks, the Arctic Council held its inaugural meeting in Ottawa on September 19th 1996, when ministers and senior representatives of the eight Arctic states signed the 'Declaration on the Establishment of the Arctic Council'. Leaders and senior representatives of the Inuit Circumpolar Conference, the Saami Council and the Association of Indigenous Minorities of the North, Siberia and the Far East of the Russian Federation were also present. The Declaration provides for the full consultation and involvement of these indigenous organisations in the work of the Council. Representatives of several non-Arctic states and NGOs were also present at the signing ceremony.[1]

The Arctic Council places emphasis on environmental protection and sustainable development, especially with regard to continuing the work begun by the AEPS. As the joint communiqué of the Council puts it:

> Ministers viewed the establishment of this new intergovernmental forum as an important milestone in their commitment to enhance co-operation in the circumpolar North. The Council will provide a mechanism for addressing the common concerns and challenges faced by their governments and the people of the Arctic. To this end, Ministers referred particularly to the protection of the Arctic environment and sustainable development as a means of improving the economic, social and cultural well-being in the Arctic.[2]

One concern raised over the proliferation of organisations and initiatives on Arctic environmental protection has been that work will be duplicated. As Chaturvedi (1996: 245) observes,

While there appears to be little disagreement among the Arctic states, at least in principle, that ecological problems require transnational strategies with sufficient regulative competence, differences persist over how best to realise the objective of ecological security for the Arctic without duplication of effort, excessive bureaucratisation and the common political problems associated with the combination of asymmetry and competition.

However, the Arctic Council does not intend to add another layer of bureaucracy or to duplicate current initiatives. To get over this potential problem it has subsumed them instead. The various programmes of the AEPS have been integrated into the work of the Arctic Council. The integration process was completed by the time of the final AEPS ministerial meeting in Alta, Norway in 1997. With the Arctic Council's emphasis on trade, improved economic lifestyles for Arctic residents, and development, environmentalist groups are concerned that environmental protection will take a back seat and point to the difficulties of reconciling conservation and development, especially as there exists no enforceable environmental law regime for the Arctic. As the Arctic Council begins to plough its first furrows, this chapter assesses the potential for sustained co-operation on Arctic environmental protection and sustainable development.

INDIGENOUS PARTICIPATION

The issue of indigenous participation in Arctic environmental politics had been firmly established since 1989 and the ICC was keen to support the idea of an Arctic Council, believing it would raise awareness of Arctic issues and of the problems and needs of Northern communities. The Arctic Council also represented an opportunity for indigenous peoples' organisations to institutionalise indigenous knowledge further and to demand a greater involvement in the process, direction and benefits of resource development. Yet, while the ICC was supportive of the initial idea to form the Council, and had contributed considerable input to the draft declaration on its establishment, the organisation was far from enthusiastic when the final Declaration of the Arctic Council was eventually signed. The ICC had hoped that more attention would have focused on sustainable development and was disappointed that indigenous peoples' organisations were only accorded the status of 'permanent participants', rather than being made full and active members of the Council, that they were not invited to sign the Declaration, that it avoids the use of the plural term 'indigenous peoples', and does not include indigenous perspectives on sustainable development (Watt-Coultier et al. 1996).

Mary Simon had argued that the direct and meaningful participation of indigenous peoples was a prerequisite for the success of the Council, and the ICC has questioned what the Council can achieve without its involvement as a full member. The Arctic Council, however, has made it clear that it is a forum for states, not peoples or organisations—aiming perhaps to test Litfin's (1994: 95) claim that,

> Only the state, standing at the intersection of domestic and international politics has sufficient authority, political legitimacy, and territorial control to influence the myriad causal agents of environmental deterioration. Thus, global ecological problems can be expected to bolster the power and legitimacy of the state in new ways.

But however dissatisfied it may be with the final declaration, the ICC could not afford to ignore the Arctic Council and has vowed to use its right to participate at Council meetings to bring indigenous perspectives on sustainable development and cultural protection to the forefront of debate.

Archer and Scrivener (in press) argue that problems may result from weaknesses in the organisational basis of the Council and over the issues of participation, funding and the scope of its activities. Several indigenous organisations representing other Arctic peoples, such as the Athabascans and Aleuts of Alaska are unlikely, as things stand, to gain the status of permanent participants—a situation they find unacceptable. The United States had insisted that the permanent participants category should be opened up to include more indigenous groups, such as the Council of Tribal Athabascan Governments, but was opposed by Russia, Canada and Denmark, who argued that the number of permanent participants should be less than the number of member states. Archer and Scrivener (*ibid.*) argue that the creation of the Arctic Council has slowed the momentum of Arctic co-operation and revived 'mutual fears of hidden agendas'.

Clearly, there are questions over indigenous participation which need to be addressed, including whether more indigenous groups, other than the three permanent participants, should play distinctive roles with regard to Arctic Council decision-making processes, and indeed whether the activities of the Council should represent all peoples (other than indigenous peoples) with Arctic concerns, rather than just state governments and specific organisations (although this may be opposed even by the three permanent participants, keen to safeguard their own interests as representing the 'indigenous voice'). Furthermore, it is notable that the Declaration on the Establishment of the Arctic Council does only refer to indigenous people in the singular, not in the plural, as if reifying the term 'indigenous' and ignoring the diversity of Arctic cultures. For example, the Declaration recognises 'the traditional knowledge of the indigenous people of the Arctic', suggesting that this knowledge is uniform and undifferentiated throughout the circumpolar north (see Chapter 4 and Chapter 7). Perhaps this is an attempt to defuse the

challenge posed by indigenous peoples' organisations and other social movements in the Arctic to the hegemony of the state. Certainly, admission to the
Arctic Council is not based on the political rights of indigenous peoples and
the Declaration is careful to point out that permanent participant status does
not mean the individual Arctic states are recognising the rights of indigenous
peoples accorded under international law.

THE ARCTIC AND THE GLOBAL ECONOMY

If other cracks are to appear in the Arctic Council then they will do so because
of conflicts over development projects which are not, in the opinion of AEPS
working group participants and Arctic Council members, sensitive to environmental protection needs and concerns for sustainability, nor indeed to the
spirit of Arctic environmental co-operation. Large-scale development continues in the Arctic, even though the excitement over the AEPS and Arctic
Council may have obscured it for a while. But it is not only the nation-states
with Arctic territory that regard the circumpolar north as increasingly important for resource development. The economic future of the Arctic depends on
global and economic processes, which makes the Arctic regions vulnerable to
the volatility of world markets.

Countries such as Japan, Korea and European Union member states constitute markets for valuable Arctic resources, thus firmly placing the circumpolar north in the world system. Densely populated parts of the world
with no or few resources of their own cannot sustain the material demands
made by their growing populations. They look to the northern regions for
fisheries development, hydrocarbons and minerals. Siberia, for example, has
some 20% of the world's forested area and about 40% of the world's conifer-
ous forests, and the Bering Sea is one of the richest fisheries on earth. Fish
stocks in the Bering Sea are threatened, however, by the commercial nature
of the fishing industry (the pollock fishery was closed in 1992 due to over
fishing), and the United States is only one of many nations contributing to the
impoverishment of the Bering Sea ecosystem. Overfishing by a large international fishing fleet is also having an impact on the marine ecosystem in the
European Arctic. There is urgent need to agree upon management regulations, but it is notable that fisheries do not seem to have provided a focus
for Arctic environmental co-operation. There is uncertainty over whether
fisheries will be a sustainable resource issue for the Arctic Council. And there
is also disagreement over the environmental impact of commercial fishing. A
report produced by the European Environmental Agency (EEA) points to
commercial fishing having the greatest impact on the marine ecosystem
(Hansen *et al.* 1996), while a Nordic Council of Ministers report contradicts

the EEA by concluding that overfishing in European waters has not depleted stocks (Bernes 1996).

The work begun by the AEPS and its various working groups, and to be continued by the Arctic Council, focuses mainly on monitoring the effects of Arctic environmental problems, seeks to produce state of the Arctic environment reports, feed this information back to politicians, scientists and indigenous communities, and make recommendations for action on environmental protection and sustainable development by government ministers. While it is widely recognised that many environmental problems facing the Arctic originate from outside the region, Arctic environmental co-operation seriously lacks a wider perspective on the regional and global dimensions of environmental change and resource pressure.

John Rayner, the Assistant Deputy Minister of the Canadian Department of Indian Affairs and Northern Development (DIAND), was correct when he said that "I think the Arctic is important for the entire globe. The Arctic and the Arctic Ocean are vital factors for world climate and what happens and impacts on the Arctic reflects what is happening around the rest of the globe" (*WWF Arctic Bulletin* 1996: 6). Yet what is happening in the rest of the globe is equally as important for the Arctic. Arctic environmental discourse reproduces the image of the Arctic as a natural laboratory for studying global environmental change (a handy phrase to use when justifying grant applications to scientific foundations and research councils), but fails to consider that it is important to understand the relevance of poverty in developing countries, deforestation in Nepal, floods in Bangladesh, or the activities of transnational corporations in South East Asia for the future of the Arctic, its peoples and its resources.

The major threats posed to the ecology of the Arctic are primarily the result of social conditions arising from human activity and interactions with the environment in local, regional and global contexts. But the remit of the working groups initiated under the AEPS has been to monitor the systemic and cumulative effects of global processes on a specific region, albeit a geographically vast one, rather than with seeking to understand the complex social, economic and political processes which are the specific underlying causes of the global dimensions of environmental change and resource pressure. Future strategies for Arctic environmental protection and sustainable development would benefit from moving beyond an Arctic-centred perspective in an attempt to conceptualise economic, social and environmental linkages between the Arctic and other regions of the globe.

Those involved in agenda-setting for Arctic environmental protection initiatives need to take into account the processes of globalisation. As with practically every part of the world, social, economic and political relationships in the Arctic have become truly globalised. In the modern Arctic virtually every aspect of life is influenced and shaped by events, trends, decisions and activities happening elsewhere. Just a glimpse of the well-stocked shelves of a Fairbanks supermarket, or drinking a cup of coffee with seal hunters on the sea ice in northern Greenland (whose wives prepare sealskins which will ultimately be exported to Japan) is enough to show how Arctic residents are very much a part of a global network of production and exchange. As the Arctic is inextricably linked to the global system, in complex cultural, ideological, economic and political ways there is a need to understand the process of globalisation and such issues as population, production, technological change, consumption and lifestyles in global perspective. A growing population places considerable demand on resources and world production is increasing to keep up with demand for consumption. This, inevitably, leads to the depletion of natural resources such as coal, oil, gas and minerals and contributes to the emission of greenhouse gases such as carbon dioxide, and to habitat loss and the extinction of flora and fauna.

Pressure is placed on the environment not only by countries of the developed world, driven by the desire for economic progress and the maintenance of affluent lifestyles and vibrant economies (for example Japanese industry is depleting the forests of Sarawak and Sabah), but also by developing countries. One legacy of colonialism has been the creation and shaping of forms of society which now not only have to adjust to post-colonial systems but are following the same trajectory of economic development as developed countries. Many of these developing countries have to find ways of broadening their economic base. Industrial development means more burning of fossil fuels and increased emissions of carbon dioxide. And not only do developing countries need to feed their growing populations, they also have to pay off massive international debts, which accounts in part for deforestation (such as in the Amazon). The growth of urban areas in the developing world is also placing the environment under greater strain. Although the majority of the population of industrialised countries live in urban areas, Africa has the fastest urban population growth and by the first few decades of the twenty-first century half the world's population will probably be found in South and South East Asia. Most people in these regions will be living in cities which cannot produce what they need to sustain themselves. Resources from rural areas, the oceans and regions such as the Arctic will be vital to an increasingly urbanised world.

The future of the Arctic regions may be linked to other, non-Arctic regional, social, political and economic interests. Osherenko and Young (1989:

60–61) point of the importance of seeing the future of development in the Arctic in terms of transnational connections rather than the classic model of core-periphery relations developed under conditions of internal colonialism. As they put it

> foreign investors can promise capital and advanced technologies for Arctic develop-
> ment as well as providing markets for which there is no local demand. With few
> exceptions…this has not resulted in colonial arrangements or even neo-colonial
> relationships. But direct investment on the part of foreign corporations or govern-
> ments is still growing rapidly and producing a complex network of transnational
> connections in the Arctic.

But understanding the processes of globalisation also means taking into account the activities of transnational corporations and the consequences of transnational practices for the circumpolar north. The sociologist Leslie Sklair (1991) has suggested a new conceptualisation of the global system as one which is defined increasingly by transnational practices (TNPs). Transnational practices cut across state boundaries but do not necessarily originate at the level of the state and Sklair calls upon social scientists to pay attention to transnational relationships that emerge under conditions of globalisation. He argues that the transnational relations or transnational connections approach (as put forward by Osherenko and Young to analyse global trends affecting the Arctic) tends to 'analyse interactions within systems rather than effects of practices and, though they claim to be transcending the state-centric model, they more often than not permit the state to set the agenda for them' (*ibid.*: 3). Sklair acknowledges that classical Marxists would not accept his analysis, as they argue that the global system is a capitalist global system where the most important and powerful actors are the capitalist classes. He contrasts this classical view, however, with contemporary Marxist theory which is state-centred.

Although he does not put forward a working definition of transnational practices Sklair distinguishes them on three levels: economic, political, and cultural-ideological. Each of these is usually, although not always, characterised by a major institution. Economic TNPs are characterised by the transnational corporation (TNC), political TNPs are characterised by the transnational capitalist class, while cultural-ideological TNPs are characterised by the culture ideology of consumerism. In developing a global sociology, Sklair (1994: 205) hypothesises '…the primacy of economic power over political and/or cultural power'.

Transnational practices have socio-economic and environmental implications and Sklair argues that TNPs create social differentiation and prevent economic and environmental sustainability. The hegemon is the main agent of TNPs and can be the state, an agency, an individual or a corporation. But the characteristic feature of any hegemon is that they are involved in some way in a struggle for resources. As Sklair points out, we engage ourselves in typical transnational practices regularly. For example, when we purchase imported goods we are engaged in economic transnational practices. Transnational practices have profound implications for environmental change. If the cultural-ideological transnational practice is to consume, then increased consumption will bring greater pressure to bear on natural resources. Greater resource extraction is needed to feed the demand from consumers, and increased resource development means such things as the construction of pipelines and deforestation.

Sklair's perspective on transnational practices is one, I suggest, which provides a more useful theoretical framework than the transnational connections approach suggested by Osherenko and Young (1989). While Osherenko and Young's stress on transnational connections is enlightening and helps us to understand the place of the Arctic in the global system, it remains state-centred, or at least implies the involvement of agencies and other parties that act on behalf of the state. It also suggests that transnational connections are an expression of the internationalisation of economic enterprise and that societies are only linked by economic interdependence, ignoring the fact that transnational connections are also political and cultural. Although Osherenko and Young do mention multinational corporations and non-governmental organisations, transnational connections is for the most part an ambiguous term, only seeming to focus on relations and interactions, not on effects.

The changing nature of political and cultural understandings that shape the use of the Arctic, the consequences of global change and resource pressure, and the conflicting political, cultural and aesthetic values concerning its future make a theoretical rethinking of the Arctic in geopolitical terms necessary. Recent geographical and political perspectives on how the Arctic regions are changing under geopolitical, economic and cultural stress have made some progress in this respect (e.g. Young 1992, Chaturvedi 1996). Beck (1989) has pointed out that as we approach the twenty-first century, research in both the natural and social sciences in the Arctic will be valued increasingly for the contribution it makes to how we can understand global issues. But it is equally important to consider global processes and their impact if we are to understand the contemporary Arctic and its place in the global system.

DEVELOPMENT AND CONFLICT

Perhaps the first real threat to Arctic environmental co-operation and solidarity, and something which could dominate immediate Arctic Council discussion, is concern over Canada's decision in August 1996 to approve conditionally the country's first diamond mine, to be located north east of Yellowknife in the Northwest Territories. While Canada argues that the mine will bring economic advantages in the form of jobs in an area with high unemployment, especially among impoverished indigenous communities, the project will also contribute a few billion dollars a year to Canada's gross domestic product and blaze a trail for further development in the Canadian Arctic (*WWF Arctic Bulletin* 1996: 12). The mine is controversial in that, like most development projects, it is feared it will have a negative impact on the environment, disturb wildlife and have an adverse effect on the indigenous Dene communities that depend on the area, especially with regard to their land claims which remain unsettled. WWF Canada claim that the environmental assessment review process was rushed and did not included adequate consideration of conservation goals. WWF argues that

> From a circumpolar perspective, Canada's handling of the mine proposal will set an important precedent for the Arctic Environmental Protection Strategy...and the Arctic Council...In their Nuuk Declaration (1993), the Arctic Environment Ministers stated that "in order to achieve sustainable development, environmental protection shall constitute an integral part of the development process and cannot be considered in isolation from it".

> (*WWF Arctic Bulletin* 1996: 14)

WWF further argues that

> Given its leadership role in AEPS and the Arctic Council, Canada stands to lose credibility outside as well as within its borders if mining and industrial activity in the central Arctic does not proceed in concert with strong action to secure long-term environmental conservation objectives at the same time.

> (*WWF Arctic Bulletin ibid.*)

Herein lies an immediate problem: how far will individual members of the AEPS and Arctic Council go with regard to the original objectives when faced with domestic and international pressure to develop their own resources, and indeed exploit (or contribute to the exploitation of) the resources of other Arctic states? This suggests that there are contested and inadequate definitions and understandings of the whole concept of sustainable development. This should hardly be surprising. Since the Brundtland Report, the dominant discourse concerning environmental management has centred on debates over sustainability. Yet apart from a small number of critiques (e.g. Redclift 1987) there has been little attempt to take sustainability at anything other than face value, rather than understanding how sustainable development strategies originate in specific social and economic contexts where diverse individual and group interests are contested (Redclift and Woodgate 1994).

As Milton (1991: 4) has argued, whatever the extent of global environmental degradation and the loss of non-renewable resources, there are '...under-lying disagreements over how problems are defined, their degree of seriousness, who is responsible for solving them, and how amenable they are to solution'. There is uncertainty over the terms of reference for sustainable development activities that the Arctic Council will adopt. Young (1997) argues that, given the elusiveness of the whole idea of sustainable development, it is no surprise that consensus has yet to be reached on the terms of reference for sustainable development in the Arctic, or what indeed is the relationship between sustainable development and environmental protection. Young (*ibid*.: 6–7) states that

> if sustainable development is to be meaningful in this context, it must be understood as the underlying concern in terms of which all other activities are evaluated. Sustainable development in the Arctic means economic and social development for northern communities that does not deplete or degrade the ecosystems within which these communities operate.

It is notable that the AEPS initiative on sustainable development clearly made the U.S. uncomfortable when work focused on barriers to trading marine mammal products imposed by the Marine Mammal Protection Act. As far as the Arctic Council is concerned, the U.S. opposes the idea of sustainable development being structured as a formal working group with clearly identified goals and specific projects, favouring instead 'sustainable development as a loosely defined, limited set of co-operative activities' (Smith 1997: 5). Perhaps the Arctic Council's decision in 1997 to support the development of a university for the Arctic is a way of avoiding, for the time being, having to reach agreement on the terms and references for sustainable development.

Canada is not the only country wishing to go ahead with what environmentalists see as megaproject development. Renewable and non-renewable resources will continue to be vital to the development of Arctic states well into the twenty-first century. Norwegian oil production, for example, could expand beyond the North Sea into the Barents Sea and other areas within the Norwegian Arctic. In Greenland the political and economic realities of self-government and the need for increased revenue at a time when the fishing industry is experiencing severe crisis has forced the Home Rule Authorities to revise their policy towards non-renewable resource development. In 1991 the Greenland Parliament passed a new Mining Act to encourage mineral exploration and exploitation. This change in policy allows for favourable taxation and more lenient concession arrangements for foreign companies to mine minerals such as lead, zinc, coal and gold. In 1992 the Danish Mineral Resources Commission announced a series of licensing rounds offering areas off the west and northwest coasts of Greenland for oil exploration, and in 1996 oil exploration took place for the first time on land (on the Nuussuaq peninsula in central west Greenland). Major zinc deposits have been found in Peary Land, which lies within the national park in northern Greenland. The exploitation of these deposits, by Platinova, a Canadian-Greenlandic company, would be vital for the Greenlandic economy. Although it has been argued that if non-renewable resource development is managed effectively, the resulting revenues could strengthen the Greenlandic economy (Poole *et al.* 1992), such development would precipitate serious opposition from those interested in protecting the environment, especially sensitive areas within the national park. WWF, for example, already claims that management problems in Greenland's protected areas are increasing and expresses concern that the Home Rule government does not enforce environmental protection legislation. But Greenland is not only looking to the commercial production of non-renewable resources. As the country attempts to lessen its dependence on imported foodstuffs, pressure is also being placed on the country's renewable resources, such as marine mammals, which threatens to conflict with traditional patterns of harvesting and sharing and brings opposition from environmentalist organisations (see Chapter 5).

Interests are not only divided over resource development. There is an unresolved sovereignty dispute between Canada and the United States over the Northwest Passage and the waters of the Canadian Arctic Archipelago—the U.S. insists the Northwest Passage is an international strait, while Canada asserts sovereignty. A disputed maritime boundary between the U.S. and Canada may also cause future controversy if exploitation of marine resources goes ahead in the area. There is also potential conflict between Canada and the United States over the Arctic National Wildlife Refuge (ANWR) issue (see below). A further controversy was generated in mid-1997 by Greenland's offer to store nuclear warheads no longer needed by the U.S. and Russia. Greenland's Premier Lars Emil Johansen was quoted in the Danish newspaper *Jyllands Posten* as saying "We don't want to be a dumping ground, but we would like to contribute to world peace". [11]

Discussion on sustainable development of renewable resources is also hampered by existing trade barriers that affect subsistence hunting and the fur trade, such as the 1972 U.S. Marine Mammal Protection Act (which, while exempting Alaska's indigenous peoples affects Canadian and Greenlandic communities), the 1973 Polar Bear Protection Act, and both the European Union ban on the importing of sealskins and furs from wild animals caught in leghold traps. These restrictions on the international trade of products from marine mammals and other fur bearing animals contribute to controversy between Arctic states, dampen constructive dialogue on environmental conservation, represent a major loss of income to indigenous peoples, place impositions on the right to self-determination and hinder the development of a sustainable base in Arctic communities (see Chapter 5). It is unlikely that the Arctic Council will be able to resolve these issues in the foreseeable future.

For those who still depend on hunting and fishing, then, the productive activities and distributive networks in which they are involved are subject both to the ebb and flow of the market economy and to globalising forces that contribute to a redefinition of subsistence, or threaten the subsistence lifestyle and its ethic of sharing. Animal-rights groups and environmentalist organisations have mobilised international public opinion and political action against the harvesting of wild animals and express concern over what they see as the development of 'non-traditional' activities. For example, one controversy in southeast Alaska centres on attempts by Native groups to develop world-wide markets for sea otter products, such as furs and reproductive organs as aphrodisiacs. Although the sale of sea otter furs in their raw state is banned under federal law, Native hunters are allowed to sell them if they are stitched together as blankets or made into handicrafts. Hunters sell sea otter products to tourists on cruise ships, but are seeking to open up markets beyond southeast Alaska. Conservationists accuse Native companies of selling raw pelts which are roughly sewn together as traditional Indian dance blankets, and point out that foreign buyers only have to unstitch the blankets to get the raw pelts which would otherwise be illegal to obtain.

One further problem hindering the commercialisation of hunting and fishing lies in regulatory regimes and management practices imposed by outside political agencies. While these aim to protect and conserve wildlife they also restrict access to resources (see Chapter 5). In Alaska state and federal policies make subsistence issues extremely complex. One long-running debate has focused on whether rural residents should be given preferential access to subsistence hunting and fishing rights, or whether urban residents should also have the right to hunt and fish for subsistence purposes (Caulfield 1992). A limited-entry system also operates for commercial fishing in Alaskan waters and some residents have lost licences, and therefore lost rights to resource use, under this system (Langdon 1984). Regulation also limits the prospects of finding markets for meat and fish. Again, in Alaska, state and federal law defines subsistence as the customary and traditional non-commercial use of wild resources. Food is often distributed through non-commercial sharing networks, and while this may mean that caribou, whale meat, salmon and other game finds its way to family, kin and friends throughout Alaska (and also living elsewhere in the United States), earning money through more commercial channels is not an option for subsistence hunters. In Greenland, government legislation and the imposition of quotas for hunting and fishing is undermining local resource management systems. In Greenland's hunting districts the complex of reciprocal rights and obligations towards the environment and animals are underpinned by unwritten customary rules and regulations. With no tradition of formal or institutionalised leadership in small Greenlandic hunting communities, those responsible for passing down knowledge about hunting and relations with the environment are people known as *piniartorssuit* ('great hunters'). These are people recognised by others in their community as having skill and prowess in hunting, and profound knowledge of animals, the weather and the environment (Nuttall 1992). The *piniartorssuit* are important for teaching hunters and 'co-operation and partnership, for imparting knowledge through instruction and experience, and for teaching the next generation' (Dybbroe 1991: 14). Increasingly, however, customary rules and the position of the *piniartorrsuit* have been eroded and have given way to more centralised forms of power and authority that leave no room for previously important politics of consensus at the local level. In this respect, Home Rule government legislation is contributing to the transformation and redefinition of human-environmental relationships (see Chapter 5).

Trade within and between indigenous communities is an increasingly apparent feature of the Arctic's economic and cultural landscape and the expansion of local, regional and inter-regional trading networks that link remote Northern communities may be one crucial way of developing informal economic activities (Young 1992). Subsistence hunters and fishermen living in small Greenlandic settlements, for example, have long sold part of what they catch and much of this ends up in supermarket freezers in the larger towns of the country's west coast, where there is an eager and steady market for whale meat and *mattak*, the skin from beluga whales and narwhals. An increase in the production, distribution and exchange of hunting and fishing products is a central aspect of the Greenland Home Rule government's policy for creating sustainable conditions in small settlements. Some indigenous communities are already exploring other potential pan-Arctic trade links, such as the prospect of Greenlandic skin and fur workshops making winter clothing for people in Alaska, Canada and Scandinavia, the sale of harp seal meat from Baffin Island to west Greenland, and the sale of the by-products of marine mammal hunting such as baleen and walrus ivory.

While the expansion of informal economic activities is attractive in that it enhances the prospects for small-scale local development and enables local initiatives to remain under local control, it is unlikely that fur workshops, community co-operatives or tourism, either alone or in combination, can provide the economic solutions to problems faced by the remote communities of the circumpolar north. The potential for economic development is still severely hampered by the small size and remoteness of many villages. Trade between Arctic communities is likely to be limited because markets are small, making the development of international markets necessary. This will do nothing to lessen dependency on southern tastes, fashions and needs.

If the Arctic is seen as the last great resource frontier, it is in Russia that some of the more spectacular development is taking place, prompting international concern for the environment and for the cultural survival of Russia's northern peoples. Gas and oil are important exports for Russia, and now that major oil and gas producing regions of the former Soviet Union, such as Kazakhstan, Azerbaijan and Georgia, are independent countries, the Russian North and Far East have assumed greater importance for Russia in terms of both economic development and environmental security. Western Siberia, the Komi Republic, the offshore areas of the Barents Sea, Beaufort Sea, Chuckchi Sea, eastern Siberia and other regions of the Russian North all have huge reserves of oil, which oil companies from the United States and other countries are eager to develop. Many have established offices in Moscow, and the Russians see oil development as a way of easing their massive foreign debt and internal economic catastrophe. Further development and opening up of Russia's Northern Sea Route as a major international marine trade corridor may also help to promote the development of Arctic resources and contribute to the growth of Russia's economy (Østreng and Simonsen 1992).[12] There is no international agreement that regulates oil and gas development in the Arctic and conservationists argue that a marine protection strategy is necessary as the Arctic Council begins its work in 1998.

To be fair, Russia is not ignorant of the environmental problems facing its northern regions and has developed strategies to protect areas of wilderness in its already country-wide system of state nature reserves, called *zapovedniki*, which will form part of a circumpolar protected area system. *Zapovedniki* were developed after the revolution of 1917 to serve as scientific research stations, or to preserve 'representative samples...of a specific type of landscape or natural zone, such as steppe, estuary, or montane ecosystems' (Pryde 1991: 136–7). Many have recently been designated as world Biosphere Reserves under the UN's Man and the Biosphere programme (MAB). In 1993 Russia doubled the area of protected Arctic landscape under its *zapovedniki* system, by establishing the Great Arctic Reserve of the Taimyr peninsula. In October 1996 the Gydansky *zapovednik* was established in the Yamal-Nenets Autonomous District to protect threatened bird species such as Bewick's swans and barnacle geese, and mammals such as polar bear. This has been welcomed by indigenous minorities in the Russian North as recognising the importance of land and resources for their survival. Nonetheless, despite these developments in environmental protection, there is concern that resource development in Russia will override plans for habitat protection and erode further the subsistence and herding lifestyles of northern minorities. For example the Koryaksky *zapovednik* was established in 1995 on the Kamchatka peninsula. However a gold deposit lies nearby and Canadian investors have been pressing the authorities of the Koryaksky autonomous district for licences to exploit the gold, estimated to have a value of 1.5 million U.S. dollars (Nikiforov 1997).

If basing small-scale community development on renewable resources is precarious, then it is non-renewable resource extraction which offers the best promise of jobs for Northern residents. Despite the controversies over the social, economic and environmental impacts, it remains that non-renewable resource extraction such as mineral development is the only industrial activity that may prove to have economic potential. In Greenland, for example, the Home Rule government inherited a post-colonial economy characterised by a relatively high standard of living and housing compared to other parts of the Arctic. But this economy had been planned and developed by the Danes through the transfer of annual block-grants and had no sound internal basis to prove viable under a newly forged Greenlandic administration. The transition to Home Rule had to be a gradual one, and the difficulties of achieving autonomy are illustrated by the fact that Greenland remains dependent on Denmark for economic support and block transfer payments. The latest agreement on block grants made between Greenland and Denmark was reached in 1995 and deals with the period from 1996–1998. Direct annual grants to the Greenland Home Rule government often make up 40% of its total revenue. Economic development in the 1980s and 1990s has focused primarily on the shrimp and cod fishery, and while this initially proved profitable since the mid-1980s the fishing industry has been experiencing severe crisis. While this can be attributed in part to the recession experienced by most countries in Europe and North America, the causes also lie with mismanagement, uncontrolled growth of the fishing fleet and subsequent over fishing. Exports, which are mainly shrimp, cod and other products, have dropped since 1989, mainly as a result of declining cod stocks and decreasing prices of shrimps. The last few years have seen bankruptcies in the fishing industry, in service industries and in the emerging private sector. Unemployment has also become a particularly acute problem in some areas.

Economic development in Greenland can no longer be based primarily on the shrimp and cod fishery. Exploitation of the country's natural resources is seen as lessening the dependence on imports and block grants as well as easing the economic crisis. The Home Rule Authorities are looking to alternative industries such as tourism (see Chapter 6) and mining, and in the future oil and gas production. This marks a significant turnabout from government attitudes during the first few years of Home Rule. Then the Home Rule authorities regarded fishing, hunting and sheep farming (the latter is pursued in south Greenland only) as Greenland's main occupations, and did not look favourably on the exploitation of non-renewable resources. Concern was expressed, by both politicians and people living in small communities, that the development and transportation of oil, liquid gas and other minerals would be harmful to the environment and would pose a threat to traditional hunting and fishing activities. However, the political and economic realities of self-government and the need for increased revenues have forced the Home Rule Authorities to revise their policy towards non-renewable resource development. The Home Rule Government Act regulates access to mineral resources in the Greenlandic subsoil. Mineral resources, which are defined as non-living natural resources, are the property of the Danish Realm and are therefore the joint property of Greenland and the Danish state. Apart from the exploitation of hydroelectric power for energy supply in Greenland, over which the Greenland Home Rule government has sole decision-making powers, the exploitation of mineral resources is subject to joint-decision making by both the Greenland Home Rule government and the Danish state, with net revenues to be divided equally.

The economic future of indigenous communities will be tied increasingly to distant markets. For example, south Greenlanders are shark fishing for export to Japan, and as we shall see in Chapter 6 the economic and cultural survival of some indigenous communities depends on their ability to sell an image of themselves to wealthy tourists. This, however, adds a complicated twist to the politics of Arctic development: resources are no longer extracted and expropriated only by colonial or neo-colonial governments and powerful multinational corporations—indigenous communities and indigenous-owned companies (some of them transnational) are now key players in the regional, national and global trade of valuable commodities such as fish, oil, gas and timber. This kind of participation is both necessary and vital if indigenous communities are to overcome problems of high unemployment, dependency, stagnation and decline. In the western Canadian Arctic, Inuvialuit corporations have been established to receive and manage the benefits from the IFA. These are the Inuvialuit Regional Corporation (established to receive the lands and financial compensation obtained under the IFA), Inuvialuit Development Corporation (whose mission statement is to fulfil the business goal of the IFA, enabling Inuvialuit to participate in Arctic, national and circumpolar economic development), Inuvialuit Investment Corporation, Inuvialuit Land Corporation and Inuvialuit Petroleum Corporation, and are controlled directly by Inuvialuit. In addition each Inuvialuit village has a community corporation. These corporations, like Alaskan corporations and Greenlandic enterprises, are not merely local or regional in scope and operation. The Inuvialuit Petroleum Corporation, for example, is based in Calgary, Alberta. It was created in 1985 to develop a medium-sized petroleum company for the benefit of Inuvialuit living mainly in the western Arctic. One of its objectives is to create employment opportunities for shareholders. However, it is a major player in the Canadian oil and gas industry, possessing substantial assets in western Canada. It has ownership of a potential gas field in northwestern Alberta and is exploring and developing other areas. These corporations, although owned and controlled predominantly by indigenous peoples, exhibit the characteristics of transnational corporations. They have substantial assets and sales. For example, in 1994 the Inuvialuit Petroleum Corporation made a profit of $29.5 million from selling many of its oil and gas assets.

Mary Simon is a tireless advocate of both trade between Arctic peoples and of the sustainable development of renewable and non-renewable resources for export to distant markets. Simon recognises the difficulty of reconciling industrial activity with environmental conservation, which both indigenous peoples' organisations and Arctic environmental ministers claim should constitute an integral part of any development process in the Arctic. However, environmentalists argue that large-scale economic development runs counter to the indigenous ideal of living in harmony with the land, an ideal that leaders of indigenous peoples' organisations politicise in order to construct for themselves an identity as original ecologists (a theme explored in Chapters 4 and 7). Indigenous participation in industrial activity undermines these claims, if it is seen as unsustainable, and makes indigenous peoples vulnerable to accusations from conservationists and environmental groups that they too are provoking and contributing to the overuse of natural resources and the destruction of wildlife habitats and fragile Arctic ecosystems.

Divisions and disagreements over resource development may not just be happening between Arctic states, but also between groups and parties (including indigenous peoples) within those states. In Alaska, for example, natural resource exploitation is necessary to sustain both the state economy and the Alaskan population's demands for an ever higher living standard and quality of life. Since oil first began flowing from the Arctic North Slope, oil revenues have supplied about 85% of the Alaskan state budget (McBeath and Morehouse 1994: 2). With production from Prudhoe Bay now in decline the search is on for viable alternatives that will ease the transition from an oil-dependent economy to one based on renewable resources. Yet, further oil development still threatens the Arctic National Wildlife Refuge (ANWR). Situated in northeastern Alaska, the coastal plain of ANWR could represent one of the last great oil discoveries in the United States.

Environmentalists argue that ANWR also contains some of the last great wilderness areas in the country, which would be destroyed if development went ahead. Canada opposes oil development in ANWR, which would threaten the principal calving grounds of the Porcupine caribou herd, a herd which the Gwich'in Indians of northeast Alaska and Yukon Territory depend on for subsistence. While Inupiat Eskimo hunters also rely to some extent on the Porcupine caribou herd, the Inupiat would stand to benefit financially from leasing lands they hold in ANWR to oil companies, resulting in friction with the Gwich'in who, in turn, are opposed by a majority of non-Native Alaskans in favour of oil development. In 1995, the Alaska Federation of Natives (with the exception of the Gwich'in) signed a declaration in support of opening up ANWR's coastal plain for oil exploration.

In Alaska, ANWR 'pits the interests of Alaska economic development against those of national environmental conservation. It also juxtaposes the consensus of opinion in the United States, which has favoured preserving the refuge, against the will of a majority of Alaskans who look to ANWR for future economic security' (McBeath and Morehouse 1994: 1). Similarly in Greenland, as the Home Rule government continues to embark on a course of nation-building and seeks ways to revitalise the country's ailing and fragile economy, resource development is contributing to a climate of ideological oppositions within the country. In terms of oil, zinc and gold, the Home Rule government hopes that Greenland may well be the Arctic's new resource frontier.

This points to one further problem: large-scale economic development and the corporate nature of business heightens or results in divisions within and between indigenous communities. In Greenland, where the economy is weak, the Home Rule Authorities will probably have to defer to increasing domestic and international pressure to exploit the country's resource base, presenting them with a dilemma: how best to avoid generating a climate of ideological oppositions as the current political agenda emphasises the need for increased revenue from resource development (Nuttall 1992, 1994).

Already in Greenland a process of nation-building and the social and economic changes this entails is threatening to result in uneven development throughout the country, perhaps best illustrated with reference to different perceptions regarding the environment and the use of natural resources (Nuttall 1997).

This is perhaps more strikingly the case in Alaska where the compatibility, or lack of it, between traditional Native and Western-style corporate values is the subject of considerable debate. While the U.S. Congress saw Native corporations created under the Alaska Native Claims Settlement Act (ANCSA) as devices for the generation of the prosperity of Native communities, critics of ANCSA have argued that the settlement has amounted to nothing more than an acculturative process imposed on the people of rural Alaska in an attempt to speed up modernisation and cultural integration. It has been suggested that the Act, which excluded those born after 1971, made Alaska's Native people shareholders in corporate-owned land, alienating them from their customary relationship with the land and shaping their future relationship with global economics (Chance 1990: 166). Huskey and Morehouse (1992: 132) have said of land claims generally that 'to the extent that they contribute to socialising and training Natives in western ways and to moving them into the economic and social mainstream, claims settlements can also be considered as instruments of assimilation'. Anders and Anders (1987: 134) point out that while the corporate approach aimed to give Alaskan Native communities greater self-control than previously possible under the Bureau of Indian Affairs, 'little effort was made by Natives or their legal consultants to evaluate the corporation against other models of organisation'. ANCSA effectively meant that profit-making activities pursued by Native corporations would be the only way that Native people could benefit from the settlement, and as Chance (1990: 163) observes, the 'lure of corporate power and wealth also held considerable appeal to some Native leaders who had been frustrated by years of political powerlessness'. Arguably, though, most Alaskan Native people did not understand the legal complexity of ANCSA, although it represented a significant accomplishment at the time.

While customary subsistence activities remain important for the economies of remote Alaskan villages, many of Alaska's Native peoples are engaged in large business ventures. The corporate ownership of land meant that Native peoples could be involved in the economic development of Alaska on an equal basis with other residents of the state. As a result of economic activities over the last twenty-five years or so, some corporations are tied increasingly to countries in south-east Asia where they export natural resources such as timber and salmon. While some Native corporations have not fared well at the corporate game and have made tremendous losses, mainly owing to limited economic potential in rural Alaska, or due to the volatility of world markets (for instance a glut in timber supplies led to losses for Native corporations in southeast Alaska), or simply because of unwise investment, others have been spectacularly successful by promoting development of their lands and resources, or by making investments outside Alaska.

Anders and Anders (*ibid*: 133) argue that the pursuit of conventional profit-making activities would only partly determine how Alaska's Native peoples would benefit from ANCSA. The success of the settlement is more likely to be measured in terms of how far traditional values have been integrated within the institutional framework of corporate management structures (the Arctic Slope Regional Corporation, for example, claims to represent success in this respect, with what it considers the non-confrontational meeting of tradition and modernity). Under the terms and agreements of ANCSA and state corporate law Native corporations are legally obliged to maximise benefits for their shareholders. One of the major ways of doing this is through involvement with the oil industry or with commercial logging.

Yet, what is often entirely consistent with corporate views of making profit is often seen by some shareholders as inconsistent with traditional values. Conflicts over priorities are common, such as disagreement over economic and social goals. Shareholders of Alaskan Native corporations do not always understand the relationship between profit and non-profit organisations. While Native corporations stress that they are established to make profit from economic activities there is still feeling in rural communities that profits should be invested in areas that have social concerns as their goal, concerns which corporations were never designed to deal with directly. Some shareholders from both urban areas and remoter villages also feel that they are not represented adequately by corporation boards that have their headquarters in Alaska's urban centres.

As shareholders become more familiar with the workings of their corporations, the activities of corporation board members and their investments are becoming subject to scrutiny and accountability. For example, in 1995 Doyon Ltd., the corporation for the majority of Alaska's interior Athabascans, was forced to call a special meeting of its board to consider a petition turned in by a group of 10% of its shareholders concerning the nomination process of Doyon's board of directors and how the corporation's money is spent. Doyon is one of the most successful of Alaska's Native corporations and manages over 12 million acres of land on behalf of 13,000 shareholders, as well as having $154 million in assets deriving mainly from land, real estate and oil-related business. Yet, on a live broadcast on Fairbanks local radio in

March 1995, where shareholders telephoned in, Doyon's president attempted to answer, and in fact dodge, thorny questions about such things as why Doyon shareholders receive a small dividend, the necessity of the board to maintain a hospitality room in an upmarket Anchorage hotel, or the need to hold a meeting (attended by only a handful of people) in Las Vegas for the corporation's shareholders living in states other than Alaska.

More than twenty five years after ANCSA there is a fundamental conflict of interest between tribal and village forms of government and the regional and village corporations that have come to resemble state and federal forms of corporation in their institutional structure. The newer formal institutions of government and leadership sit uneasily with traditional leadership and the politics of community consensus. Anders and Anders (*ibid.*) describe the tension as stemming from conflict between the corporate culture of individualism and profit-making and the traditional village culture of communal and kinship-oriented values. These tensions splitting Native communities in Alaska illustrate the complexity of the social and political landscape of the contemporary Arctic, where conflict between and within Native communities is an increasingly apparent feature.

There are signs that the excitement of multilateral co-operation on the Arctic environment may now just be simmering away on the back burner. Some of the initial momentum has been lost. This is currently the case with relations between Canada and Russia. Nor do Arctic issues provide the basis for daily interaction between Canada and the United States. Some states may attempt to emerge as leaders in Arctic co-operation. For example, Canada is acting as chair of the Arctic Council for the first two years and clearly sees itself as occupying a key role in setting the agenda for Arctic affairs well into the next century. For this reason, a Canadian House of Commons Standing Committee on Foreign Affairs and International Trade carried out a study in 1996 of Canadian interests in expanding circumpolar international relations, as a way of achieving Canadian foreign policy objectives. The Committee's work was in two phases: a) it obtained views within Canada on the directions government policy should take on issues such as sustainable development and environmental protection, giving recognition to indigenous peoples and other non-state actors, promoting circumpolar trade and enterprise, and b) the Committee obtained international perspectives on the priorities that should guide future circumpolar co-operation activities by visiting the United Kingdom, the Nordic countries and Russia (Graham 1997).

Arctic politics could be characterised by conflict in what may soon be seen as a post-environmental co-operation period. Although co-operative efforts between Arctic states are being encouraged across a range of common Arctic interests, such as environmental protection, sustainable development, trade, human health, and communications, and as Arctic states continually construct and define for themselves identities in a global context of political, economic, cultural and environmental flux, national interests may override broad circumpolar concerns. This will especially be the case as the future of the Arctic regions is linked to non-Arctic social, political and economic interests.

Alaska and eastern Siberia now form part of an emerging North Pacific rim that includes Japan, Korea, parts of northern China, as well as Pacific Canada and the western seaboard of the United States. Since 1988 there have been direct air links between the Russian Far East and Alaska, while during autumn 1989 a telephone link between Gambell on Alaska's St. Lawrence Island and Provideniya in Chukotka was established, providing an extensive communications network between Alaska and the entire Russian Far East (Krauss 1994: 375–76). There are numerous examples of foreign investment in this region. The Canadian-based multinational corporation Cominco has been developing zinc deposits of the Red Dog mine north of Kotzebue in northwest Alaska (Cominco formerly controlled the Danish firm Greenex A/S, which operates in Greenland). Alaska has also long experience of Japanese-owned companies operating in the state, such as the Alaska Pulp Corporation which exploited timber from the Tongass forest. Currently three British companies are investing in oil, tourism and mining in Alaska. British Petroleum is spending an extra $1 billion over the five year period from 1997 to increase production at Prudhoe Bay and to bring new fields on line, Princess Tours is investing in cruise ships, while RTZ-CRA has reopened a silver mine. The importance of this region may be highlighted by the emergence of the North American Free Trade Agreement (NAFTA) and the emergence of Pacific Asia. Both Alaska and eastern Siberia are suppliers of timber to Japan and Korea.

Greenland, although having left the EEC (now the EU) in 1985, remains inextricably linked to Denmark and may develop its connections with the European Union in the future. When Greenland left the EEC it negotiated Overseas and Countries Association status. This allows favourable access to European markets and a fishing agreement is re-negotiated every five years. Europe constitutes one of Greenland's biggest and most valuable overseas markets for fishing products. Withdrawal from membership of the European Community meant that the Greenland Home Rule Authorities lost much-needed grants from the EC's development fund. However the Home Rule authorities currently receive an annual payment of 37.7m ECUs for allowing member countries fishing rights in Greenlandic waters. And since the early

1990s Greenland has sent an observer to the EU in order to strengthen Greenlandic and European links. But Greenland is also looking to other trade partners such as Japan. The future of western Siberia may also be bound up with Europe, especially as EU interest is focusing increasingly on eastern Europe and Russia. The Arctic regions of Sweden and Finland will now also be tied to the European Union after those two countries voted to join the EU in 1994. By setting common standards in areas such as trade and environmental protection, the EU has restricted the independence of its member states.

The surrender of sovereignty by individual states to international bodies will surely have consequences for the AEPS and the Arctic Council. How far, then, will individual states be able to follow guidelines for environmental protection and sustainable development when they will be expected to toe the line with regard to the demands and expectations of other international political and economic bodies? If the Arctic Council has no firm powers of policy enforcement, then individual states may be unable to follow its recommendations in the face of economic and political pressure in a rapidly changing world. It also remains to be seen just how far indigenous concerns will continue to dominate the agenda for environmental protection and sustainable development—this will be dependent on who formulates procedural rules and maintains control over their application. As we have seen, in the case of the Arctic Council participation by indigenous peoples' organisations has already been limited.

1 The following observers were present at the inaugural meeting of the Arctic Council: the Standing Committee of Parliamentarians of the Arctic Region; the Nordic Council of Ministers; the Nordic Council Finnish Secretariat; Great Britain; Germany; Japan; Poland; the Netherlands; International Union of Circumpolar Health; International Arctic Science Committee; International Union for the Conservation of Nature; Advisory Committee on Protection of the Sea; United Nations Environment Programme; and the World Wide Fund for Nature.
2 Arctic Council (1996) 'Joint Communiqué of the Governments of the Arctic Countries on the Establishment of the Arctic Council', Ottawa, September 19, 1996.
3 'Greenland offers to take warheads' *The Independent* 23 June 1997, p.9
4 The Northern Sea Route follows the northern Russian coastline, between the Atlantic and Pacific Oceans. The Soviet Union invested heavily in a marine transportation network used by powerful ice-breakers to help the development and extraction of Siberian natural resources and to supply northern settlements. Russia now hopes the Northern Sea Route will be attractive as an international marine route because it will cut distances between European and Pacific ports (which are usually routed via the Suez and Panama canals) by anything up to 60%. Germany is eager to play a major role and is currently developing new icebreaker technology.

Chapter 4

WAYS OF KNOWING, WAYS OF ACTING:
THE CLAIM FOR INDIGENOUS ENVIRONMENTAL
KNOWLEDGE

The claim that indigenous peoples are original ecologists, wise and responsible users of natural resources, 'people who for centuries have lived in harmony with nature' (Lynge 1992: 5) is at the heart of indigenous discourse on Arctic environmental management. Faced with threats to cultural survival, indigenous peoples' organisations such as the ICC argue for greater awareness of the effectiveness of indigenous resource use systems for the conservation of natural resources. Indigenous perspectives on Arctic conservation are also used by indigenous peoples in order to construct for themselves an identity as custodians of the Arctic environment, and to challenge 'dominant ideological formulations and practices that support environmental degradation' (Breyman 1993: 127). The successful outcome of struggles for self-determination depends on indigenous peoples regaining and reasserting control over both lands and resources and establishing strategies for sustainable resource exploitation. Furthermore, growing international recognition of the limits of conventional resource management based on rational, reductionist, objective science has, over the last decade in particular, focused interest in what has been called traditional or indigenous environmental knowledge.

Through practical engagement with land and sea, indigenous peoples have extensive, detailed, intimate and complex knowledge of their environments and the resources they depend upon. In the Arctic the gathering of indigenous knowledge involves the collection of local place names which contain information about subsistence activities and about mythical and real events that have significance for individual, family and community history (e.g. Kleivan 1986, Nuttall 1992, 1993), knowledge about plants, animals and landscape, and information about climate change and local resource management systems. Once gathered, indigenous knowledge is put to use in, among other things, environmental impact assessment, participatory approaches to subsistence and environmental management, land claims, climate change studies, cultural heritage programmes and the design of appropriate education programmes for Native children.

Research suggests that the application of indigenous knowledge in Arctic development projects, environmental management and impact assessment both enhances the likelihood of success and acknowledges that indigenous peoples are environmental experts who possess and have access to empirical and qualitative information unavailable or denied to scientists (e.g. Nakashima 1990). As the previous chapters discussed, the AEPS and the Arctic Council have institutionalised indigenous environmental knowledge and constructive dialogue aims to incorporate it with scientific perspectives on resource management.

This chapter examines the claim made for indigenous environmental knowledge and looks at both anthropological accounts and indigenous perspectives on what value this knowledge has. Because of the cultural and geographical diversity of the Arctic, and as a consequence the diverse forms of knowledge in this vast region, rather than seeking to analyse the actual construction, content and nature of indigenous knowledge my aim is to explore some of the discourses on indigenous knowledge, in particular by considering how these discourses stress the contrast between concepts of a fixed body of knowledge (science), and concepts of knowing and acting in a local context, which form the basis for appropriate systems of resource management. In later chapters I provide some illustrations of indigenous knowledge in action, by showing the local potential for innovation, sustainability and empowerment through the political use of indigenous knowledge.

THE CLAIM FOR INDIGENOUS ENVIRONMENTAL KNOWLEDGE

Indigenous environmental knowledge is usually defined as knowledge unique to a given culture or society (Warren *et al.* 1995). Johnson (1992: 4) sees it as

> a body of knowledge built up by a group of peoples through generations of living in close contact with nature. It includes a system of classification, a set of empirical observations about the environment, and system of self-government that governs resource use.

As countless ethnographies show, indigenous knowledge systems are often detailed and complex, developed and enhanced through long-term experience and generational transmission, demonstrating profound understanding of local conditions, wildlife, resource availability, plants and crops, land use, climate, and human interactions with the natural environment. Indigenous environmental knowledge is primarily behaviour-oriented, drawing on precise information about where to locate resources and how to exploit them.

This wealth of knowledge, which contains both cosmological and practical information, is often encoded in song, myth, ritual, storytelling, anecdote, place names, unwritten regulations and everyday discourse. Such knowledge includes denotative statements—'know-how', 'knowing how to live', 'how to act', 'how to listen', 'how to behave'—practical, pragmatic rules that bind society together (Lyotard 1979). Indigenous environmental knowledge is holistic and integrative, it is shared, passed on to children through stories, narratives, participation and experience, and provides the foundation for economic, cultural, spiritual and ethical concerns that guide the use and management of natural resources by and for local communities.

This is knowledge, like all knowledge (including that of science), which is acquired, nurtured and shaped within particular social situations and social contexts (Berger and Luckmann 1984). In this way, indigenous knowledge systems can only make sense within local contexts of social relationships and productive activities. People acquire environmental knowledge by moving through the world, living and acting in it, breathing the air, drinking the water, hunting, harvesting, fishing rivers, lakes and the sea, tilling soil, growing crops, and so on. Furthermore people engage with others in productive activities so that local knowledge of a resource or of a particular environment is one aspect of a complexity of social, economic and ecological relationships. In Arctic hunting communities, for example, knowledge is transmitted within and between households and children are brought up within a social environment defined by hunting and sharing (Nuttall 1992). People, their knowledge and the environment exist 'within each other' (Croll and Parkin 1992: 1). Ethnographic accounts of Arctic cultures often point out that people remark that they are 'part of the land' and that land has a strong spiritual value (e.g. Freeman 1976, Brody 1981). In this sense knowledge is a relationship with the natural world, 'that is constitutive of both the knower and the known' (Hornborg 1996: 55). But this relationship is a negotiated one, and knowledge not only represents human-environment interactions, it brings them into being and reconstructs them (Bird 1987).

Indigenous knowledge is most commonly referred to in the literature on Arctic resource management as traditional environmental or ecological knowledge (TEK). Berkes (1992), however, prefers the use of 'indigenous' to 'traditional', and argues that the term 'traditional knowledge' suggests that knowledge is static, whereas 'indigenous knowledge' 'helps avoid the debate about tradition and explicitly emphasises indigenous people' (Johnson *ibid.*: 4). Chambers (1983: 82–3) sees problems with the use of both 'indigenous' and 'tradition' arguing that it implies something originates from and is naturally produced in an area. This ignores the fact that local forms of knowledge are 'added to, influenced by, and destroyed by knowledge from outside the area' (*ibid.*: 83). Instead he prefers to use 'rural people's knowledge' as an all inclusive term as this does not exclude people living in rural areas who may not be defined as indigenous. For Chambers (*ibid.*) the 'people's' part of the term emphasises that much of the knowledge is located in people and only rarely written down. 'Knowledge' refers to the whole system of knowledge, including concepts, beliefs and perceptions, the stock of knowledge, and the processes whereby it is acquired, augmented, stored, and transmitted.

Advocates of the use of indigenous environmental knowledge argue that, despite its obvious value in offering a constructive perspective on resource management, it has long been under-utilised, ignored or subverted and rendered unscientific by reductionist science (Brokensha *et al.* 1980, Cruikshank 1984, Warren *et al.* 1995). By the standards and paradigms of Western scientific rationality, the legitimacy of indigenous environmental knowledge is questioned. It is not considered to be empirically-verifiable, and because it is not seen to be acquired as the result of experiments in laboratory settings, indigenous knowledge is regarded as inaccurate or irrational, or based on superstition. Scientific knowledge on the other hand is generalisable, addressing universal phenomena, 'a type of knowledge which tends towards disinterestedness...openness, accumulation...' springing from 'constructed, operative frameworks, which are justified by the results obtained' (Gurvitch 1971: 33). Alternative, environmentally-benign systems of knowledge which can provide solutions to global environmental problems are often derided by reductionist science. Scientific epistemology does not allow for a plurality of knowledge and rejects other forms of knowledge, such as myth, ritual and folk knowledge, as 'non-knowledge', or as simply false (Foucault 1976). By not accepting the validity of statements drawn from local narratives or myth, and by questioning their legitimacy, science establishes itself as legitimate, 'true', 'genuine knowledge' (Lyotard 1979).

But there are political as well as epistemological reasons for the rejection of other forms of knowledge. Benton (1994: 37) argues that 'posing the solution to environmental problems in terms of the invention of technologies directs attention away from gross global inequalities in power and resources'. Because science and technology are products of particular cultural and political interests, a technocentric form of environmental management informed by scientific knowledge is, as Benton argues, 'a global strategy for securing and regulating the conditions for the long-term sustainability of a *particular kind* of human culture and its dominant economic and political interests' (*ibid.*).[1] Foucault (1976), by rejecting the idea that science is pursued for its own sake, links knowledge to power and argues that the very aim of science is to gain power and so assert hegemony over other forms of knowledge. Local knowledge may be rejected because it poses challenges to conventional scientific theories and could potentially undermine institutionalised knowledge. An elite professional bias has undermined indigenous knowledge because it does not conform to scientific models and accepted ways of acquiring knowledge about the world.

In this way it is claimed that scientific environmental management acts as a form of continuing imperialism, with former colonial powers determining the way that the natural resources of other countries are developed and managed. Wynne (1994: 172) accuses scientific knowledge as being the 'handmaiden to political attempts by the rich countries to impose a policy consensus on the developing countries', and as Redclift and Woodgate (1994: 64) put it

> In the North, countries have adopted their own language to describe environmental problems in the South. This language has become 'globalized', and has served the purposes of the international agencies which have taken the lead in economic development. It frequently conveys the idea that 'environmental problems', and the cost of addressing them, represent a brake on 'development' for countries in the South.

Critics claim that this language was very much in evidence at the United Nations Conference on Environment and Development (UNCED) held in Rio de Janeiro in 1992, a conference which was in the end more about economics than protecting the environment, and only served to highlight deep and pervasive differences between the rich nations of the North and the developing countries of the South. As was widely reported in the press and in post-conference critiques (e.g. Chatterjee and Finger 1994), leaders from developing countries saw UNCED as continuing the imperialist legacy of developed states in its treatment of sustainability and discussion of strategies for environmental management. Chatterjee and Finger (*ibid.*: 3) argue that UNCED reasserted an anthropocentric development paradigm underscored by the authority of rational scientific knowledge and 'boosted precisely the type of industrial development that is destructive for the environment, the planet, and its inhabitants'.

While some argue that there is a 'need for the state to step in to protect the ecosphere and maintain ecological balance' (Young 1981: 4), a Western scientific, or technocentric view of environmental management and sustainable development is narrowly defined in biological and economic terms and is said to devalue indigenous knowledge and the environmental management systems of local peoples, such as rural populations in the tropics and hunters and herders in the circumpolar north. As Shiva (1988: 233) puts it:

> to prove itself superior to alternative modes of knowledge and be the only legitimate mode of knowing reductionist science resorts to suppression and falsification of facts and thus commits violence against science itself, which ought to be a search for truth.

State control of resources can also manifest itself as conservation by coercion, a particularly insidious form of environmental management that rides roughshod over local people and their interests. The promotion of participatory approaches to development and environmental management based on the use of local knowledge is seen by some states as a way by which the rural poor can organise themselves and therefore is considered as ultimately dangerous and subversive. For example, by focusing on elephant conservation in Kenya and forestry management in Indonesia, Peluso (1993) argues that some states 'appropriate the conservation concerns of international environmental groups as a means of eliciting support for their own control over productive natural resources' (*ibid.*: 47). As she argues,

> The state's mandate to defend threatened resources and its monopolisation of legitimate violence combine to facilitate state-apparatus-building and social control. "Legitimate" violence in the name of resource control also helps states control people, especially recalcitrant regional groups, marginal groups, or minority groups who challenge the state's authority.

Yet despite the political and epistemological reasons for rejecting local perspectives, current thinking does stress the significance and value of indigenous knowledge for environmental management and sustainable development. Johnson (1992: 3) remarks that a 'growing body of literature attests not only to the presence of a vast reservoir of information regarding plant and animal behaviour but also to the existence of effective indigenous strategies for ensuring the sustainable use of local natural resources'.

The value of indigenous knowledge as a vital way of conserving biodiversity and cultural diversity has gained global recognition in recent years through IUCN's *World Conservation Strategy*, the Brundtland Commission report *Our Common Future*, and UNCED. Agenda 21, the final document from UNCED intended as a blueprint for action on sustainable development and the environment by governments, NGOs and international organisations, emphasises that indigenous knowledge systems should be incorporated into research and development programmes for biodiversity conservation and natural resource management. Several agencies responsible for sustainable development and environmental management programmes, such as the UK's Overseas Development Administration (ODA) and the United Nations Development Programme (UNDP), actively promote participatory and community-based approaches as ways of environmental protection, while at the same time recognising human rights and supporting strategies for community empowerment. How far this is actually put into practice is another matter, however.

Despite the official sanctioning of the significance and importance of indigenous environmental knowledge, there remains scepticism concerning its validity vis a vis rational scientific experimentation, data collection and analysis. And biases of an elite scientific professionalism are hard to erode meaning that indigenous knowledge is still denigrated. Scientists looking for biological truths are often sceptical when environmental problems or fluctuations in a resource are attributed to sorcery or witchcraft, for example. Too often scientists do not have an understanding of the cultural dynamics, institutions, decision-making processes and value systems of local communities. Anthropologists who romanticise indigenous communities also hinder dialogue. Epistemological issues aside, a further problem centres on the development of appropriate methodology for integrating indigenous perspectives on resource management with scientific perspectives. Questions arise as to how best local knowledge can be gathered, synthesised, systematised and empirically verified as proven knowledge.

And while Agenda 21 makes it clear that indigenous peoples are seen to have a role to play by contributing their 'knowledge' to conservation and development, the UNCED process reaffirmed a form of global sustainable development guided ultimately by scientific knowledge, envisaged by leaders of developed nations as necessary for economic growth. The ICC and the Saami Council had failed to get participating nations at UNCED to recognise the Arctic as a 'fragile ecosystem'. But not only did Agenda 21 not consider the Arctic directly, indigenous peoples (along with women and children) were not treated by the UNCED process 'as full agents to whom authority and decision-making power should be handed over' (Chatterjee and Finger *ibid.*: 53). Representing an indigenous voice, the Inuit Circumpolar Conference prepared a draft document in response to Agenda 21. Clearly disappointed with what it saw as only a token nod towards indigenous peoples, the ICC responded to Agenda 21 by claiming that

> It was a common view among indigenous peoples that they had been manipulated by the UNCED process. They were often used as a symbol of what the UNCED process sought to achieve, but in the end, their ability to control their own destiny was contested and their rights and role in the process were subsumed under the control of state governments by including them as a vulnerable group in a separate chapter of Agenda 21.
>
> (Inuit Circumpolar Conference 1993: 2)

Chatterjee and Finger's (*ibid.*: 58) critical evaluation of Agenda 21 also lends support to this view:

> the recognition of indigenous peoples is blunted by the fact that it addresses them as 'indigenous people', which legally means that they have individual rights. But the concept of 'indigenous peoples', which legally recognises their claims as sovereign nations with rights of self-determination, was struck from every page of the

document by the Brazilians and the Canadians. Both these countries face considerable pressure from their indigenous communities who want to have more say in the use —or rather the destruction—of their own lands and resources.

Such attitudes do little to remedy the neglect and marginalisation of indigenous peoples and their knowledge, nor to foster conditions for participatory approaches to development and environmental management.

While the differences between indigenous knowledge and scientific knowledge have long been stressed and may now be widely recognised, there are also differences between 'indigenous' and 'local' knowledge. As will be explored later in this book, the rhetorical use of 'indigenous' and 'traditional' by Arctic peoples both politicises the debate over resource management and relates it to issues of self-determination. 'Indigenous' and 'traditional' are used synonymously and are more culturally and politically potent terms than 'local'. The ICC's definition of indigenous knowledge as information and concepts about the environment and ecological relationships, for example, marks it out as belonging to people who are members of a cultural group inhabiting a specific locality for several generations (Brooke 1993). This definition seriously ignores the diversity of different forms of knowledge held by local, non-indigenous peoples, such as Norwegian and Icelandic whalers and fishermen, who also have detailed and complex knowledge systems that are 'traditional' in the sense of being deep-rooted in local culture. Indigenous knowledge is the politicisation of local knowledge and local knowledge can become 'indigenous' knowledge if people choose to see it as such.

Whatever the differences and arguments over appropriate terminology the claim for indigenous (or traditional, or local) knowledge is that it offers an alternative to scientific and technological approaches to environmental management. Throughout the world, indigenous communities, anthropologists and resource managers argue increasingly that central government agencies responsible for resource management and development should recognise indigenous peoples as a legitimate source of environmental knowledge (e.g. Freeman 1979, Freeman and Carbyn 1988, Nakashima 1990, Sallenave 1994). Indigenous peoples' association with a specific place, locality and environment has led them to be described as members of a 'natural resource community', which Dyer, Gill and Picou (1992: 106) define as 'a population of individuals living within a bounded area whose primary cultural existence is based on the utilisation of renewable resources'. People dependent on natural resource utilisation are said to be culturally integrated with those resources. Hunters, fishers and herders have an intimate familiarity with the environment and with the resource, possessing knowledge unavailable to biologists and environmental managers.

Local knowledge, it is claimed, can be tapped as a resource to provide the basic and essential components and strategies needed for sustainable livelihoods. Shifting cultivation is widely considered to be ecologically-sound, for example, in the way it differs from intensive commercial agriculture and allows the soil to recover its regenerative capacity.[2] Writing of the importance of local knowledge for fisheries management, Dyer and McGoodwin (1994: 2) argue that it includes strategies for regulating fishing and enhancing the productivity of fish stocks and 'differs little in practice from biologically-based modern fisheries management'. Similarly, indigenous forestry management allows for conservation and replenishment of trees. Anthropologists have shown that tribal peoples who depend on forests demonstrate both profound respect for the resources they rely on and have systems of environmental knowledge that guarantee the continuity of both culture and the natural world (e.g. van Beek and Banga 1992).

Such practices correspond to what Palsson (1996) calls the paradigm of communalism which, rejecting the separation of nature and society, emphasises contingency and dialogue and stresses reciprocity as a guiding principle in human-environment relations. For Palsson, who is careful to point out that he is not advancing a romantic view of primitive peoples living in harmony with nature, the paradigm of communalism, 'with its emphasis on practice, reciprocity and engagement...provides an avenue out of the modernist project and current environment dilemmas' (ibid.: 78). External influences and the introduction of new technology do not make bodies of local knowledge any less 'traditional' or redundant. Local knowledge systems are enhanced and continually improved and elaborated through experience and by incorporating new influences. Effective management and sustainable use of natural resources can only come about if environmental managers take note of the knowledge and management strategies of local people and encourage their participation at every stage in the formulation of management policies.

Anthropological accounts

In the Arctic, anthropological and archaeological research shows that indigenous populations have consistently developed significant flexibility in resource procurement techniques and social structure to deal with fluctuations in climate, resource availability, social and economic change, and the introduction of new technology. It is often assumed that in pre-modern Arctic cultures environmental problems were perceived as having only local consequences. For example, the needs of herders and pastoralists to find adequate annual grazing lands were met within the group, while climatic change or over exploitation affecting animal and fish populations meant that Arctic hunting bands would have been forced to move to another area in search of game, or to have adapted their range of subsistence techniques. Historical, archaeological and anthropological evidence suggests that Arctic peoples had elaborate ecological knowledge and knew how to survive and adapt to changing environmental conditions. Archaeological research in particular has attempted to shed light on the strategies of successful Arctic hunting populations in long-term environmental adaptations.

Odner (1992), for example, has argued that the Saami of northern Norway coped with the periodic scarcity of wild reindeer in the sixteenth and seventeenth centuries by diversifying their subsistence activities and intensifying the exploitation of other resources, such as fish, by moving on to exploit another area, developing techniques of animal husbandry, or by storing meat. In the eastern Canadian Arctic, Sabo (1991) has examined how, over an 800-year period from about 1100 AD, prehistoric Thule and historic Inuit groups living in the Lake Harbour/North Bay region of southern Baffin Island responded to and coped with the effects of climatic change on the population dynamics, distribution and availability of the terrestrial and marine resources they depended upon. Developing an ecosystem model and reviewing evidence for climatic change in the central Canadian Arctic over a 1000-year period, Sabo demonstrates how the rescheduling of resource procurement systems and the continuation of a flexible arrangement in Inuit settlement patterns and demographic organisation ensured both the availability and production of food and act as regulatory social mechanism that respond to environmental change. Sabo argues that, while there is paleoenvironmental evidence to suggest climatic change did affect Inuit subsistence activities on Baffin Island during this period, climatic change is only one of several factors contributing to adaptive responses. Rather than resulting in environmental determinism, the ecology and climate of southern Baffin Island enabled successive human populations to develop long-term strategies of environmental diversification. Through the use of a variety of resources and habitats the prehistoric population and historic Inuit retained a resilient human ecosystem during a long period of continuity and change.

Pre-modern Arctic peoples were perhaps also aware of the consequences of human interaction with the natural world, perceiving their environments to be environments of risk. The problem of human survival had to be met within the constraints and opportunities of the environment, which represented daily dangers. For example, poor weather, famine, illness and accidental death were common hazards. Resources were often elusive and difficult to procure, times of scarcity were a constant threat and the element of risk was ever present because human action was considered to have a major influence over natural phenomena. Daily life was precarious because failure to act correctly in relation to the natural world would result in misfortune and harm.

For the Inuit, human-environment relations were underpinned by an elaborate system of beliefs and moral codes that acted to regulate a complexity of relationships between people, animals, the environment and the spirit forces believed to be inherent in natural phenomena. The environment was indeed one of risk (compared with the modern perception of it being *at risk*), fraught with danger and uncertainty. Part of this danger was due to the fact that the Inuit relied on hunting animals that had souls that needed to be propitiated by the hunter after being killed. Lack of success in hunting, illness, misfortune, famine and bad weather were all understood to come about because this elaborate moral code had been contravened in some way, resulting in a violation of the relations between Inuit and the natural world. Offences by an individual against animals and spirits in the natural world would put the entire community at risk. The transgression of the complexity of taboos necessary for ensuring the regulation of relationships between the human and natural worlds would either cause pain to the souls of recently killed animals, or could cause vindictive and malevolent spirits to bring illness. A return to human well-being was possible through the intervention of the *angakkut* (shamans), who acted as curers of illness, affliction and misfortune (e.g. Oosten 1997).

Lending support to the archaeological record, the argument that contemporary indigenous peoples practice sustainable resource management finds support in the anthropological literature (e.g. Berkes 1992, Freeman 1979, Usher 1987). Anthropologists, however, have often regarded Arctic hunting, fishing and herding peoples as particularly fine examples of how human populations adapt to and exploit an environmental niche. As such they have been special objects of study for those anthropologists and archaeologists influenced by evolutionary ecology. The ability of human beings, especially the Inuit, to survive and adapt in the Arctic, and to remain there to this day has inspired generations of researchers, prompting Fienup-Riordan (1983: xi) to remark that 'the students of Malthus and Darwin have long been attracted to the study of the inhabitants of the Arctic'.

Studies of Arctic hunting peoples which are influenced by evolutionary ecology have focused on environmental adaptation, optimal foraging, risk and uncertainty, and cost/benefit analysis. The sharing of game, for example, is often viewed as an adaptive strategy to ensure against the over exploitation of scarce resources, while concepts of risk and uncertainty are utilised in explaining the differentiation of inter group relations and the variations inherent in social behaviour (e.g. Smith 1991). Smith prefers to see hunting and gathering as 'foraging' and is concerned with analysing the material investments and material outcomes of a foraging mode of production. For Smith, such an approach requires and entirely objective and straight-forward empirical inquiry from the anthropologist, who in this case considers the anthropological endeavour to be one of applying optimal foraging theory to the study of hunting and gathering activities. In a quantitative study of the hunting economy of the Inujjuamiut of northern Quebec, Smith takes a neo-Darwinian position in discussing contemporary foraging patterns, prey choice, co-operative foraging, patch choice and time allocation and the place of foraging within the modern cash economy (Smith 1991). Smith considers natural selection to provide an important framework for explaining and understanding ecological and behavioural variation in human societies (*ibid.*:31), and particularly for the formulation of theory to help explain variation in specific socio-economic contexts.

Recent anthropological approaches to understanding Arctic hunting societies have challenged and overturned many previous theoretical assumptions and popular stereotypes by attempting to gain insight into how Arctic peoples conceptualise their own relationships to their environments and to the animals they hunt and depend on for food. There has been a move away from viewing subsistence activities in materialistic terms to understanding social agency and cultural imagination. The emphasis on evolutionary ecology and stress on hypotheses in order to make quantitative predictions of hunter-gatherer behaviour is one that many anthropologists have rejected in favour of more humanistic approaches and a concern with understanding the construction of cultural meaning (e.g. Bodenhorn 1997, Riches 1982, Nuttall 1992, Kwon 1997). These approaches argue that the use of foraging theory for prediction and explanation leaves out the person of the hunter as a conscious agent interacting with his social and natural environment and hardly considers the subtle and complex interplay of culture, social structure, kinship, ritual and belief, exchange relationships and prestige.

The complexity of human-environment relations can only be understood by looking at how humans engage with the natural world and by examining the significance of human intention, action and purpose in economic production (e.g. Ingold 1986, Palsson 1991, Croll and Parkin 1992). Within anthropological theory generally, there is increased interest in how people's conceptualisation and understanding of human-environment relations underpin and inform everyday social life. That individuals constitute themselves as social persons through mutual involvement with others has long been a central theme in sociology and anthropology, and can be traced back at least to the writings of Marx. Added to this is the view that individuals also constitute themselves as social persons through mutual involvement with the natural world, a view which represents a radical departure from sociological accounts of the natural world as a mirror image of the social world, and differs from structuralist concern with a narrow culture-nature polarisation. Ingold (1992: 40) suggests that, rather than focusing on how humans evolve cultural systems which adapt to environmental conditions and even accepting perspectives that human environments are cultural constructs, 'an adequate ecological anthropology' must be adopted that 'proceeds from a notion of the mutualism of person and environment'. The approach taken is to focus on the distinctive ideas and understandings that people themselves have of their environments, ideas and understandings which result from continuous and mutual interaction.

Some of the most imaginative recent attempts to revise existing thinking on how hunter-gatherers relate to their environments have been explored in the writings of Bird-David (1990, 1992) and Ingold (1996). While Ingold elaborates the Lévi-Strauss axiom that animals and the environment are 'good to think with' to being 'good to relate to', Bird-David (1990) has argued that hunter-gatherers perceive the environment as a 'giving environment' and that the metaphor of sharing provides a key for understanding how they not only conceptualise both the natural and social worlds, but how this conceptualisation informs human agency and social action. Bird-David argues that hunter-gatherers are distinguished from other peoples by their particular views of the environment, and of themselves, and by a particular type of economy which she calls a 'cosmic economy of sharing'. Arctic hunting peoples are very much aware of this distinction and do much to stress it as forms of political discourse—as examples below from Telekova, Lynge, Kuptana, Kawagley and the ICC illustrate. Not only is the environment regarded as giving, the economic systems of hunter-gatherers are themselves characterised by relations of distribution and property constructed in terms of giving, instead of principles of immediate return or reciprocal expectation.

Furthermore, Bird-David argues that the relationship between hunter-gatherers and the environment is a generic one. For example, in her own work on the Nayaka of India Bird-David shows how the Nayaka regard the forest as a parent and themselves as siblings who are engaged with each other through giving and requests to be given. As Bird-David puts it

> Nayaka...are engaged in giving with people they regard as siblings, and their transactions reaffirm and reproduce the close and immediate ties between them (*ibid*. 194).

Sharing is thus a social event that demonstrates relatedness, affection and concern (Bird-David 1992: 30), and Bird-David says of hunter-gatherers generally that

> Through their close interaction with the natural environment they have come to perceive it, and act with it, as with a friend, a relative, a parent who shares resources with them (*ibid*: 31).

A great deal of anthropological work in the Arctic has demonstrated that indigenous peoples perceive their environments as inherently spiritual, believing that animals are an 'infinitely renewable resource' (Brightman 1987) 'possessing both immortal souls and awareness comparable to that of human persons' (Fienup-Riordan 1990: 172), rather than finite resources. Human-environmental relationships are commonly conceptualised in terms of gift-giving and reciprocity. The cosmology of indigenous peoples is underpinned by an elaborate system of beliefs and moral codes that act to regulate the complexity of relationships between people, animals, the environment and spirits. Fine ethnographies of such religiosity and intimacy between the human and natural worlds include Nelson's (1983) acclaimed study of Koyukon views of the forests of interior Alaska, Tanner's (1979) insightful account of Cree hunters, Bodenhorn's (1989) work among Inupiat on Alaska's North Slope, Fienup-Riordan's (1983, 1990) research amongst Yup'ik Eskimos, Ingold's work on forest and identity amongst Finnish Saami (1976), and Wenzel's (1991) discussion of the organisation of ecological relations between Inuit and animals in the eastern Canadian Arctic. And with greater opportunities to carry out long-term fieldwork in the Russian North, non-Russian anthropologists are now documenting the ecological knowledge and environmental relationships of Siberian peoples (Anderson 1995, Kwon 1993, 1997).

A sense of social relatedness, then, is a central feature of human-environmental relations as conceptualised by Arctic hunters, fishers and herders. Wenzel (1992: 43) has commented that for the Inuit Bird-David's notion of the giving environment 'translates at the societal level into an interest in each member's security', and points out that while Inuit live in a materially-poor environment, theirs is a socially-rich one. Describing this sense of social relatedness and complexity of rights and obligations to persons and the environment on Baffin Island, Wenzel (1991: 60–61) has described how

> Animals share with humans a common state of being that includes kinship and family relations, sentience and intelligence. The rights and obligations that pertain among people extend to other members of the natural world. People, seals, polar bear, birds and caribou are joined in a single community in which animals give men food and receive acknowledgement and revival.

Here then, is an identity that is founded upon and derives meaning from a culturally-embedded system of shared relations (Wenzel *ibid.*), and something which is common to Inuit culture generally (Nuttall 1992). In communities which depend on hunting, the sharing and distribution of meat is guided by an obligation to give which is central to the customary ideology of subsistence. This structures social organisation and contributes to its reproduction. Hunting encapsulates relations which are posed in ideological, natural and cultural terms. Reciprocal rights and obligations towards the environment and towards animals are underpinned by customary rules and regulations. Central to subsistence hunting in Siberia, Alaska, Canada and Greenland is the sharing and distribution of meat, which expresses and sustains social relationships, and reaffirms fundamental values towards animals and the environment. Animals are believed to give themselves up to hunters and it is incumbent on the hunter to give them in turn to other people.

In this sense, humans, animals and the environment contribute, through reciprocal exchanges, 'to the general equilibrium of the cosmos' (Descola 1994: 89). Hunters give meat to others, including those who are unable to hunt for themselves or their families, and those who lack the means, or do not have the equipment to hunt. As well as providing food necessary for survival, the sharing and distribution of meat from the hunt defines, expresses and sustains social relationships, as well as reaffirming fundamental values that guide attitudes towards animals and the environment (Nuttall 1992, Wenzel 1991). Hunters have practical knowledge of the animals they hunt, their habits, habitats, and feeding cycles. From the perspective of the hunter there is no distinction between nature and society, and an understanding of animals and the environment is fundamental to the understanding of the hunter's notion of self. There is also an implicit assumption that such indigenous perceptions of animals and nature suggest that indigenous peoples possess a conservationist ethic.

Indigenous perspectives

Emphasising these anthropological accounts, in political arenas the Arctic's indigenous peoples argue that the harvesting of renewable resources such as seals, whales and caribou is sustainable. Indigenous perspectives on the Arctic environment commonly emphasise an awareness and understanding that spiritual forces exist in nature, compared to Western science which stresses the inanimate nature of things. The indigenous representation of the environment as 'an aware world', where animals and geographical features are endowed with consciousness (Kawagley 1995), was endorsed by the United Nations Experts Seminar on Indigenous Land Rights and Claims, held in

Whitehorse, Canada in March 1996. The seminar concluded that indigenous peoples have a distinctive spiritual and material relationship with their homelands, with the air, waters, coastal sea, ice, flora, fauna and other resources that sustain cultural and economic life. From an indigenous perspective, all life—human and animal—is interdependent. Indigenous peoples are in meaningful dialogue with the environment and with the animals they depend on for survival. As one account of indigenous views of the Arctic put it, the relationships between Arctic peoples and the natural world

> are characterised by exchange, reciprocity, mutual respect and friendship. They believe that animals give themselves to human beings out of pity or desire. In exchange, people have to obey certain rules and regulations about how to treat animals properly and to show them respect.

> (IWGIA 1991: 11)

For example, the Nenet of Siberia, who depend on reindeer herding, are described by a representative of the Nenets Autonomous District as

> ...children of nature. The tundra gives them food and clothes and helps heal and raise them. The Nenet people treat animals, plants, stones and natural phenomena as creatures that are capable of understanding humans. For example, a man who meets a bear while hunting doesn't kill it at once, but first talks to it.

> (Telekova 1995: 33)

Animals, then, are not inferior beings to be exploited and killed for the benefit of humans without respect. Indigenous peoples have elaborate taboos and rituals which recognise that animals give themselves to humans as food. In turn these rituals, together with gift-giving and reciprocity, serve to maintain harmonious ecological relations.

While it is common in the literature to find writers stressing the difference between indigenous knowledge and scientific knowledge, critiques of reductionist science are explicit in indigenous discourse that underlines the value and importance of indigenous knowledge.[3] Over the last two decades Native leaders and politicians have argued forcefully that the Western understanding of the Arctic environment remains divergent from the views held by its indigenous peoples. Such indigenous discourse posits that the dualism between mind and body, and between object and subject, remains prevalent in Western thought and that this shapes non-Native ideas and attitudes towards the Arctic and its development.

This argument has come about partly because, in response to the anti-harvesting campaigns of European and North American animal-rights groups, indigenous peoples such as the Inuit have been forced to reconstitute their own world views and redefine human-environmental relationships as a philosophy which emphasises harmony, rather than conflict, between humans and the natural world. Indigenous peoples are part of the natural world, so the argument goes—it does not make sense in their eyes to see humans and nature as discrete, mutually-exclusive and potentially irreconcilable categories. The Greenlandic politician and human-rights activist Finn Lynge (1988) drove this point home rather prosaically in response to the activities of Greenpeace and other anti-sealing campaigners in the 1980s, by saying that Greenlanders are a carnivorous sub-species of homo-sapiens and should be respected as such. Indigenous environmental discourse has responded to external threats to Native culture, such as animal-rights campaigns, by reconstituting human-environmental relations, whether real or imagined, as coterminous with the ideologies of environmentalist groups.

Lynge elaborated this argument in his elegant defence of Inuit subsistence hunting and polemic against opposition from international groups such as Greenpeace (Lynge 1992). In Lynge's account, human-environmental relations, as conceptualised by Inuit, are reconstituted as a 'philosophy'. Running through his argument is the idea that the separation of human consciousness from the natural world results in the loss of the kind of subtle interplay between imagination and landscape that can only be realised through intuitive awareness. A central theme in Lynge's book is the importance of myth as an expression of the intuitive mind of the Inuit and one way through which the relationship between Inuit and the land is expressed. This theme is also found in the work of many Inuit intellectuals, artists, writers and poets. Inuit myths are used as the basis for poetry, novels and theatre to illustrate how the dialectic between human nature and landscape is not only revealed in the resonance between experience, thought and intimacy, but provides a fundamental grounding for the continuity of Inuit culture.

Indigenous peoples have reacted against the Arctic being labelled a 'frontier' or 'wilderness' and have called instead for recognition of Arctic lands as indigenous *homelands*. Indigenous perspectives on Arctic conservation have been put forward by organisations such as the ICC and Indigenous Survival International (ISI) at international conferences and working groups on environmental management and protection. Whatever their form and specific themes, the texts and documents produced by indigenous organisations almost always emphasise the importance of indigenous participation in Arctic policy making, the value of traditional environmental knowledge, and the importance of promoting sustainable development.

As will be discussed further in Chapter 7, one consequence of the politicisation of indigenous culture has been the emergence of an indigenous environmentalism that appeals to and emphasises enduring spiritual values.

Anthropological texts on human-environment relations in the Arctic, which draw on fieldwork mainly with hunters and their families, are increasingly mirrored (some would say are being replaced by) indigenous political discourse. Rosemary Kuptana, a spokesperson for Inuit Tapirisat of Canada (an organisation representing Canada's 35,000 Inuit) has said that traditional subsistence practices are 'based upon a dynamic and interdependent relationship between humans and other living beings that must be continually renewed and sustained' (Kuptana 1995: 39),

> This relationship is better understood by explaining Inuit views on seal hunting. The seal willingly gives itself to the hunter who shows the proper respect for the natural world and its living beings. By following certain harvesting rituals and sharing with kinship and community, the hunter demonstrates proper respect....the soul and spirit of the seal is allowed to return to the sea and be reborn. The relationship between human beings and animals, therefore, sustains and renews both human and animal populations.

> (Kuptana *ibid:* 39–40)

And a recent ICC report on circumpolar sustainable development claims that

> Inuit have a special relationship to the land, water, and wildlife in their homelands. Out of this special relationship comes a unique philosophical perspective, based on a deep understanding not only of each individual environmental component, but also of ecological interrelationships and the role of humans within the natural world. From an Inuit perspective, sustainability is not simply conservation and protection, with conventional regulations, standards and management plans. Rather it means using resources in a sustainable, balanced way to meet human needs. *Inuit have practised this for centuries, using their intimate knowledge of environmental systems and inherent conservation values and practices to protect their resources from overexploitation.*

> (ICC 1994: 2, my emphasis)

If from this reading outsiders fail to get the message, the ICC document goes on to explain how 'cultures based on harvesting living resources in the Arctic have shown themselves to be sustainable over thousands of years. *No non-renewable-resource-based culture is able to make the same claim*' (ICC *ibid.*, my emphasis). The ICC places indigenous perspectives on subsistence at the very centre of debates on sustainability, self-determination and resource management. Claims are made that 'subsistence emphasises an ethic of sharing and mutual support, community cohesion, and a commitment to stewardship of the land and its resources, based on a perspective of many generations, both past and present' (IWGIA 1991: 42). By emphasising indigenous resource ethics, the ICC constructs an identity for Inuit generally as stewards and defenders of the Arctic, prudent users who have 'developed management systems to assure sustainable yields of renewable resources from their environment' (IWGIA *ibid.* 43).

The claim advanced for indigenous knowledge by indigenous peoples is that, despite its traditional and culturally-specific nature, it can be used to inform local, regional and global discourses on environmental protection and sustainable development. Advocates of indigenous knowledge also advance claims for recognition of its scientific nature. There is a certain amount of ambivalence in this claim. On the one hand, advocates of indigenous knowledge criticise science as a field of inquiry that separates nature and society and for underpinning forms of development and systems of environmental management that impact upon and fail local communities. On the other hand, there are increasing references to indigenous knowledge as 'indigenous science'. This reassertion of tradition, values and knowledge as 'science' is, however, part of the process by which indigenous peoples construct a rhetorical vocabulary to challenge the Western scientific perspectives they see as influencing their lives and placing an imposition on their rights to self-determination.

The construction and assertion of an indigenous scientific tradition is used to influence decision-making processes and promote strategies for community-empowerment. This is illustrated by current initiatives to reconfigure the place of education in the circumpolar north as a means for perpetuating indigenous cultures. Under conditions of colonialism and policies of assimilation schools became institutions for the effective transmission of cultural values that were foreign to, came into conflict with, and suppressed both traditional knowledge and indigenous languages (Christianity and socialist ideology also replaced and subverted indigenous world views and religious beliefs). For example, during the first half of this century Canadian Inuit children were sent to mission schools where they were forbidden to speak Inuktitut (the Inuit language), and were often subjected to corporal punishment and sexual abuse by priests and teachers (Creery 1994: 131). In the Russian North many children from indigenous nomadic tribes were sent to boarding schools because of a policy of Russification. They were expected to go through the same education system as Russian children from urban areas, and 'to assimilate a totally new view of the world and their place in it' (Slezkine 1994: 241). Vakhtin (1994: 61) describes how

> children became fully state-dependent in many places and deprived of a family upbringing. They also lost their mother tongues. At the ages of 15 or 17 they returned to their families as complete strangers, with no knowledge of traditional culture or of home life. Parents also suffered since, in many cases, they lost all their feeling of responsibility towards their children and delegated it to the state.

Until the mid-1970s, the education system in rural Alaska's Native communities was also assimilationist in aim. Native children were to be educated as U.S. citizens and many had to leave villages for a high school education. In 1975 a revision in the administration of education established regional school districts and village high schools, and while this went some way to empowering communities with regard to education, the education curriculum remained the same. Native schoolchildren have learned the same subjects as children elsewhere in the United States. While schools are effectively under local control they remain institutions that are not really part of the social and cultural fabric of Native communities. It is only in Greenland and northern Quebec where the indigenous population has achieved a degree of autonomy over the education system in terms of being able to develop school curricula and to have their own languages as the medium of instruction. As such they provide a model for other Native groups who wish to assert control over education.

The work of Angayuqaq Oscar Kawagley, a Yupiaq writer and educationalist from southwest Alaska has been highly influential in recent years as attempts are made to strengthen cultural identity through education. Kawagley argues that his work also has universal applicability in that we need to use the elemental spirit, values and cultural perspectives of indigenous peoples such as the Yupiaq to create a new way of knowing and acting in the world that will achieve the balance and harmony necessary for a sustainable way of life. Kawagley's book *A Yupiaq World View: a pathway in ecology and spirit* has been used to inspire a new education curriculum in rural Alaska that attempts to incorporate indigenous science.

In rural Alaska, despite the creation of regional school districts and the greater political control that rural communities now exercise over the education system, schools still remain alien institutions in Native villages and people have no influence over the kind of curriculum their children are taught. Academic achievement among children from Alaskan villages is low, perhaps explained in part by the conflict 'between the objectives of education for community use and education for success in Western culture' (Korsmo 1994: 101–102). The Alaska Native/Rural Education Consortium has implemented a five-year programme which aims to document indigenous knowledge systems in Alaska. One intended outcome is to develop educational practices which integrate indigenous knowledge into the educational curriculum in Native schools. Kawagley has attempted to identify what he sees as core values and principles of human-environmental relations that are essential to the well-being and cultural integrity of Native peoples, determining how to make them a vital part of a newly constructed school curriculum that would revive and reorient indigenous peoples to a 'more harmonious and sustainable life' in a context of rapid social change (Kawagley 1995).

For Kawagley, the education system, with its imposition of foreign values and ways of learning, dehumanises Native people, takes no account of Native forms of consciousness and is in its way a form of 'cognitive imperialism'. Greater indigenous control over schools and the education system is the goal of many Native communities. Elders, community leaders and schoolteachers are concerned that indigenous knowledge is being lost amongst younger members of indigenous communities. An imported education system, which does not suit the needs of Arctic living, prevents children from participating in customary subsistence pursuits. One way of reshaping education so that it is best suited to Arctic residents is to incorporate indigenous knowledge into the school curriculum. The challenge for Yupiaq and other indigenous peoples is to take control of the education system that suppresses them and reconstruct it in terms of indigenous ways of knowing, language and culture. But recognising the near impossibility of rejecting modern values and institutions, a blending of the traditional and the modern is necessary (Kawagley *ibid.*).

Significantly, Kawagley explores Yupiaq knowledge systems and illustrates how Native peoples practice their own form of 'science'. When Yupiaq are involved in subsistence practices, such as fishing or hunting seals, they are 'doing science'. Unlike Western science, however, Kawagley argues that Yupiaq science is not compartmentalised knowledge. Rather, it is a way of learning about, acting in and adapting to the environment. Knowledge of natural 'laws' is acquired through direct experience of living in and moving through the natural environment, not in a laboratory situation removed from nature. At the same time, Kawagley suggests that Yupiaq knowledge is constantly being tested within the context of daily survival. In a sense, what one needs to know to survive is not based on some predetermined system of ideas and fixed body of measurable knowledge. Competency is about knowing and acting in a local context where one is required to put knowledge into practice (Nuttall 1998). People learn through direct participation with the environment. But Kawagley argues that through this participation they construct precise bodies of knowledge which are general and specific. In this way, Native people have their own forms of meteorology, and knowledge about climate, chemistry, physics and earth science, as well as spiritual knowledge.

Sustaining core values and principles of human-environmental relations is the Yupiaq conception of *Ellam Yua*, or Creative Force. For the Yupiaq, argues Kawagley, nature is their metaphysic. It is only through first learning the Yupiaq way that Yupiaq children can hope to succeed in learning the vocabulary and concepts of an alien education system, and also learn how to be full constituent human beings living in and with the natural world. Kawagley attempts to identify what he sees as critical elements of the values and principles that guide Yupiaq relations with nature. In doing so his aim is to see how these values and principles will allow Yupiaq to reconstruct a view of human-environment relations that will empower them. Kawagley's project is to restore a sense of place and sense of sacredness in the lives of Yupiaq people—what he calls a 'gift of the spirit'. Yupiaq ways of knowing, he argues can teach us all about how to live comfortably and sustainably with nature.

To achieve this, Kawagley advocates the use of the community and the environment as sources of teaching and learning. In this way, elders would visit classrooms to talk about the skills needed to live on the land, and children would go to summer fishing camps, what Kawagley calls a 'fish-camp science odyssey curriculum', or take part in environmental development projects which would teach children how to be 'ecologically aware'. At fish camps, which would be periods of introspection as well as formal learning, students would be told stories of creation (both Yupiaq and Biblical). Fish camps and environmental development projects would also be times for considering scientific methods as a way of exploring the world.

An imposed education system has not only had a negative impact in rural Alaska, it has been one of the most effective means of altering the cultures and lifestyles of indigenous peoples elsewhere in the circumpolar north and both schools (often seen as 'foreign institutions') and the education system have long been resented. Because of rapid social change, in many Arctic communities it is getting harder to teach customary activities within kinship groups and within families. Indigenous knowledge is applied increasingly to the development of culturally-appropriate educational curricula in other areas such as Canada and Greenland. Until relatively recently attempts have not met with much success. For example, in Canada, the policy of assimilation began to change in 1967 when the government of the Northwest Territories was established. A 'cultural inclusion' programme was set up in some schools in Inuit communities, where

> the older Inuit would come into the schools regularly to teach the boys how to build *qamutit* (wooden sleds), and the girls how to sew *kamit* (sealskin boots). This programme had only limited success, because it was not associated with a systematic attempt to rework the approach to education.
>
> (Creery 1994: 132)

Despite such early difficulties incorporating indigenous perspectives into schools is becoming widespread throughout the Arctic—the persistence of Native parents and community organisations in their demands for change in schools has largely paid off. For example, in Canada's Northwest Territories, Dene schoolchildren are using indigenous knowledge databases and taped interviews with elders to sharpen their language skills and learn about traditional medical knowledge. In this way they are able

> to hear colourful tales of traditional life sprinkled among the descriptions of rat root tea or cloudberry poultice. The interviews and database include elders' discussion on spiritual healing, healthy lifestyles and traditional surgical procedures, including tracheotomies.

> (Latta 1994: 13)

Native languages are also being revitalised in some areas through innovative education programmes and Native children are now receiving instruction through their Native languages. Attempts are made for education to be broad-based. Elders are invited into classrooms to talk to schoolchildren about life on the land in the past and to share stories or teach handicrafts, art, kayak-building, or how to make skin clothing. It is now being demonstrated that innovative education systems based on culturally-appropriate criteria and suitable for the needs of Native people can be developed. One example from the Canadian Arctic is Piniaqtavut, an integrated education programme set up by the Baffin Island Divisional Board of Education. Piniaqtavut aims to offer Inuit children an education which reflects the cultural and linguistic strength of the Inuit heritage on Baffin Island. Children learn about Inuit history and traditional culture, while at the same time developing skills necessary for survival in contemporary Canadian society. Inuktitut is used as the language of instruction, although Inuit children are to become bilingual in both Inuktitut and English. The system meets the needs of Inuit living in the circumpolar north who want to become more informed of the issues of the contemporary Arctic. Piniaqtavut is not a curriculum, but a programme that aims to provide the basis for future education in Nunavut.

Indigenous and scientific perspectives on the workings of the environment and the complexities of ecological relationships are not necessarily mutually exclusive and therefore irreconcilable. In his classic text *The Social Frameworks of Knowledge*, Gurvitch (1971) argued that the cultural evaluation and hierarchical importance of different types of knowledge (such as political, technical, and common-sense knowledge) vary from one social context to the other. So technical and political knowledge may be valued more highly in some societies, and while types and forms of knowledge may be opposed to one another, they also often overlap. Thus in some societies technical knowledge may also be esoteric and mystical. In the Arctic, as the example of education shows, attempts are being made to integrate the indigenous metaphorisation of human-environment relations with Western scientific tradition. Indigenous world views are important as a basis for a conceptual framework in schools, especially as a way of relating Western science to indigenous knowledge of the environment.

Although, from an indigenous perspective, science may be viewed as a way of compartmentalising the environment, asserting control over it, and suppressing local ways of knowing, indigenous peoples are not rejecting it. The survival of indigenous cultures relies to some extent on indigenous knowledge systems being able to incorporate scientific perspectives, rather than resisting them. Similarly, the success of science as an effective method of dealing with environmental problems may well depend on its practitioners developing 'new sympathy for and interaction with the insights and perspectives of other, less formalised bodies of knowledge' (Grove-White *et al.* 1992: 247). Scientific data can be augmented and enriched by local knowledge of resources. As will be explored in the next chapter, the success of indigenous knowledge for renewable resource management can depend on this successful integration with Western scientific knowledge.

1   Benton traces the contemporary view of technocentric environmental management, in part, to the Club of Rome's report *The Limits of Growth* (1972): 'the model developed by the *Limits* team was a specific *use* of scientific method and their proposals for a steady-state economy, in which growth in production would be contained with limits set by environmentally-improved technologies opened the way for a "managerialist approach to the environment"' (Benton 1994: 33).

2   Agribusiness is often cited as a good example of a capitalist economic enterprise that not only utilises science and the latest technology to increase production and profits, but as a consequence has an adverse effect on the environment. Much of the world's agricultural production is controlled by concessionary companies that were originally established by colonising powers to have a monopoly on production. These concessionary companies have since developed into large and powerful agribusiness firms which control and dominate the global production and export of agricultural foodstuffs. The intensive production of food has been criticised as not only having an impact on the environment in terms of land degradation and loss of biodiversity, but having deleterious effects on human health.

3   It is an understatement, at the very least, to say that science, technology and industrialism are not without their critics. As Alvares (1988: 70) has argued, while modern science offers the opportunity and promise of technological achievement and improvement in the quality of life of human beings it is not a benign force, but rather more alarmingly brings tragedy and destruction, as 'violence is intrinsic to science' (illustrated by the disproportionate amount of scientific activity devoted to defence and military technology), as well as resulting in pollution and environmental damage. Shiva (1988: 23) elaborates on the link between modern science and violence, but is careful to point out that conventional models of science., technology, culture and society 'locate sources of violence in politics and ethics, that is, in the application of science and technology, not in scientific knowledge itself'. Shiva's critique of reductionist science is levelled at its applied nature and association with profit-

based economic systems. Thus, desertification, deforestation, climate change and health problems are taken to be the effects of modern science and technology in action.

4   Such an approach is due in part to a tradition in anthropological thought and practice that tended to regard hunters and gatherers as isolated remnants of the stone age. In this way, peoples such as the İnuit, Australian Aboriginal and the San peoples of southern Africa were held to be a living record of human history.

Chapter 5

HUNTING AND THE RIGHT TO DEVELOPMENT:
THE CASE OF ABORIGINAL SUBSISTENCE WHALING

The remote communities of the circumpolar north face challenges in finding forms of sustainability that are possible within local and regional diversified economies. By emphasising the importance of indigenous knowledge attempts are made to establish small-scale locally-based economies as a way of escaping cycles of boom and bust, to overcome constraints to self-determination and seize opportunities for local empowerment. Both this and the following chapter provide examples from Greenland and Alaska that contribute to discussion about the enhancement of political, economic and cultural sustainability in the circumpolar north through expansion of informal economic activities. This chapter examines aspects of the aboriginal subsistence whaling issue as an example of co-management and how the development of renewable resources is seen as a way of constituting a sustainable economic base, while Chapter 6 focuses on the involvement of indigenous peoples in tourism.

The hunting of seals, whales and other sea mammals provides the mainstay for many Inuit coastal communities in Greenland, Canada, Alaska and Chukotka. Sea mammals are not only a vital source of meat necessary for satisfying dietary, nutritional and economic needs. Like all other forms of subsistence activity vital to the production and reproduction of Inuit culture, sea mammal hunting also has powerful ideological and symbolic value (Nuttall 1992, Wenzel 1991). And as Caulfield (1997) and (Dahl 1990) have observed of whaling in Greenland, its significance lies in the contribution it makes for the continuity and cultural viability of local communities. But for all its obvious cultural importance as a subsistence activity, indigenous peoples are looking to the hunting of marine mammals as a way to enhance opportunities for economic development. It is this which has placed aboriginal subsistence whaling at the very centre of debate over appropriate approaches to conservation and renewable resource harvesting in the Arctic. On the one hand, indigenous peoples claim the right both to continue whaling and to develop domestic and international markets for whale products. On the other hand, environmentalists and animal-rights groups express concern over depleting whale stocks and abhorrence at the commercial nature of whaling.

In recent decades, owing to intensive commercial whaling by non-Native peoples, many Arctic whale species have become seriously endangered or threatened. Whaling has become one of the most potent symbols for conservationists of the negative aspects of the human exploitation of the natural world. But just as commercial whaling has declined as an economic activity, so Inuit subsistence whaling has attracted more attention over the last few years from the International Whaling Commission (IWC) and environmental organisations concerned with whale conservation. As a consequence, aboriginal subsistence whaling faces increased regulation, while the very meanings of aboriginality and subsistence are undergoing critical re-evaluation and rethinking.

By way of response Inuit themselves have acted to counter the extent of management by the IWC and currently exercise a degree of control over the regulation and management of subsistence whaling. Inuit have formed their own organisations concerned specifically with the importance of subsistence activities for the survival of Inuit culture, or co-operate with other whaling communities in marginal areas to produce community-based strategies for whale management. These organisations, namely the Alaska Eskimo Whaling Commission (AEWC), the Greenland Association of Fishermen and Hunters (KNAPK), the Inuit Circumpolar Conference (ICC), and the North Atlantic Marine Mammal Commission (NAMMCO) work to ensure that subsistence whaling in the Arctic is monitored and controlled by and for the communities that depend on it, thereby safeguarding its future. This work has set a precedent for the management of marine resources by and for indigenous peoples elsewhere, for example Inuit in Chukotka, and demonstrates how indigenous knowledge may be used to feed into political action. Whales and whaling have assumed symbolic potency as indigenous peoples claim the right to hunt marine mammals in a sustainable way.

After outlining the main issues, I examine subsistence whaling in Greenland as a specific case study. Because of the complexity of cultural and political meanings associated with marine mammal hunting in Greenland, and because the country is undergoing tremendous political, cultural and economic transformation, local and national understandings of resource use, and of traditional and culture are diverse and often contested. In turn these changes influence how whale management bodies, conservationists and environmental organisations perceive and interpret the contemporary nature of subsistence hunting.

PARTICIPATION AND CO-MANAGEMENT

Since Brokensha *et al*'s (1980) seminal volume on indigenous knowledge, a steadily expanding literature on the sociology and anthropology of development argues and stresses the need for the increased participation of local people and the incorporation of their knowledge in the defining, working out and implementation of resource management programmes that affect their communities and their ways of life (for examples of recent work see Agrawal 1995, Chokor 1994, Dewalt 1994, Osunade 1994a, 1994b, Warren *et al.*, 1995). Rejecting a simplistic distinction between human settlement and the natural environment, and critical of the dominance of scientific management, supporters of participatory approaches tackle questions of how human knowledge of the environment is actually constructed, and demonstrate how it used as a foundation upon which decisions relating to the effective local management of natural resources are made.

In many parts of the Arctic, Africa and India, for example, it has been demonstrated by anthropologists and development economists that environmental and development projects are more likely to succeed if a participatory approach is adopted, and indeed when a degree of decision-making power is given to local communities (e.g. Drijver 1992, Freeman and Carbyn 1988). Anthropologists have shown how local communities have their own pest-control methods or forest regeneration strategies, their own effective systems of soil classification and fertility management, or have pointed out that religion and ritual is important for conserving the environment. Explicit in much of the literature is the suggestion that local economic practices are environmentally benign. As Wolfe (n.d.: 12) has observed of seal and sea lion hunting in Alaska,

> we find that only a small number of potential hunters actually hunted seals and sea lions; that harvest levels were intentionally limited, substantially below production potentials; that many hunters chose not to hunt sea lion at all; that many hunters intentionally selected for adult seals and adolescent sea lions and chose to protect pups and pregnant females; and that hunter-seal interactions resulted in the selection of males over females. All these practices may have good conservation effects.

Furthermore, as Wolfe (1989: 18) has also argued,

> Most subsistence communities have customary rules for treating the land and the ecosystem. These rules have been passed on through the generations: "Do not waste," "Take only what is needed," "Treat the animals with respect," "Do not damage the land without cause", among others. It is believed that if the rules are followed, then the land will continue to provide. Subsistence peoples are the original conservationists, although they may not use the word, because their very lives depend on it.

The claim then, and as was discussed in Chapter 4, is that indigenous peoples have first-hand knowledge of ecological relationships and are good managers of common-property resources. Ideally, when a participatory approach is adopted, officials of environmental and development agencies act as catalysts, intermediaries and advisers (Drijver *ibid.* 133), aiming to let local people define and work out projects, plans and sustainable management schemes that would best meet their own needs and incorporate local systems of management. The incorporation of indigenous knowledge into resource management regimes allows managers to gain more insight into patterns of change in local production systems, whether those changes are the result of climatic factors, technological innovations, or fluctuations in the population dynamics and ecosystem interactions of the resource.

In many cases the inclusion of indigenous communities in Arctic resource management has met with a remarkable degree of success, despite the difficulties of incorporating indigenous knowledge into co-management systems (see Chapter 7). For example, co-operative wildlife management schemes have been effective for several years in Canada and Alaska (e.g. Berkes 1982, Freeman 1989), ensuring the continuity of local subsistence activities. Usher (1995: 197) defines co-management as

> institutional arrangements whereby governments and aboriginal entities (and sometimes other parties) enter into formal agreements specifying their respective rights, powers and obligations with respect to the management and allocation of resources in a particular area. Comanagement is a form of power sharing, although the relative balance and the means of implementation vary from case to case.

The argument put forward for the co-management of wildlife is that by integrating indigenous knowledge and Western scientific knowledge, the resulting resource management system is better informed and suited to the resource, the people who rely on it, and to the needs of scientists and conservationists (e.g. Berkes *et al.* 1991). Much of this has been based on principles of power-sharing, with the creation of wildlife commissions and boards made up of representatives from indigenous communities and state, federal and provincial agencies. Success stories include the co-management of caribou herds in Canada's Northwest Territories, waterfowl management schemes in southwest Alaska, and indigenous whaling in northern Alaska and Greenland. Co-management programmes have also transcended national boundaries, such as a polar bear management agreement between the United States and Russia which involves both governments as well as indigenous associations in Alaska and Chukotka.

Despite the success of some participatory approaches to the management of subsistence hunting in the Arctic, community-based approaches to environmental management and the use of indigenous knowledge are not without their problems. As Usher (1995) points out, co-management arrangements are more likely to succeed and further the local community interest if they are central features of comprehensive land claims agreements, rather than ad hoc, or temporary co-management arrangements. Co-management does not necessarily mean that local user groups are involved in the planning process from the beginning and wildlife management is still often considered to be the primary responsibility of the state, with regimes and systems defined and implemented according to scientific advice.

Any form of co-management, however, will only work if there is a shared understanding in a community of what management is and if efforts are made to include gender and generational aspects of indigenous knowledge (see Chapter 7). Whatever the institutional arrangement, conservation and management remain concepts and approaches defined and shrouded in technical and scientific language, which are often difficult to translate to an aboriginal context. Similarly, it is also often a problem to translate aboriginal concepts so that they make sense in terms of a Western scientific paradigm. Co-management is, as Usher (*ibid.*: 205) points out a compromise, 'much less than self-determination or self-regulation, which is what many aboriginal harvesters actually want'. For indigenous peoples the success of co-management regimes will be measured in terms of how far they not only conserve the resource and at the same time allow continued harvesting, but how far they will allow expansion and development of the mixed economies of Arctic communities, as will be explored in the rest of this chapter.

INTERNATIONAL REGULATION OF WHALING

World-wide, during the nineteenth and early twentieth centuries, intensification of commercial whaling by nations such as Great Britain, Holland, the United States, and Norway, together with developments in whaling technology, resulted in the depletion of whale stocks. This over exploitation occurred at a time when whale oil was required for a variety of industrial purposes. Traditionally, commercial whaling was unregulated and no quotas were imposed on the numbers of whales to be taken. The method involved exhausting the whaling grounds and then moving on to new areas. While the Atlantic Gray is believed to have become the only species of whale to have become extinct because of this kind of intensive exploitation (Freeman 1990), the management of commercial whaling became a necessity, in order to protect both whales and the industry.

The International Whaling Commission (IWC) was set up in 1946, at a time of expansion in the whaling industry, as a regulatory body to ensure against the mismanagement of whaling and the depletion of whale stocks.

Its remit was to serve the interests of commercial whaling and ensure its continuity by managing the resource. However, in the 1970s and 1980s increased international opposition from environmentalists and non-whaling nations towards whaling politicised the issue of whale management and led to the IWC imposing a moratorium on commercial whaling from 1986. At its annual meeting in 1993 in Kyoto, Japan, the IWC decided to extend the moratorium for a further year, although Norway defied the ban and claimed the right to resume hunting for minke whales and to set its own national catch limits for its coastal whaling operations. This again precipitated opposition from environmental organisations and from animal-rights and animal welfare groups who argue that killing whales is immoral and offensive and a threat to the natural world.

So far, the moratorium on commercial whaling has not been lifted at subsequent IWC meetings and small-type coastal whaling has come to dominate much of the organisation's deliberations. At the annual meeting in Aberdeen in 1996, the IWC agreed to hold a workshop to consider the importance in commercial and socio-economic terms of community-based whaling in Japan's four coastal whaling communities, an issue that looks likely to remain unresolved for some time. Significantly, the IWC delegates could not reach a consensus on a proposal submitted by the Makah Indian Tribe of the northwestern United States to allow them to hunt five gray whales, nor on a request by indigenous peoples from Chukotka to take five bowhead whales. Russia withdrew its request for a quota of five bowheads when it became clear that it would not achieve a clear majority and later announced that, regardless of IWC recommendations, it would allow indigenous communities in Chukotka to catch two bowhead whales.

At the 1997 meeting in Monaco the IWC allowed the Makah to kill four whales during the 1998 whaling season, a decision that was not without some controversy. The Makah had not hunted whales for over seventy years and argued for a resumption of whaling on cultural grounds. Tribal leaders had argued that hunting whales once more would help Makah communities reclaim part of their heritage, rediscover aspects of cultural identity and strengthen tribal ties in order to offset social problems caused by alcoholism, unemployment, violence and crime. Opposition to the Makah resuming whaling came from conservationists who claim that the Makah do not, unlike Inuit communities, need to hunt whales to provide for subsistence needs and fear that the meat will be sold to Japanese restaurants. Critics also say that the decision breaks the IWC provisions for aboriginal subsistence whaling and has set a precedent for Canadian tribes from the Pacific coast who also wish to resume whaling and will now seek a similar 'cultural quota'.

Whatever the moral and ethical arguments over species survival and environmental damage, many coastal communities in the Arctic depend on whaling and hunting of other marine mammals for subsistence. Indeed, for the Inuit, subsistence hunting of marine mammals such as seals and whales provides the only, or sole means of survival in some areas. Recognising this, the IWC has, since its foundation, authorised aboriginal subsistence whaling and has so far exempted it from any moratorium (with one exception, as will be discussed below). The IWC (IWC 1981: 83) defines aboriginal subsistence whaling as

> whaling for the purposes of local aboriginal consumption carried out by or on behalf of aboriginal, indigenous or native peoples who share strong community, familial, social and cultural ties related to a continuing traditional dependence on whaling and the use of whales.
>
> Local aboriginal consumption means the traditional uses of whale products by local aboriginal, indigenous or native communities in meeting their nutritional, subsistence and cultural requirements. The term includes trade in items which are by-products of subsistence catches....Subsistence catches are catches of whales by aboriginal subsistence whaling operations.

When coming up with this definition, the IWC Ad Hoc Technical Committee Working Group on the development of management principles for aboriginal subsistence whaling was divided over the application of separate management guidelines that would apply to aboriginal subsistence whaling and commercial whaling. Because both types of whaling involve the same kind of interaction between humans and whales, and as it could be argued that commercial whaling is deep-rooted in the history of whaling nations just as subsistence whaling is embedded within the cultural life of indigenous peoples, some members of the Committee argued that the same principles and management objectives should apply to both forms (IWC 1981). Other Committee members argued that there was a qualitative as well as quantitative difference between the two types of whaling. Put simply, commercial whaling is intensive, large-scale, and potentially unsustainable if mismanaged. Commercial whaling also aims to maximise profits. Subsistence whaling, on the other hand, is considered to be small-scale, sustainable and aimed at satisfying local needs. Furthermore, there is no profit incentive that drives subsistence whaling—it is inextricably linked to and underpins the culture and economy of aboriginal peoples.

The IWC definition of subsistence fails to take account of the complex interplay between informal and formal economic activities. A more encompassing definition of subsistence would be Ellen's view that it is 'all the uses to which a species may be put' (1982: 175), while a mode of subsistence would be, again following Ellen (1988: 133), 'the aggregate of extractive processes characterising a particular population'. In this sense, subsistence is a way of life bound up with the harvesting of renewable resources. Subsistence encapsulates an intricate web of human-environmental relations, irrespective of what kinds of technology are used, or whether the food that is produced is consumed by the hunters and his household directly, or whether it is shared, traded or sold beyond the local community.

However, while acknowledging the importance of whaling for Inuit, the IWC has not allowed it to continue unregulated. In particular, the IWC has been concerned in recent years with the exploitation of the humpback whale by Greenlanders, the Beaufort Sea bowhead whale by Alaskan Inupiat and Yup'ik Eskimos, and the Eastern Pacific gray whale hunted by Siberian Inuit. Since 1985 the IWC has not allocated any quota for humpback whaling in Greenland, but the hunting of both fin and minke whales by Greenlanders is subject to a quota system. Canada withdrew from the IWC in 1982 and bowhead whaling was resumed by Inuvialuit in the western Canadian Arctic in 1991 (Freeman *et al.* 1992). Inuvialuit hunters landed a male bowhead whale off the eastern Beaufort Sea, and the meat was distributed to all six Inuvialuit communities within the region. The hunting of beluga whales and narwhals, which takes place mainly in Greenland and the Canadian East Arctic, is not currently regulated, but a real possibility exists that a quota system may be imposed in the future, despite doubts cast on the IWC that it has the expertise to manage hunting of small cetaceans. Problems may also arise because Canada is not a member of the IWC. The West Greenland wintering population of beluga has declined by 30 percent over the last decade, with Baffin Bay stocks declining by 60 percent over the same period (Mikkelsen 1996). The threat of the imposition of quotas for belugas and narwhals rests on a 'rational' science-based management approach that does not consider the hunting of whales by Inuit to be self-regulatory. Regardless of any possible IWC interest in beluga hunting, the Greenland Home Rule authorities intend to impose quotas for belugas on the recommendation of a Joint Greenland-Canada Commission on Beluga and Narwhal report, reducing the numbers taken from about 769 a year to 250 a year. It has been suggested that IWC interest in aboriginal subsistence whaling has increased precisely because the IWC's role in regulating commercial whaling has diminished since the moratorium was imposed in 1986 (Faegteborg 1990: 124–125). Faced with the demise of commercial whaling, or with the refusal of whaling nations such as Iceland and Norway to comply with its recommendations and management procedures, the IWC is casting around for a new role as a regulatory body.

The IWC affected Inuit subsistence whaling directly in 1977, when it removed the hunting of the bowhead whale by Alaskan Eskimos from its exemption for aboriginal whaling and imposed a moratorium. This resulted from IWC concern over scientific evidence which suggested declining numbers of bowhead whales in the Beaufort Sea, together with pressure from North American and European conservationist organisations. The response of the nine Inupiat and Yup'ik Eskimo villages dependent on the bowhead was swift, and led to the formation of an indigenous organisation, the Alaska Eskimo Whaling Commission (AEWC), to fight to have the moratorium lifted. Essentially, the AEWC disagreed with the IWC estimate of less than one thousand bowheads and, determined that whaling should continue, undertook its own biological studies and census projects.

Based on these studies, and combining indigenous knowledge of whales and whaling, the AEWC argued that the Beaufort Sea bowhead population probably numbered over ten thousand, and that continued hunting could not possibly harm stocks (Chance 1990: 177). Immediately, the AEWC drew up its own management plan, in collaboration with the U.S. National Oceanic and Atmospheric Administration (NOAA), and in 1978 the IWC agreed to lift the moratorium and allowed the Alaskan whaling communities a kill of twelve whales annually, or a strike of eighteen whales. While annual quotas are still set by the IWC, the AEWC are responsible for observing and actually managing the quota, and for providing the NOAA with information on each whaling venture collected from the whaling captains. The result has been regarded as a successful co-management programme because, here at least, indigenous environmental knowledge and traditional resource management has been taken seriously by advocates of rational science-based systems (Freeman 1989a). By integrating indigenous knowledge and western science the resulting resource management system for Alaskan bowhead whaling is better informed and better suited to the protection of the whale stocks, the needs of Alaska's Eskimos and to the needs of scientists and conservationists.

The success of the Alaska Eskimo Whaling Commission and its politically advanced view of indigenous knowledge has an additional twist. Alaska's Inupiaq Eskimos see themselves in the vanguard of the politics of aboriginal whaling. In the mid-1990s Alaska's North Slope Borough set up a project, together with the American-Russian Centre of the University of Alaska Anchorage, to help Inuit in Chukotka who had appealed to Alaskan whalers for assistance in obtaining appropriate whaling technology and training in how to go whaling. Marine mammal hunting has become vital to the coastal communities of the Russian Far East to remedy extreme food shortages and the crisis affecting the regional economy. Since the collapse of the Soviet Union and the resulting tenuous links between Chukotka and the rest of Russia, Native peoples in Chukotka have found themselves needing to rely more on traditional subsistence hunting techniques. However, knowledge and skills surrounding whaling have almost disappeared in the small communities in Chukotka. Until 1993 a specialised Russian whaling vessel fitted with a harpoon gun was responsible for catching the Russian quota of gray whales and distributed part of the quota to each village in Chukotka. Although the IWC were aware that much of the meat was used to supply fox farms, gray whale quotas were allocated on the basis of calculating the nutritional needs of the marine mammal hunting communities in the region. Economic reforms and problems in supplying spare parts and equipment to the whaling vessel ended its operations. Local hunters who had not harvested whales for many years had no other choice but to resume hunting. However, they did so with inadequate equipment and many of them had lost the knowledge required for successful and safe hunting. Early landings of gray whales were at a price— lives have been lost and boats and equipment damaged.

The 'Alaska-Chukotka Program for Encouragement of Native Involvement in Policy and Decision Processes' aims to strengthen Native organisations in Chukotka, encourage Native hunters to engage and participate in wildlife management policy-making processes, and to document local knowledge in Chukotka about the use of marine mammals so that Native people in Chukotka can use it to empower themselves and to carry out successful whale hunts. The North Slope Borough is currently carrying out this work with the Eskimo Society of Chukotka and the Naukan Native Company. Funds from the project have been used to establish Native whale observer posts along the coast of Chukotka, and local hunters are relearning long-forgotten hunting skills from Alaskan whalers. Yet while the aim is to empower the Native people of Chukotka, there are also advantages for Alaska's Eskimo communities.

The initial reason for the project stemmed from the North Slope Borough's need to know more about the bowhead whale population that migrates into Russian waters and is therefore unknown to the observers at the whale census station at Point Barrow. Both the AEWC and the North Slope Borough have long claimed that not all the bowhead whales migrating to the Bering Straits during spring have been counted. These claims are based on the observations made by hunters on St. Lawrence Island that some bowheads move towards the coast of Chukotka. Local hunters are observers in situ: they are better placed than scientists to monitor the migratory habits of whales. Since the IWC bases is quota largely upon the AEWC estimate, and since Eskimos in Chukotka and the Inuvialuit of Canada's western Arctic wish to resume hunting bowheads, the North Slope Borough's argument that there are more bowheads than current estimates suggest is an astute political and cultural move, one that aims to increase the number of bowheads allowed by existing quotas.[1]

In Greenland, the allocation of IWC quotas to specific municipalities is the responsibility of the Home Rule Authorities after consultation with KNAPK (Kalaallit Nunaat Aalisartut Piniartullu Kattufiat; the Greenland Association of Fishermen and Hunters), an organisation which represents the interests of all those dependent on hunting and fishing for a living. The municipal authorities are then responsible for distributing their share of the quota to individual whaling vessels. The municipal authorities must inform the Home Rule Authorities about the numbers of whales caught as well as struck but not killed, and about any infringements of the whaling regulations. In turn, the Home Rule Authorities are responsible for providing the IWC with an annual report on all whaling activities in Greenland, and this forms the basis for the working out of the quota for the following year. KNAPK presents the case for aboriginal subsistence whaling in Greenland at the annual meetings of the IWC. It challenges the scientific knowledge that the IWC uses to work out its regulatory policies as inadequate, and carries out its own whale counts, as well as participating with scientists from the IWC. The Greenland Fisheries Survey initiated the first aerial surveys of minke and fin whales off the Greenland coast in 1988. Studies of the population and distribution of minke whales have been carried out off the coasts of west and east Greenland, while aerial surveys have been made of fin and humpback whales in west and south Greenland (Greenland Home Rule 1989).

Both the IWC and Inuit agree that sound management programmes cannot be implemented without sufficient knowledge about the size and distribution of whale populations, together with a greater understanding of their exploitation. In fact, some biologists would even agree that there is insufficient knowledge about the biology and dynamics of whale stocks to implement satisfactory management plans based on scientific information alone (e.g. Heide-Jørgensen 1990). Yet scientists would also argue that owing to demographic transitions in Inuit communities, changes in hunting technology and methods, and transformations in the economic infrastructure of indigenous societies, with its associated reconfiguration of human-environmental relations, the self-regulation of whaling by Inuit communities themselves is not an option. A compromise needs to be reached and agreed upon. To ensure a participatory approach to the management of subsistence whaling and that IWC decisions take into account the subsistence, nutritional and cultural needs of local communities, Inuit organisations stress the importance of undertaking more user-based research. Much of this is currently carried out across the Inuit area with the support and co-operation of the Inuit Circumpolar Conference. The ICC aims to defend Inuit subsistence whaling and has had observer status at IWC meetings since 1980. The attitude of individual IWC member countries towards Inuit hunting is not always clear and the ICC position is that many member countries do not understand fully the nutritional and cultural significance of whaling for the Inuit. The ICC argues in the Inuit defence that the contemporary threat to whales comes not from hunting, but from other environmental problems, such as marine pollution, which are harming the biological reproductivity of whales and the health of whale populations as a whole.

The Inuit are challenging what they regard as insufficient scientific data with indigenous knowledge, claiming that local resource harvesters who involve themselves with the environment on a daily basis are more likely than scientists to have reliable knowledge of the resource based on regular observation over long periods. At the same time they recognise that both indigenous knowledge and science are complementary and vital to successful whale management. But to be effective in the international arena, Inuit have to demonstrate to the IWC and environmental groups concerned with marine mammal conservation exactly what that indigenous knowledge is, what it is founded upon, and how it can be used to inform subsistence whaling management programmes. Recognising this, the ICC has established a data bank on renewable resources and gives priority to the collection of information from scientific sources and from hunters and fishermen. This work requires the participation of Inuit communities and organisations throughout the Arctic.

Of particular concern is that research projects should focus on both scientific and local knowledge of wildlife and ecological conditions. This kind of research programme has been under way in Greenland for several years, where the Inuit population has a greater degree of decision-making power concerning environmental management than elsewhere in the Arctic (Nuttall 1994). The Home Rule Authorities have implemented (sometimes unpopular) legislation to restrict hunting and fishing, have given protected status to certain areas, aim to gather as much information as possible on the human use of natural resources, both in historical and contemporary times, and invest heavily in projects to monitor hunting and assess the population status of key species. Greenlandic and foreign researchers work in close collaboration with local people and while recent anthropological research on subsistence hunting, for example, has concentrated on traditional and modern hunting techniques, and on cultural factors and social relations in local communities (e.g. Caulfield 1991, Nuttall 1992), more research is required on changing distribution patterns, the internal trade of hunting products, the ideology of subsistence and changing human-environmental relations.

WHALING IN GREENLAND: SUBSISTENCE OR COMMERCIAL?

In recent years, scientists and environmentalists have claimed that the distinction between commercial and subsistence whaling has blurred, with the unsurprising result that definitions are now contested. Whaling in Norway, Japan and the Faroes, while defined by the IWC as commercial, is considered by some commentators as having a subsistence element as well as being a fundamental part of culture at both local and national levels (e.g. Kalland 1990, Sanderson 1990), while there have also been recent arguments from animal-rights groups that subsistence hunting of whales and seals has become commoditised and 'non-traditional'. For example, in Greenland subsistence whaling is now not only said to have a commercial element, which has removed it from a purely subsistence context. It is also doubtful whether whaling in Greenland can really be defined as aboriginal. This is because Greenlanders are the only population of Inuit origin to have achieved Home Rule, and it is no longer tenable to construct for them (or for Greenlanders to construct for themselves) an identity as an oppressed minority in relation to a dominant nation-state (Nuttall 1994). The Greenland Inuit have embarked on a course of nation-building and, because of the extensive system of self-government that has developed under Home Rule, they have more constitutionally-protected rights than many other indigenous peoples (Nuttall *ibid.*: 1).

Greenland Inuit are permitted to hunt minke and fin whales because the IWC recognises them as aboriginal people. Yet much of the meat is sold and finds its way into supermarket freezers, which makes Greenlanders vulnerable to accusations that their form of whaling is commercial. There is already a market for Greenlandic foods within Greenland, mainly in the large west coast towns where many people do not have the time, means or ability to hunt, yet value and rely on Greenlandic meat and fish products as the basis of their diet, or look upon Greenlandic foods as delicacies. The Greenland Home Rule Authorities wish to see the expansion of this market and the corresponding increase in production necessary to meet demand. The increase in the production, distribution and exchange of hunting and fishing products is also a central aspect of the Home Rule government's policy for creating sustainable conditions in the settlements, and in the process easing the subsidies that make it possible for many villages to survive. Supporters and

representatives of Japanese, Norwegian and Icelandic whaling have highlighted this and ask repeatedly at IWC meetings why their type of whaling should
be regarded as any different from Greenlandic whaling, especially when most
of the distribution and sale of whalemeat is confined to specific localised
regions and hunting is carried out by relatively small-scale fisheries.

Greenland's whaling communities
Subsistence hunting underpins the social and economic life of people in small
communities in Greenland's hunting districts of Upernavik, Uummannaq,
Avanersuaq, Ammassalik and Ittoqqortoormiit, despite the development of
capital-intensive fishing along the west coast. In these areas hunting households remain primarily units of production and consumption and people rely
on hunting marine mammals, especially seals, as the sole or principal occupation. Ringed seals, harp seals, hooded seals and bearded seals are hunted. In
addition, beluga, minke and fin whales, narwhals, walrus and certain species
of small cetacean and seabirds are also harvested. The latter include guillemots, eider ducks, little auks, barnacle geese and kittiwakes. Subsistence
fishing is also of vital importance. Apart from those districts where hunting
remains the principal mode of occupation, subsistence activities are carried
out by a significant number of people who live elsewhere in Greenland.
While commercial fishing is dominant from Disko Bay in central west Greenland, down to the Nanortalik area in the far south, the hunting of seals and
other sea mammals is important all along the west coast either as a full-time
occupation or as a supplement to wage labour. Currently, over three thousand people hold licences which entitle them to make a living from subsistence hunting and fishing, while over four thousand hold recreational or part-
time licences (Greenland Home Rule Government 1995). [2]

Hunting settlements in Greenland enjoy a localisation of resources and the
continued use of a particular area means that each community has its own
recognised territory, known as the *piniarfik*, or *piniariartarfik* ('the hunting
place'). The use of a specific area by a community is reflected in the place
names given to features in the landscape which contain information about
hunting, other subsistence activities and about mythical and real past events
(Kleivan 1986, Nuttall 1992, 1993a). Place names not only refer to physical
features and are geographically descriptive, they tell of the use of both land
and sea resources. Other place names in the landscape hint of religious
beliefs and practices in pre-Christian times. But the *piniarfik* is also a per-
sonalised landscape, having significance for individual and family history,
and descriptions of places are shaped and framed by human purpose, values
and meanings. Greenlandic place names are mnemonic devices, triggering

recollection of events that happened at those places, even though the name may not reflect those events (e.g. 'Kangeq [meaning headland] is the place where I once caught a polar bear', or 'Saattut ['thin flat stone islands'] is the place where my father was once stormbound', or 'Ulua is a frightening place because ghosts steal from hunters who camp there'). People talk about places in this way, and regularly tell stories that are associated with those places, whether they are travelling on long hunting journeys by boat in summer, or dog sledge in winter, when living in summer camps, or when they are confined to the warmth of their houses during the long dark winter. Places are part of a well-defined trajectory along which a person travels. People use place names to think their way across both the landscape and chronological time, and places are as much a part of daily discourse as they are a key component of a sense of identity.

Access to the resources of local hunting and fishing grounds usually depends on affiliation to the local community. In Greenland there is a conflict between, on the one hand, an individual's right to hunt where he chooses, and on the other the right to hunt in an area as regulated by the community and where membership or affiliation to the community is a prerequisite. While there is extensive individual appropriation of resources and even individual custodianship rights to seal, beluga whale and salmon netting sites and to campsites, this is grounded within and dependent upon notions of collective appropriation and communal rights. The allocation of netting sites, campsites and storage sites to individuals is done so on a communal basis. Individuals then have rights to exclusive tenure only so long as they continue to use those sites. In this way, sites can be inherited by the relatives of previous users, but the rights to tenure can be allocated to another person if use is discontinued by the present custodian. In customary Inuit tradition, and also enshrined in the modern legal system, no-one in Greenland owns land.

Collective appropriation of the *piniarfik* is also reflected in patterns of sharing and distribution, in particular by communal claims to catch-shares from large sea mammals such as walrus, whales, narwhals and bearded seals harvested by an individual hunter. Just as the use of both sea and land does not entail any exclusive individual ownership rights, so no one individual hunter can claim ownership and control over the means of production (Dahl 1989). The sharing and distribution of meat is guided by an obligation to give which is central to the customary ideology of subsistence. Because animals are believed to give themselves up to hunters it is incumbent on the hunter to give them in return to other people. As well as providing food necessary for survival, the sharing and distribution of meat from the hunt defines, expresses and sustains social relationships, as well as reaffirming fundamental values that guide attitudes towards animals and the environment (Nuttall 1992).

Rather than describing hunting communities in Greenland as whaling communities, it is more accurate to see them as communities that hunt whales at certain times of the year. In the far north and on the east coast, people hunt beluga whales and narwhals in spring and early autumn. Elsewhere, in the south and west, hunting for minke and fin whales is important during summer and autumn. Whaling is not only confined to the villages and small settlements, it is also an activity in which people from the towns engage themselves. For example, in the town of Qerqertarsuaq on Disko Island, Inuit continue to hunt for minke whales (Caulfield 1991), while narwhals and beluga are hunted from Sisimiut northwards. For most of the year, communities that whale are engaged in other economic activities and other forms of subsistence. People hunt seals, they fish or work in paid employment. Fishing and casual labour in fish processing plants or for the municipal authorities are often seen as activities necessary for supplementing the subsistence economy. For example, in more than two thirds of families dependent on subsistence hunting and fishing, at least one partner is a wage-earner, while in less than one third of hunting families, both husband and wife work in hunting and fishing activities (Greenland Home Rule Government 1995). Most families derive little income from hunting. The market value of sealskin prices has dropped considerably over the last few years, partly as a result of the activities of animal-rights groups, and the trade in sealskins is only made possible because it is subsidised by the Home Rule government.

In most communities including the larger towns, whales provide a vital supply of meat for many people and although whaling is a seasonal activity its social and economic significance should not be underestimated. While people like to enjoy fresh whale steaks, much of what is caught is prepared for the winter. People make *nikkut*, by hanging strips of whalemeat outside their homes to dry, or *mattak*, the skin of the whale, is frozen for winter consumption. With the imposition of quotas for minke and fin whales, whaling has become a strategically-planned activity, although Caulfield (1991: 76) has observed that in Qerqertarsuaq in central west Greenland minke whaling is more opportunistic. As I was able to observe in Nanortalik in south Greenland in 1991 and 1996, and in east Greenland in 1992, hunters meet to discuss when and where they will hunt their quota for that year. Several hunters will travel out in open boats to identify pods of migrating whales. One whale will be singled out and its movements will be then be tracked. A decision is made when to hunt the whale and plans are made for the hunt. Fin whale hunting must be done from larger fishing vessels (which are often owned by members of the same family) mounted with a harpoon cannon, while several hunters go out in small skiffs to hunt minke whales. Minke whales will be surrounded by these boats and the hunters shoot the animal with rifles before harpooning it.

Catch-shares are divided out among the hunters who participate in catching the whale. Whaling crews are often members of the same household or family (the *ilaqutariit*). Families, especially in the smaller villages, are usually independent units based on subsistence, at least in terms of production for the household economy. Hunting, together with the preparation of meat and skins, is the exclusive preserve of each household, with daily tasks the concern of individual members carrying out their allotted roles within local systems of the division of labour. In many villages in north, south and east Greenland, as I have observed on numerous occasions, whale meat is often shared and given away as gifts to people who do not participate in the hunt as well as being given to unrelated households. Meat from seals, whales and other marine mammals is not regarded as a commodity but as something inalienable, containing an element of the giver when it is shared or given away as a gift. When meat from the hunt is shared it expresses the relationships people share with one another and helps to strengthen ties of kinship and community (Nuttall 1992).

Whales, meat and cash
While whale meat is shared between the hunters and their families, or given away as gifts to people who may not have participated in the hunt, a large proportion of it is also sold, which goes against the IWC provisions for aboriginal subsistence whaling. So far the IWC has turned a blind eye to this. Hunters need to pay for the running costs of their boats, they need money to buy imported foodstuffs and clothes for their families, as well as having to pay for essential amenities such as electricity and fuel. In short, they need to earn money in an increasingly market-oriented economy. During summer 1996, for example, hunters from Nanortalik landed a minke whale. It was butchered and divided down at the harbour and the choicest cuts were shared between the hunters who had participated in the hunt. Their wives and other relatives crowded the harbour, armed with plastic bags and plastic tubs and buckets, which were quickly filled with meat. Once the meat had been divided and shared in this way, individual hunters discussed with their wives what meat they should keep for themselves and what cuts they should sell. Some hunters and their families had more need to keep as much meat as they could, while others preferred to sell a larger share. Some hunters put meat on sale at the *kalaaliaraq* that same day, others turned up with meat for sale the following day (Nuttall 1996).

The *kalaaliaraq* (lit. 'the little Greenlander') is a small market comprising one or two stalls which can be found near the harbour in most Greenlandic towns, where hunters and fishermen sell the day's catch. Depending on the area and according to seasonal availability, one can purchase seal meat, caribou meat, seabirds such as guillemots and eider ducks, and fish such as salmon, halibut, catfish and Arctic char. While Greenlandic foods (*kalaalimernit*) such as seal meat and seal blubber, frozen *mattak*, and frozen whale meat are available in supermarkets, the food put on sale at the *kalaaliaraq* always sells well. Prices are fixed by the local hunter's and fishermen's association and usually undercut the price of Greenlandic foods which can be purchased in the supermarkets—sometimes it may cost slightly more than the supermarket price, but there is a ready demand and people are prepared to pay the price. The hunters prefer to sell their catch in this way, rather than to Royal Greenland (see below), because they receive immediate payment and can avoid paying tax. People prefer to buy their meat and fish at the *kalaaliaraq* because it is often cheaper and fresher than buying it from the supermarket. If they are early enough to get down to the harbour soon after a hunter has brought in his catch, people can also choose which cuts they want. The *kalaaliaraq* is also a place of active social interaction, where hunters and fishermen discuss the day's hunting and fishing, the availability of seals and fish, the migration routes of whales, and the weather.

The sale of hunting products in Greenland has brought criticism from antisealing and anti-whaling groups which claim that this illustrates how hunting has undergone a transition from a purely subsistence activity to something that has more of a commercial rationale. However, when people sell seal and whale meat and fish at the *kalaaliaraq* they are participating in forms of exchange which have long been part of the subsistence economy, as several writers have remarked (Caulfield 1997, Dahl 1989, Marquadt and Caulfield 1996, Nuttall 1992, Petersen 1989). Animal-rights groups consider money to sit uneasily within the context of traditional subsistence whaling. To some extent, this is in keeping with a negative attitude to the corroding power of money generally (see Parry and Bloch 1989). But, as Lynge (1992: 48) sees it, marine mammals are caught and landed by Inuit 'to be eaten and sold to whoever wants the meat, but not with the aim of earning money'. In Greenland, for example, where subsistence sealing and whaling are considered to be activities integral to a modern and rapidly industrialising society (Dahl 1989, Lynge *ibid.*), money is a supplement to the subsistence economy generally and is part of a symbolically constructed framework that emphasises cultural continuity rather than being based on large-scale profit (Nuttall 1992). And if money is a necessary part of subsistence hunting, replacing customary practices of sharing in some places, then it has been argued that new distribution systems are not disruptive, but allow continuity (Petersen 1989).

Nonetheless these kinds of changes are grist to the environmentalist's mill. Animal-rights opposition to subsistence whaling and sealing is fuelled partly by claims that the incentive to hunt has become moneterised, and that the introduction of modern technology has removed subsistence activities away from a previously 'traditional' context. Greenpeace, despite having made a public apology to Greenlandic hunters for its anti-sealing campaigns, is still opposed to indigenous hunting if it is commercial. Here, the definition of 'traditional' is tenuous, invoking images of a romantic idealised past before the days of Euro-American contact. While accepting Inuit hunting of sea mammals if there is minimal outside influence in technology, the animal-rights position rejects contemporary whaling and sealing for two main reasons. Firstly, hunters now use motorboats and larger whaling vessels, high-powered rifles and harpoon guns. Secondly, because the Inuit trade whale meat (at least in Greenland) and sell sealskins, they are seen as being implicated and involved in commercial hunting as part of their participation in a capitalist cash economy: their need for meat is considered secondary to their need for money. Conservationists express alarm that the participation of hunters in the cash economy is contributing to overharvesting of marine mammals and seabirds. The WWF position, for example, is that the decline in the population of key animal species 'is principally the result of local hunting. Increased exploitation of belugas and narwhals is due to the spread of a cash economy to even remote areas of the country' (Mikkelsen (1996: 17).

While falling back on arguments to do with conservation and endangered species, environmental and animal-rights groups have turned Inuit whaling into an ethical issue. They question the necessity of whaling for Inuit in the modern world, arguing that traditional hunting and the ideology of subsistence have become secularised and that Inuit no longer care about the animals they hunt. Furthermore, they point to how whaling by aboriginal peoples is unacceptable when modernity and technological change strains the definition of what is and what is not 'aboriginal' (e.g. because Alaskan Eskimos have been made rich by oil money, they have no need to hunt whales). Recently, the activities of Yup'ik and Chuckchi whalers in the Russian Far East have come under intense scrutiny from the Humane Society, which questions whether they can claim to practice what the IWC regards as aboriginal whaling. The society presented a report to the 1997 IWC meeting in Monaco detailing how Yup'ik and Chuckchi were defying IWC rules by using inappropriate hunting technology when hunting gray whales, such as Second World War rifles and traditional harpoons that did not kill the whales swiftly and humanely. The society's report also claimed that the Siberianss were in defiance of the IWC provisions for aboriginal subsistence whaling by hunting more whales than they actually need (including female whales nursing calves) in order to provide feed for fur farms.

The activities of animal welfare groups have provoked passionate and forceful response from Inuit themselves, who consider such organisations as cultural imperialists '…who have slid off the road and settled in sentimental animal protection postures that have little or nothing to do with species survival or ecological balance' (Lynge 1988: 18). Inuit have been forced to defend and redefine subsistence activities in accordance with contemporary perspectives. Lynge, a Greenlander and indigenous rights activist, has argued that the Inuit world view regarding the sustainable use of marine resources is consistent with the views of international environmental organisations, believing it to be an urban arrogance stemming from alienation from nature on the part of those who would have it otherwise:

> when the hunter respects the ancient rules and taboos, he is led to an attachment and reverence for the prey that can best be likened to the sentiments a man feels for his beloved. Just as, in a human relationship, love can wither, so can the hunter become insensitive to the animals upon which he feeds; his feelings can die away, and with them, alas, his own self-esteem as well. But love between man and woman can also thrive, and among the true leaders of the small hunting community one can always find those whose ways and sentiments are dictated by respect for the prey and the rules of the hunt. Those hunters' families will never go hungry: the animals will seek them out as if asking to be taken.

(Lynge 1992: 39–40)

Such poetics are multi-layered. On one level, Lynge acknowledges that not all hunters carry the mantle of Green primitivism, yet on another, there are still *real* and *genuine* hunters who know how to act in relation to nature, who know how to set out on the hunt observing all the rules and taboos necessary so that the hunted animal recognises the skill and prowess of the hunter, deferring eventually to his superiority by giving itself up. By slaking the thirst of the dead animal's spirit, that spirit will be free to find a new body, only to return eventually to the *same* hunter and give itself freely once more. In this way, the hunter is the embodiment of wise, responsible, sustainable resource-use. And the message is clear: marine mammals really are renewable resources if their souls are respected and recycled.

Criticisms levelled at the nature of whaling in Greenland are perhaps unjust, and demonstrate a profound misunderstanding of the way of life of Inuit in the modern world. For the most part, in those communities dependent on hunting today, changes in technology or the mixing of informal and formal economic activities have not altered the cultural, emotional and spiritual interplay between the human and animal worlds (Nuttall 1992). Opponents of whaling by indigenous peoples in the modern world see informal and formal economic activities as non-complementary and view a subsistence-based society as simple, primitive and traditional, isolated from the rest of the world and unaffected by modernity. Further controversy was generated recently by the Danish economist Martin Paldam (1994) who has asked if subsidising the costs of small settlements in Greenland is justified. Paldam and other critics of small-scale hunting fail to understand the cultural and economic importance of domestic production. As Wenzel (1991: 98) argues 'the socio-economic "closure" that defines Inuit subsistence requires that we reconsider our ideas about formal and informal economic behaviour as forming two distinct and exclusive functional categories'. Although money is very much a vital part of the subsistence economy it is not necessarily inconsistent with it. Indeed, money and the commercial sale of marine mammal products has long been incorporated into an already flexible and variable range of subsistence techniques. Money is necessary for subsistence-based activities in the remote communities of Greenland—communities with no alternatives to hunting and fishing—and indeed makes the subsistence economy possible.

THE RIGHT TO DEVELOPMENT

The sale of whale meat and other Greenlandic foods, such as seal and fish, is also being encouraged by the Greenlandic Home Rule Authorities, although on a larger scale beyond the local level economy. Although the Home Rule Authorities aspire to greater political, financial and economic independence from Denmark based on the exploitation of natural resources, Greenland remains in an economically vulnerable position because it relies to a considerable extent on imports. Greenland is heavily dependent on other countries for trade and, excepting hunting and fishing products and a few private and public services, all goods used by private households, private and public institutions and businesses are imported. The country has only twice had a positive balance of external trade since 1980 (in 1989 and 1990), and this almost permanent deficit is only made possible because Greenland is supported by block grants from Denmark.

As well as other goods, Greenland relies to a great extent on imported foodstuffs, mainly from Denmark. To ease this reliance, hunters are being encouraged to sell part or most of what they catch to Royal Greenland, the country's meat and fish processing and marketing company. The Home Rule Authorities consider the production, distribution and exchange of food and products from hunting and fishing as vital to the development of local, small-scale sustainable community development (Greenland Home Rule Government 1995, Marquadt and Caulfield 1996).

As Marquadt and Caulfield (*ibid.*:115) point out, the promotion of this system by the Home Rule government 'reduces the need for imports, promotes indigenous hunting practices, offsets the need for government subsidies to smaller settlements, and encourages consumption of nutritious and culturally valued foods'. There is no doubt that extensive research on the viability of this system is essential. An increase in the internal trade in hunting and fishing products will also benefit Royal Greenland, the Home Rule-owned company responsible for Greenland's fishing, production and export business. Royal Greenland owns the majority of land-based production facilities, as well as owning 16 large and more than 40 smaller processing plants, and employs almost 3000 people world-wide as a consequence of its global processing and operating offices. Royal Greenland's activities are becoming increasingly globalised. But the company's role in the commercial trade of hunting and fishing products highlights a fundamental clash between the culture of the market economy, which has come to define and shape the course of development in Greenland, and the small-scale, kinship-oriented subsistence culture that persists despite widespread social change, upheaval and economic restructuring.

In many parts of Greenland there is local opposition, or reluctance, to sell seal and whale meat to the Royal Greenland processing plants which are to be found in many villages. For example, the Home Rule government has already invested 12.6 million Danish kroner in a new processing plant in Kuummiut, a village in east Greenland, where there is a lot of active hunting of sea mammals. It was hoped that hunters and fishers from settlements throughout the district would travel to Kuummiut and sell their catch to the plant. However, as of summer 1996 hunters were not doing as Royal Greenland had forecast. An article in the national newspaper *Sermitsiak* reported how hunters were failing to sell meat from narwhal and seal hunting, as well as the meat from successful polar bear hunts. The thrust of the article, and the response of the manager of the processing plant, was that Royal Greenland had been let down by local hunters and that the plant was threatened with closure as a result, thus placing 100 jobs at risk.[3] Hunters in east Greenland, like their counterparts on the west coast, sell part of what they catch at the *kalaaliaraq*. They keep the rest for themselves and their families. Royal Greenland has failed to recognise the essence of sharing as a fundamental part of the hunting culture, as well as understanding the immediate gains for a hunter who sells meat privately rather than to the Royal Greenland processing plant.

Royal Greenland not only caters for demand for hunting and fishing products, its marketing and development strategies may possibly increase demand for seal and whale meat and other Greenlandic foods. Pressure on the local resource base of hunting communities may be a direct consequence of ensuring a regular supply of hunting and fishing products for an internal country-wide market. Increased hunting may threaten beluga and narwhal stocks leading to management guidelines imposed by the IWC. But the production, distribution and exchange of hunting products on a larger scale may also threaten to conflict with the traditional or customary ideology of subsistence. In many parts of Greenland today, much of the meat which is sold is surplus and the money earned is essential for the economic viability of the hunter's household. Although some hunters do see the incentive to earn money as overriding other concerns such as sharing, for the most part when hunting is done to satisfy a market demand beyond the household, local community or regional economy, then the customary ideology of subsistence is disrupted and threatened (Nuttall 1992).

Despite the difficulties of supply, Greenlanders are looking to open up new markets outside the country for marine mammal meat and sealskin clothing. But such plans are further hampered by how international organisations perceive Greenlanders as aboriginal people in the modern world. As Chapter 7 explores Arctic peoples use terms such as 'tradition', 'aboriginality' and 'indigenous' politically and rhetorically. These terms can also be used against them in negative ways. In recent years it has been argued that the IWC category of aboriginal subsistence whaling is a static category, implying that indigenous cultures are traditional and unchanging. Kalland (1994) has criticised the concept of aboriginal subsistence whaling for its imperialist associations, arguing that it not only excludes whalers in Japan, Norway and Iceland, but imposes strict definitional criteria on indigenous peoples and allows outsiders to say how indigenous peoples are to be defined, and indeed how they are to act and behave. In this case, it seeks to define and perpetuate an image of true 'aboriginal' peoples as those who continue to live within a non-commercial economy and utilise simple technologies. As long as Greenlanders and other indigenous peoples conform to this image, then they are seen as having a legitimate right to continue whaling.

At a whaling seminar held in Greenland in early 1995 the chairman of KNAPK said that while Greenland's domestic market for whale meat had been met it was time to consider exporting it. The KNAPK position is clear: Greenlanders, as indigenous peoples, have an indisputable right to exploit resources including whalemeat, on a commercial scale.[4] Following Kalland, the definition of Greenland whaling as aboriginal subsistence whaling has actually proved to be an imposition. It restricts Greenlanders from developing their resources in ways that seem appropriate and defined in terms of their own cultural and economic needs. Furthermore, the concept of aboriginal subsistence whaling allows a policy consensus to be imposed on ethnic minorities and keeps them in a position of subordination and dependency (Kalland 1994). Meat and other products from marine mammals cannot be exported. The U.S. Marine Mammal Protection Act (MMPA) of 1972, for example, provides a trade barrier for Greenlandic hunting products. The ICC and KNAPK have been persistent in their efforts to persuade the American authorities to lift the ban on importing marine mammal products imposed under the Act, arguing that it is a contravention of the international trade agreement GATT. Greenlanders argue that the MMPA restricts the rights of Inuit to develop sustainable and equitable economic conditions in Arctic communities:

> US policy is violating the basic human rights of the Inuit peoples. It is unacceptable because the local Arctic people are not allowed to develop their own economic base and in this way secure the development of their own culture.
>
> (Jakobsen 1994: 55)

It is notable that Norwegian whalers, who wish to export whale blubber to Japan, also find this ban on trade morally unacceptable. Such sentiments are reactions to globalist models of environmental management based on 'the perceived need to assess and sanction the environmental activities of others' (Milton 1996: 186). Far from preserving the environment and conserving resources, Milton argues that globalist models promote unsustainable development, allow wealthy developed states to further their own interests, and replace indigenous perspectives on resource use with environmentally-destructive practices. In this way, as far as the hunting of whales by Arctic coastal communities is concerned, by defining modern whaling as practised by indigenous peoples as environmentally-unsustainable and unnecessary environmentalists and whale management organisations seek to extend their own power and influence over the lives of people who acquire environmental knowledge and develop local systems of resource management by living and acting in the environment.

Economic activity is, in essence, the production, distribution, exchange and consumption of the material necessities that make human survival possible. For Arctic peoples it is embedded within, and cannot be separated from, the social bases of survival. For this reason, co-management and small-scale community based development has aimed to integrate the values, perspectives, opinions and environmental knowledge of indigenous peoples with scientific approaches to resource management. In the past seals, whales, caribou and other animals may have come to the hunter who observed the correct rituals before the hunt, and who not only respected the animals he hunted, but who shared what came freely to him. If ritual was not observed or the taboos were broken, then the animals would not give themselves to him. Today, hunters are not only obliged to observe customary rituals and taboos, but modern regulations and quotas imposed by outside agencies as well. If these regulations are flouted then wildlife boards and international commissions will withhold or tighten the quotas. Hunters have never before had so many interests to appease and placate. And although animals may still reveal themselves to hunters in dreams, knowledge of where to find them is now also based on aerial surveys, census counts and computerised maps.

This chapter has pointed to some of the difficulties of basing small-scale community development on the commercialisation of marine mammal products. As the example from Greenland shows, there is a fundamental clash between two cultures: one small-scale, emphasising kinship, reciprocity and cultural identity; the other market-oriented within a context of nation-building. There are also concerns within Greenland that development based on marine mammal products would be uneven and contribute to the process of social differentiation that is currently underway in the country as a consequence of modernisation. Some hunters and communities claim that the Home Rule Authorities do not give them a fair share of the IWC quota, while others feel that even when they do participate in whale hunts then they do not always get a proper share of the meat. Tensions also arise when larger fishing vessels compete with locally-based hunts for beluga whales. Local people in Upernavik in northwest Greenland, for example, feel that the annual visits by boats from further south and with no affiliation to local communities in the district is a form of trespassing (Nuttall 1992; 142). While recognising that beluga hunting is economically lucrative, they nonetheless mistrust the changing attitudes that prompt beluga hunting on a commercial scale and mistrust those hunters who wish for a financial return from the hunt, rather than sharing meat and *mattak*.

This situation is arising elsewhere in Greenland. For example, Dahl (1990) has noted the intrusion of fishing vessels from the larger towns of Disko Bay in the beluga hunt at the small community of Saqqaq. Dahl calls beluga hunting in Saqqaq a 'well-defined communal or collective activity' and local hunters are aggrieved when other hunters interfere with a community event of economic, cultural and symbolic importance. These are by no means isolated episodes, and they point to an increasing competition for resources. This competition not only threatens to deprive local communities of their resource base, it also threatens the customary ideology of subsistence and disrupts notions of sharing and giving (Nuttall 1997). Dybbroe (1991: 14) argues that this competition 'is symptomatic of the kinds of oppositions evolving in Greenland today, which are not between local communities but between interested groups on a national scale'. At the same time, these tensions are heightened when both domestic and international markets fluctuate. This volatility makes development based on the commercial sales of renewable resources precarious (cf Young 1992).

Although this chapter has focused specifically on whaling in Greenland, it illustrates Arctic-wide concerns relating to development and cultural survival and the clash between indigenous and non-indigenous attitudes towards the environment and resource use. It seems that the exploitation of marine mammals will continue to be at the forefront of environmental debate concerning the importance of hunting and its role in providing a sustainable economic base for Arctic coastal communities (Nuttall 1993b, 1994: 26). The animal-rights campaign, for example, shows no sign of relenting and is bound to continue to undermine the subsistence economy. Furthermore, the IWC itself has been accused of moving towards an explicit anti-whaling stance, rather than maintaining its original role as a regulatory body (Freeman 1990). Scientists and environmentalists fear that increased hunting by indigenous peoples will threaten whale stocks unless appropriate forms of management are put in place. From the perspective of indigenous peoples current co-management practices only offer a compromise by regulating access to resources and do not hold the promise of allowing greater self-regulation in the near future.

Faced with such threats to cultural survival from environmentalist action and globalist models of environmental management, Inuit communities are under increasing pressure to defend subsistence hunting. This defence relies on the ability to increase international awareness of the effectiveness of indigenous systems of resource use as regulatory and management mechanisms, rather than allowing conventional science-based management to determine what Inuit can and cannot hunt. But the future of subsistence hunting, especially whaling, is also dependent on working out appropriate definitions which will allow hunting activities to exist within the framework of the market economies that characterise the modern Arctic. When environmental organisations such as Greenpeace say that they are not opposed to subsistence hunting if the meat and by-products of the catch are utilised by the family, household and community, but are vehemently against commercial hunting, they fall into the trap of reifying subsistence hunters as traditional peoples. Likewise the IWC category of aboriginal subsistence whaling is not based on any real substantive definitions of what the IWC understands by 'aboriginal' and 'subsistence'. Indigenous peoples are represented as 'traditional' if they only hunt for their own consumption, yet 'modern' if they wish to sell the products of the catch.

Worldwide, resource agencies need to take into account the environmental values of local people and adopt a participatory approach to resource management. In the Arctic, the Inuit have found themselves a new role as resource conservationists and have initiated user-based research. As such they provide a model for the inclusion of indigenous values and environmental knowledge. Although it is not without its problems, so far a participatory approach to the management of subsistence whale hunting has tended to work in the Arctic, in the sense that Greenlanders and other indigenous peoples are still able to hunt whales. In Greenland and elsewhere, indigenous peoples would rather have self-management than co-management and the power to decide on the quotas that they feel they should be able to set themselves. The future of whaling and other forms of subsistence hunting, however, relies on reconciling the interests of those local communities dependent on hunting, and those environmental and conservationist organisations that express a sincere concern for wildlife and the environment, yet do not understand fully the cultural dynamics of the mixed economies of Arctic settlements, the interconnectedness of hunting peoples and the environment, nor their rights to self-determination, to define their own future and to develop renewable resources in a sustainable way.

1   Delegates at the IWC meeting in Aberdeen in 1996 could not reach a consensus on Russia's request to allow indigenous peoples in Chukotka a kill of five bowhead whales annually under the IWC provisions for aboriginal subsistence whaling. A kill of one bowhead whale in the Canadian Arctic was also voted against.

2   Since January 1993 hunters in Greenland must be in possession of a formal hunting licence. There are two kinds of hunting licence: one for people who hunt full-time in order to make a living (i.e. occupational hunters whose sole or principal occupation is subsistence hunting and fishing), and one for those who wish to hunt part-time, but who make a living from other forms of employment. These are people who live in the towns rather than the villages, have salaried employment, and do most of their hunting and fishing at weekends or during holidays. This category of hunter also includes Danes living and working in Greenland. The allocation of quotas and issuing of licences takes place in Nuuk, Greenland's capital.

3   'Fangere svigte Royal Greenland' ('Hunters let down Royal Greenland'—my translation) *Sermitsiak* 23 August 1996, p.7. The article described how in August a hunter had caught five narwhals and three polar bears, while two other hunters had together hunted eight narwhals, but none of the meat was sold to the factory in Kuummiut. The manager of the Royal Greenland factory was reported to complain how, despite hunters coming home with several tons of meat, he could not satisfy orders for whale and seal meat from several shops in west Greenland.

4   *High North News* No. 10, May 15, 1995.

Chapter 6

CULTURAL PRESERVATION THROUGH CULTURAL PRESENTATION: INDIGENOUS PEOPLES AND ARCTIC TOURISM

As the previous chapter discussed, attractive as it may be for providing a basis for small-scale sustainable development and for supporting subsistence economies, the commercialisation of marine mammal products is not without controversy. As well as international management regimes and opposition from animal-rights groups and whale conservation societies, protectionist legislation such as the U.S. Marine Mammal Protection Act restricts cultural and economic development through the use of renewable resources. While international agreements on acceptable levels of renewable resource harvesting may be a long way off, other less controversial locally-controlled enterprises, such as adventure tourism and eco-tourism, are being developed that may guarantee employment and income for residents of small Arctic communities. This chapter discusses the development of tourism in the Arctic and, with particular reference to Alaska, considers indigenous involvement in the tourism industry and assesses its prospects for community development.

Arctic tourism depends on images of wild nature and frontier history. Increasing numbers of tourists visit the Arctic attracted especially by the idea of experiencing wilderness, but also by idealised images of traditional indigenous cultures. The emergence of locally-owned and controlled tour companies has given many indigenous communities opportunities to capitalise on this and develop cash-earning enterprises. At the same time they have begun to gain control of an industry that outsiders have otherwise dominated. Leaders of indigenous peoples' organisations stress the importance of tourism for remote communities and argue that tourism will form part of diversified local economies as traditional subsistence activities become more marginalised. For some, the attraction of tourism lies in its potential for protecting both indigenous cultures and the Arctic environment. Writing of eco-tourism development on Alaska's Pribilof Islands, Merculieff (1997: 140) has called it 'one of the most successful economic development programs in rural Alaska', not only generating sizeable revenues but helping young people to rediscover traditional ethics and values that have made indigenous peoples the stewards of their immediate environment.

From an indigenous perspective, local control of tourism allows communities to regulate the numbers of visitors to indigenous community-owned lands and develop environmental conservation initiatives. A tourism industry owned and controlled by indigenous communities is also linked to the politics of community empowerment, with some companies arguing that cultural preservation is only possible through cultural presentation and by educating visitors about indigenous ways of life. The claim is made that this form of tourism is non-consumptive and environmentally-sensitive, yet provides economic opportunities for remote communities. Nonetheless, concerns are expressed that excessive tourism degrades Arctic ecosystems and results in the commoditisation of culture, leading to calls for the development of appropriate codes of conduct for Arctic tourism to minimise its environmental and cultural impact (Mason 1996). Such concern sees local communities as passive victims of global economic processes and social trends of leisure and consumption rather than as active political agents in the development of tourism. This chapter shows how people are actively involved in Arctic tourism and how, in the process, they construct indigenous views of the environment and renegotiate their perceived cultural identities.

TOURISM, DEVELOPMENT AND CULTURAL PRESERVATION

Tourism is the world's fastest growing industry and is increasingly seen by many countries as a basis for sustainable development. The variety of tourist activities is bewildering, ranging from sightseeing in urban areas, to specialised adventure tourism such as white water rafting or hot air ballooning. Different labels have been applied to reflect this diversity of types of tourism, such as 'cultural tourism', 'eco-tourism', and 'sustainable tourism'. Tourism is also truly global in its scope and extent and is not confined to well-worn tourist trails, but is expanding into peripheral areas of the world. Whatever form tourism takes, even relatively isolated and inaccessible parts of the world, such as the polar regions and high mountain areas, are not immune to its inexorable spread (e.g. see Hall and Johnston 1995, Michaud 1995). Remarking on the industry's global nature, Lanfant (1995a: 26) has called tourism an 'international fact' which

> makes itself felt at every level and in all sectors of collective life—economic, political, geographic, ecological and technological—as well as in the less visible and tangible areas of social reality, such as its systems of signs and symbolic processes. Tourism furnishes our conversation, and its discourse fills our fantasies. There is nowhere *a priori* which might not be brought into its embrace.

Of course, tourism and travelling for pleasure, adventure or geographical and personal discovery is not just a modern phenomenon. Travellers from different lands can be identified for most historical periods and many produced written accounts of their journeys, whether real or imagined. As Waters (1995: 151) suggests, however, travel for leisure would have been an unusual practice,

> undertaken only in relation to such biographically unusual events as military service, pilgrimage, trade or diplomacy. Partly because transport was slow, it was costly in terms of time. It was also regarded as risky, and those who travelled (explorers, crusaders, pilgrims) were regarded as courageous or saintly or perhaps foolish.

Similarly, Urry (1990: 16) points out that until the development of mass tourism travel was socially selective, 'available for a relatively limited elite and was a marker of social status', most apparent in eighteenth century Europe in the form of the aristocratic civilising process known as the 'Grand Tour'. Modernisation and industrialisation changed all this by institutionalising leisure and travel as central features of social life. The separation of home and work, the conceptualisation of space and the expansion of trade all contributed to the routinisation of travel for ever larger sections of industrial capitalist society.

Mass tourism is generally understood to have developed in nineteenth century industrialised Britain as a working-class phenomenon, most notably with the development of the seaside resort (Urry 1990, Shields 1991)—as 'holy days' became secularised 'holidays'. According to Urry, this development represented 'a democratisation of travel' (*ibid.*: 16). By the late twentieth century leisure and travel have become integral aspects of modern lifestyles, often making statements about affluence and the assumption of cosmopolitan identities. It is no longer the fact that people travel, but *where* they travel to and what they do there that matters. As Turner and Ash (1975) point out, tourism has become globalised in response to the tastes and fashions of Western metropolitian tourists. Tour companies manufacture new exotic destinations, while middle-class independent travellers seeking experiences not available on a package holiday 'blaze the trail to the remaining untouched corners of the planet for mass tourism and so, inevitably, consume the planet in the fullest sense' (Waters *ibid.*: 154). Lanfant suggests that the development and global spread of mass tourism in the second half of the twentieth century is not the result of spontaneity, but rather it is due to purposeful, active, deliberate and aggressive promotion by tour companies, tourism transnationals and international organisations such the United Nations and the World Bank. Furthermore, most countries now promote themselves as tourist destinations through government-run departments of tourism, many of which make use of modern technology and advertise themselves on the Internet. Greenland Tourism has been especially vigorous in this regard.

Tourism is increasingly seen as a solution to social and economic problems, particularly in rural areas, by bringing prosperity and employment when industry and agriculture or fishing declines (e.g. Villepontoux 1981). Tourism is also considered to play an important role in strategies for both sustainable development and environmental conservation. However, it is a commonplace remark that tourism contributes to social change and the destruction of the very things that the industry both promotes and depends upon, such as local cultures and the natural environment. Sociological and anthropological approaches that focus on the negative aspects of tourism have been concerned with, among other things, tourism as an extension of capitalist economic interests which involves the commoditisation of culture (e.g. Greenwood 1989), tourism as a form of imperialism (Nash 1989) and the impact of tourism on the environment (Budowski 1976, Parnwell 1993).

Tourism can also be used by states for political purposes, as part of a process of cultural assimilation or internal colonialism. For example, Michaud (1995) argues that tourism development in the Indian Himlayan region of Ladakh and in the border areas of northern Thailand is, in both cases, a state strategy to maintain a population base in contested frontier and border regions. The Indian and Thai governments, both aiming to integrate rural populations into wider society, use tourism as a way of increasing the dependency of minority groups on the national economy. As well as contributing to national economic development, tourism is promoted at governmental level as an alternative economic activity for ethnic minorities being sedentarised by the state and who are, in the process, losing traditional means of subsistence such as herding and trading.

It has also been noted that tourists themselves are often embarrassed by each other's presence (Jedrej and Nuttall 1996) and alternative travel destinations are sought out by those disillusioned with the development of mass tourism in previously remote and 'untouched' areas such as the Himalayas and southeast Asia. Tour companies capitalise on this desire and so endeavour to compete with one another in offering 'travellers' the chance to visit places not yet accessible to the 'tourist'. Ironically, this has the effect of making the adventurous traveller in remote areas acutely aware of both the area's inaccessibility and its vulnerability. Regions like the Arctic which are at once 'remote' and 'untouched' are also threatened by the inevitable encroachment of mass tourism which will destroy forever what is vital, real and different. This emerges as a dominant theme in much contemporary travel writing and is now placed firmly on the agenda of environmental and conservation organisations such as the World Wide Fund for Nature.

In many parts of the world, as more tour companies offer 'cultural' and 'anthropological' holidays, there are fears that this form of tourism will erode traditions and ways of life, and will come into conflict with local culture. Furthermore, when tourism involves the exploitation of local resources, such as fish, wildlife and even the landscape (when it is appropriated as scenery), there is often a direct threat posed to local residents who depend upon those resources. And when local culture is appropriated by outsiders and then exploited as a resource for economic gain (especially if income from tourism goes outside the local area), for some local people tourism development and the presence of tourists can only nurture a sense of alienation and imminent social change (Jedrej and Nuttall *ibid.*).

Despite recognising that local cultures can be and are disturbed and affected by tourism, not all sociologists and anthropologists involved in researching tourism subscribe to the view that it is necessarily negative for all host communities. Lanfant (1995b: 6), refusing to see tourism as simply an exogenous force imposed on local people, has argued that some communities are not always passive but 'often seize upon tourism as a means of communication to display their existence and to establish their own power'. In the presence of tourists, the receiving society can reflect upon its on traditions and values, and in the process can evaluate and reaffirm identity (Lanfant *ibid.*). In this way, local communities can use tourism to develop strategies for self-determination and cultural survival, as the rest of this chapter discusses.

ARCTIC TOURISM AND ECONOMIC DEVELOPMENT

As elsewhere in the world, and as has been remarked on by numerous scholars, tourism is growing throughout the circumpolar north (e.g. Burton 1983, Hall and Johnston 1995, Nickels *et al.* 1991). As with other parts of the world, early Arctic tourism was probably socially-selective, although most tourists would have seen themselves as 'adventurers' or 'explorers'. Modern tourism is partly made possible by a combination of factors, such as an expanding and extensive transportation network, increased interest in visiting wilderness and 'exotic' cultures, the creation of national parks, and aggressive marketing. Tourists have, however, been travelling in the Arctic for well over a century. Alaska, for example, has been on the tourist map ever since it became a possession of the United States in 1867. John Muir, the Scots-born naturalist who was almost a zealot in his worship of the natural world, was one of the first travellers to popularise southeast Alaska in his written accounts of his journeys, calling Alaska 'one of the most wonderful countries in the world' for the 'lover of pure wildness' (Muir 1915: 13). By the mid-1880s, the Pacific Coast Steamship Company was operating regular trips through southeast Alaska's Inside Passage, carrying as many as 5,000 passengers in a summer season. Annual shiploads of tourists to southeast Alaska helped to generate a local industry of Native crafts and curios by the beginning of the twentieth century (Lee 1991). Following the Gold Rush of 1889, more tourists (including among their number many vacationing gold prospectors) ventured to the Far North, while Eskimos from the coasts of Seward Peninsula and the Bering Strait were attracted to new settlements of pioneers and seasonal visitors where they found a ready market for ivory carvings. And as more steamer services became available on the Yukon River, as well as more extensive coastal routes, tourists were able to visit parts of Alaska, such as Nome, the Aleutian Islands, and the interior, that had previously been accessible only to explorers, scientists, the military and government officials.

Tourism increased steadily during and after World War I, and the building of roads and the completion of the Alaska Railroad enhanced the possibilities of travel within Alaska, enabling more tourists to catch a glimpse of Mt. McKinley, North America's highest mountain and the very symbol of Alaska's wild nature. During World War II, the Alaska Highway was constructed to provide, through Canada, a land link for the military between Alaska and the rest of the United States. Following the war and since the 1960s especially, it has become an adventure in itself to drive the Alaska Highway— and some 13 per cent of summer visitors enter Alaska by road from Canada. Alaska has steadily become a popular tourist destination for both independent travellers and those who visit on a package tour. Since the mid-1980s the number of tourists has increased by 50 per cent to over one million a year. And it is now possible to visit virtually any part of the state. For example, day trips to Barrow, the most northerly town in the United States, offer the tourist a chance to walk on tundra and dip their toes in the frigid waters of the Arctic Ocean, while for the more adventurous Alaska offers opportunities for cross-country skiing, dog mushing, climbing and wildlife watching. Many areas, such as remoter parts of the Brooks Range in northern Alaska, are being opened up to tourism for the first time as popular destinations such as Denali National Park become overcrowded and people have to make reservations for accommodation several months in advance.

Elsewhere in the Arctic, tourism has been given a boost over the last decade by not only the ease of travel, but by the popular writings of people such as Barry Lopez (1986). As in Alaska, more regions are becoming accessible to the tourist as a result of expanding transportation infrastructures. Despite the expense of getting to and travelling in the circumpolar north, during summer tourists are as common as scientists and migrating birds. Some tourists are more casual visitors than others. During summer for example, one or two-day tours to east Greenland are available from Iceland, while cruise ships sail regularly through the North West Passage, Russia's Northern Sea Route, and also break their way through the ice to the North Pole. Hall and Johnston (*ibid.*: 11) have claimed that Arctic tourism will increase 'as the appeal of opportunities for eco-tourism, adventure tourism and cultural tourism continues to grow'. And it is not just the large tour operators who capitalise on this, Native organisations offer tours to those interested in Native culture.

As attempts are made to find ways of reconciling environental protection with sustainable development, tourism's appeal is that it is non-consumptive, environmentally-friendly, fosters understanding of local cultures, and provides economic opportunities for remote Arctic regions. For example, tourism is currently Alaska's major growth industry, generating $1.4 billion in revenues each year, with over $50 million of direct revenues going to the State of Alaska (Alaska Division of Tourism 1995). And with a work force of 20,000 people (including seasonal employees), the visitor industry (as tourism is officially known in Alaska) is one of the state's main sources of employment. Although tourism in Alaska accounts for only about 1 per cent of gross state product, it contributes more to the state's economy than the timber industry (Alaska Division of Economic Development 1994). Anticipating the national White House Conference on Travel and Tourism, called by President Bill Clinton and held in Washington D.C. in October 1995, the Alaska Division of Tourism sponsored a state summit on tourism and travel in Alaska in April 1995 which underlined the state government's commitment to expanding further the visitor industry.[1]

While tourism is confined primarily to the months between mid-May and mid-September, there is also a modest number of winter visitors. Japanese tourists are attracted to interior Alaska, especially the area around Fairbanks, in the coldest, darkest months to view (and to consummate their marriages under) the *aurora borealis*. The demand is such that a specialist Japanese-owned tour operator, Japan-Alaska Tours, (which is based in the small town of North Pole, a place renowned in Alaska for both its Santa Claus House and its religious fundamentalism—neither of which is apparently linked) caters exclusively to intrepid Japanese. But tourism industry officials wish to develop Alaska as a winter destination for people from other countries as well, and are beginning to encourage investment in winter sports as well as marketing annual dog sledding races such as the Iditarod and the Yukon Quest as international events.

In the Canadian Northwest Territories tourism employs about one third of the region's active workforce (Butler 1992), while in northern Fennoscandia, tourism has long been well-established and both local Scandinavians and indigenous Saami people rely heavily on the industry during the summer months. As Pretes (1995: 5) has shown, Lapland appeals to different kinds of tourists:

> Lapland provides a place to escape from a routine and mechanized life and to find solace in the forest... Other tourists find Lapland an ideal place for recreational activities... Adventure travel also brings tourists to Lapland, with such attractions as snowmobile safaris, ski races and treks, and cruises on ice-breakers in the Gulf of Bothnia. Foreign tourists, especially, see Lapland as a remote, exotic land suited for adventure.

Ironically, as Beach (1994: 183) points out the tourist who sets out to experience the last great wilderness in Europe

> does not always appreciate that this wilderness is infact the immemorial homeland of Saami and the stamping grounds for a highly developed traditional reindeer herding. The Saami have in fact been instrumental in creating their environment which some conservationists wish to label as purely natural.

As mentioned in earlier chapters, in Greenland economic development can no longer be based primarily on the shrimp and cod fishery and the Greenland Home Rule Authorities are looking to alternative industries, such as tourism and mining, and possibly oil and gas production. While future exploitation of non-renewable resources is as yet uncertain, tourism is seen to provide a lucrative and immediate source of revenue, and as something that can be developed into a viable industry as part of a diversified economy. In many parts of Greenland tourism is already quite well developed, albeit on a small scale. In the 1990s Greenland has been receiving over 3,000 tourists annually, but the Home Rule Authorities wish to see this figure increase to some 35,000 annually by the beginning of the 21st century. In 1992 Greenland Tourism, a Home Rule-owned company, was established to develop and coordinate tourism in the country. A development of this scale requires major infrastructural changes, for example in transportation and accommodation. At present, most visits are short-term, with the majority of tourists arriving on cruise ships or on guided excursions. Tourism also tends to be specialist in nature, with many tourists buying adventure holiday packages that have a particular interest, such as mountain walking, ornithology or wildlife. Although an increase in tourism would bring much-needed revenue to the country, it could also result in specific problems if allowed to go unchecked. This is true for other parts of the Arctic. Research into the possible environmental, economic and cultural impacts is necessary and appropriate management structures and policies need to be adopted if tourism is to proceed in the best interests of communities and the environment.[2]

The appeal and attraction of Arctic and sub-Arctic regions as tourist destinations is to some considerable extent attributable to an enduring image of northern landscapes as polar wilderness. In the popular imagination the circumpolar north is a vast forbidding wilderness, a land of perpetual cold and darkness. Much of this imagery has been shaped by the literary writings of people such as Jack London, the verse of Robert Service, or by journals and popular accounts of exploration, adventure and whaling voyages. Such literature has helped to produce what have become predictable stereotypes of the Arctic.

The tradition may have started when Pytheas of Massilia made the first recorded voyage into the Arctic around 300 BC, considered it unsuitable for human habitation and saw only a desolate icescape enveloped in fog. On the other hand, a belief in the balmy waters of the Arctic related to the ancient Greek legends of the Hyperboreans, a people living in the far north beyond *Boreas*, the north wind, continued to fascinate the Romantics. For example, the narration of Mary Shelley's *Frankenstein*, published in 1818, is set on board a ship on a voyage of Arctic exploration. At the beginning of the novel, the leader of the expedition writes to his sister from St. Petersburg how he tries in vain

> to be persuaded that the pole is the seat of frost and desolation; it ever presents itself to my imagination as the region of beauty...the sea is for ever visible, its broad disk just skirting the horizon, and diffusing a perpetual splendour.

Similarly, in his poem *Revolt of Islam* published in the same year, Percy Bysshe Shelley regards Hyperborea, with its 'Mountains of ice, like sapphire, piled on high', as a land of warmth with '...waters azure with the noontide day'. The Shelleys were hardly writing at a time of geographical ignorance of the Arctic. But despite voyages of geographical exploration, such as Scoresby's expedition north of Svalbard in 1806, Buchan and Franklin's attempt to reach the North Pole in 1818, and Ross and Parry's effort to discover the North West Passage in the same year, what lay beyond the icy polar seas continued to fascinate writers who found much in the metaphors of whiteness and inverted landscapes.

The development of modern tourism in the polar regions continues to play on this image. Tour companies market the Arctic as a land of superlatives and extremes, where nature can still be experienced as raw and pristine. The brochures they produce (as brochures are apt to do, e.g. Selwyn 1993) entice the visitor with descriptions of untrammelled wilderness, fascinating Native culture and adundant wildlife, so that a trip to the Arctic is promised to be an unforgettable encounter with majestic scenery, cathedral-sized icebergs, the midnight sun or a mystical aurora borealis, friendly indigenous people, and with whales, bears and other animals. As the official brochure produced by Greenland Tourism claims, 'travelling in Greenland in like travelling for the very first time'.

While the wildness of nature is packaged as something to be experienced, parts of the Arctic are perhaps more famously marketed as 'the last frontier'. This is especially true for Alaska and the Canadian North. Several writers have commented that the image of Alaska as the last frontier has long been a potent one for many Alaskans and for people living elsewhere in the United States. For example, Nash (1982: 272) has written that Alaska has long been valued 'as a permanent frontier where Americans could visit their past both in person and as an "idea"'. The image of life on the last frontier is funda-mental to the construction of Alaskan cultural identity. At opposite ends of the social and cultural spectrum of the state are categories of 'Native Alaskans', who are usually and for official purposes defined as the indigen-ous peoples (such as Eskimos, Athabascans and Aleuts), and 'non-Alaskans', who are either recent arrivals or transient residents (known as Cheechakos), and tourists and visitors. In between there are categories of 'genuine Alaskans', people of long-term residence born in Alaska of Euro-American or other parentage, and often called 'sourdoughs'. The history of Alaska is also one of migration and residential mobility and newcomers have in common the fact that they are migrants to the last frontier and this contributes to the defining and working out of a sense of identity amongst them (Cuba 1987).

Synonomous with the idea of the frontier is the history of gold mining, and tourism development in towns such as Skagway, Nome and Fairbanks has capitalised on nostalgia associated with the gold rush and the social character of the pioneer. Although abandoned mining machinery litters many hiking trails, gold mining is still an active industry in Alaska and tours of active gold dredges are available during the summer months of operation. Panning for gold in Alaskan rivers and streams is often mentioned in tour brochures as one of the many activities available to the tourist. In Fairbanks, visitors can attend turn of the century dance-hall revues in Alaskaland and listen to daily readings of the poetry of Robert Service in rustic bars such as the 'Malemute Saloon'. Writing on tourism in Canada's Yukon Territory Jarvenpa (1994: 29) has argued that the imagery and mythology of the gold rush, in particular the lore associated with the heroic pioneer, has contributed to a process of cultural commoditisation, which he calls 'Klondikephilia'. In Whitehorse and Dawson City, visitors can experience the thrill of old-time gambling and the performances of can-can girls. Jarvenpa (*ibid*.: 42) has remarked how 'there is a pilgrimage-like quality to Klondike tourism as thousands of Americans journey to the remote locale each summer, in essence, to witness a re-enactment of a chapter of their own history'.

But the Alaskan frontier is also a modern industrial frontier and the 800-mile Trans-Alaska Pipeline, once at the very centre of debate about the future of Alaska (Coates 1993), is now marketed as a tourist attraction, while several companies offer one-day tours from Anchorage and Fairbanks of the oil production complex of Prudhoe Bay on the Arctic coast of the North Slope. Just as visitors consume the image of the lone pioneer who endured isolation in a harsh environment, while imagining themselves to be modern-day pioneers as they travel Alaska's roads in their camper vans and recreation vehicles, they can also see for themselves the power of late twentieth century technology that harnesses resources vital for the economy of the nation. The Dalton Highway, a rough dirt road linking Prudhoe Bay with roads just north of Fairbanks, and which was constructed for the exclusive use of pipeline and oil-industry related vehicles, has recently become part of the state highway system and has been opened to the public, making it possible for anyone with the time, inclination and money to drive to the North Slope of Alaska from virtually anywhere in the United States.

Yet, while responding to the call of the Arctic wild, it seems that tourists driving the Dalton Highway wish to be reminded that they are still in the United States of America. During summer 1995, a local Alaskan newspaper, the *Fairbanks Daily News-Miner* published articles reporting on tourists using the road, many of whom complained about the lack of facilities and out-houses. One article related how 'Wisconsites Emil and Dorothy Pedersen, on their way back to Fairbanks, described sleepless nights in the omniprescent sunlight and sightings of grizzly bears, musk oxen herds, countless caribou and moose....As for the facilities at the north end, Emil Pedersen said, "There isn't any. You want to buy a quart of milk, you can't buy a quart of milk," he said.[3] While the opening of the Dalton Highway has democratised access to the far north of Alaska, such public access continues to inform heated debate between developers, who see wilderness as a resource to be exploited in return for more tourist dollars, and environmentalists who fear the day when hamburger restaurants will open to cater for tourist demand along the road.

ARCTIC REALITIES

The circumpolar north is not an inaccesible part of the world, but is linked inextricably to the global system. Herein lies one of the ironies for the Arctic tourist. Johnston (1995: 29–30) has remarked that as

the entire northern circumpolar world is ringed with the legacy of past and continuing military and industrial activity....in some locations, tourists are confronted
with the discrepancy between the image of a pristine, untouched environment and
the reality of military installations, and oil and gas exploration....requiring them to
adjust their expectations.

But are tourists really so naive? Does travel in the Arctic represent an educating experience for tourists as they stumble over rusting military hardware,
see broken down snowmachines and outboard engines piled outside the
homes of Native people, or watch hunters cutting up seals on the beach? Do
many tourists actually hope to find the 'authentic' and the 'real', or are they
shocked and disillusioned by conditions in Native villages? Hall seems to be
following an argument in the sociology of tourism, which is based on ideas
suggested by Boorstin (1964) and Baudrillard (1988), that tourists are unable
to experience reality as they travel. Rather, as they wander through tourist
space in their guided groups, they are insulated from reality and truth, and
are happier just to witness the inauthentic from the comfort of air-condi-
tioned buses and in the company of like-minded people.

Cohen (1979, 1988), however, has warned against generalising the nature
and type of tourists and tourism and has pointed out that there is a variety of
types of tourist with each seeking a variety of experiences, especially those
denied to the conventional tourist in a group. The sociology of tourism is
concerned with how tourism as both industry and process results in the production of inauthenticity, but rather than stressing the contrived in tourist
attractions some writers have focused on how tourists themselves view their
own lives as somehow inauthentic. The search for what is 'genuine' and
'real', and to be changed by the experience of encounters with people and
landscape, become the very reasons for travelling (McCannell 1976,
Zurick 1995).

In his seminal work *The Tourist* (1976), McCannell argued that all tourists
are seeking authenticity, are wanting to experience something which is lost
in their own culture, and 'desire a deeper involvement with society and culture to some degree; it is a basic component of their motivation to travel'
(McCannell 1976: 10). To this can be added that tourists also desire a deeper
involvement with landscapes. But tourists are often criticised and 're-
proached for being satisfied with superficial experiences of other peoples
and other places' (McCannell *ibid.*) Perhaps many tourists who visit the Arctic *are* striving to experience reality and to have less superficial contact with
people and places, but it is noticeable that in much academic research on
tourism it is the tourists themselves who are considered to be the problem.
But little attempt is made to consider how tour companies, agencies and local

communities actively construct the contrived and superficial nature of tourism and conspire together, often unwittingly, to deny the tourist an authentic
experience.

Tourists, in their search for the authentic, only experience what McCannell has called 'staged authenticity'. So, the Arctic *is* a last frontier, it *is* a land
of adventure, colourful and hardy indigenous people, and it *is* the home of
Santa Claus, even if agreement about his exact nationality is not easily
reached, because those involved in Arctic tourism produce and reproduce
images and stereotypes. Even the 'reality' of the Arctic as an industrial frontier can be used to good effect in tourism development. Pipelines, oil production complexes and military installations can be packaged as industrial
heritage for touristic consumption. Tourists visit the Far North as an idea
and, to paraphrase McCannell (1976: 111), do not in any empirical sense *see*
the Arctic, 'they see elements of it which are symbolic markers', just as when
tourists cross the Arctic Circle, they do not see it, they see a sign, a symbolic
marker which they can photograph (Pretes 1995).

IN SEARCH OF NATIVE CULTURE

Increasing numbers of tourists to the Arctic now cite indigenous culture as the
main attraction after scenery and wildlife. Some visit the Arctic with the sole
aim of having an ethnographic experience. For instance, one tourist to
Alaska, a London investment banker who travelled to Fairbanks, Barrow and
Nome during summer 1995, said quite simply of his reason for visiting Alaska,
"I want to break bread with the Inuit." Having experienced an organised tour
to a Native community and having visited Denali National Park, through local
contacts he was able to travel to Inupiaq Eskimo villages on the Bering Strait
coast, often in the company of local people. Along the way he was able to
learn something of the social and political situation of Alaska's indigenous
people—and he fulfilled his ambition of meeting people in their homes. As
has been well documented by anthropologists, this kind of ethnographic
tourism is increasingly popular. Linked to the continuing preoccupation
amongst tourists from Europe and North America with visiting non-Western
countries (Zurick 1995: 113), there is a growing market eager to consume
images of indigenous peoples and to understand something of their relationship with the environment. As Zurick puts it, 'If contemporary Western society no longer holds a valid myth…then that may be why people search other
cultures—to discover that which may be lost in their own' (*ibid*. 133).

The peripherality of Arctic villages (many of which are only accessible
by air) and traditional Native culture is attractive to tourists in search of

authenticity. Recognising this, the tourism development agencies of Arctic countries have long used images of indigenous people as a marketing strategy (e.g. Hinch 1995). Tourist brochures stress the ancient relationship between indigenous people and the land and contain photographs which, following Cohen (1993: 36), amount to nothing but 'ethnographically idealized pictures of colourful natives, intended to titillate the prospective visitor'. Cohen is writing generally of how indigenous peoples are represented for touristic purposes in anachronistic fashion, without reference to their contemporary social, economic and political situation, which is often uncomfortable for the tourist to accept. As Beach (1994: 184) observes of tourism in northern Scandinavia

> The tourist who desires a wilderness challenge is often willing to accept a leather-clad herder living in an old traditional tent, tending his herd on foot, but should the herder, garbed in synthetic materials, fly to his modern cabin by helicopter, the tourist can become indignant and demand restrictions.

Unlike the experiences of the investment banker mentioned above, it is very difficult for travellers to visit Native villages independently. The Alaska Native Claims Settlement Act of 1971 made many villages and their lands in effect private reserves, making it necessary for visitors to have permits before entering a community. Concerned with alcohol and illegal drugs entering communities, village elders often meet aircraft that land and check people's baggage. Together with a suspicion and distrust of strangers (perhaps because many visitors to Alaskan villages are representatives of state and federal agencies), tourists can encounter hostility if arriving unannounced and with no local contacts. As well as the expense of flying to a village there is often a scarcity, if not a complete absence of visitor accommodation and tourists can place strain on local stores which have limited supplies and are used to supplying local demand only. The easiest and safest way is to travel on an organised tour.

From the end of World War II the development of organised tourism in rural Alaska, where tourists could 'experience' Eskimo culture was started by non-Natives. Many local people were also disinterested in being involved in it as a business and remained exotic attractions rather than entrepreneurs (Smith 1989). Smith (*ibid*.: 63–4) has commented on some of the insidious aspects of tourism in rural Alaska when, in the mid-1960s, tourists visiting Kotzebue offended Eskimos with endless, repetitive questions and disturbed local people in their daily work. Smith noted how 'Eskimo women began to refuse photographers, then erected barricades to shield their work from tourist eyes, and some finally resorted to hiring a taxi to haul seals and other game to the privacy of their homes for processing'. Tour companies are sensitive to the intrusive activities of tourists and, before landing in Kotzebue today, Alaska Airlines requests that people on its tours to the village refrain from taking photographs of the Native tour guide as they disembark the aircraft.

Taking photographs of the locals is only one of many exploitative touristic pursuits, however. Residents of many Alaskan communities express concern over the increasing numbers of visitors who use Native-owned lands for recreation and sports hunting. Subsistence and sports fishing often come into conflict, for example. On Alaska's Kenai Peninsula south of Anchorage, the runs of king salmon in June and July each year bring several thousand fishermen to the Kenai River, making it the most heavily fished river in Alaska. Known in Alaska as 'combat fishing', fishermen jostle for elbow room on the riverbanks while speedboats crowd the water. Fish that are caught are weighed and then thrown back into the water, only to run the risk of being caught as they make their way upriver to spawn by several more fishermen. The sports fishermen come from many parts of North America as well as from Alaska's growing and sprawling metropolitan area of Anchorage and they disrupt the traditional subsistence fishery of the Kenaitze, a Dena'ina Athabascan tribe. The Kenaitze argue that the practice of catching, weighing and then throwing back the fish does not respect the spirit of the fish, which may then refuse to be taken by Native fishermen who fish primarily for food.

The appearance of tourists in Alaskan villages is also seasonal When tourists do arrive in the summer months, tourism may involve a high proportion of local people in servicing directly, and indirectly, the needs and demands of tourists, rather than indigenously generated needs. In this way tourism produces dependency relationships and local people may also become dependent on outsiders for seasonal or long-term employment when primary industries, such as fishing decline. Tourism often develops in areas at the same time as they are experiencing rapid social change, and while it contributes to social and economic transition, as Gilligan (*ibid*.) has observed, the success of tourism can become necessary for the economic survival of some areas. Wenzel (1995) deseibes how Inuit communities on Baffin Island see ecotourism as having the potential for expanding the wage-labour sectors of the local economy and replacing income lost through the European Community boycott on sealskin imports. Similar attitudes are probably found elsewhere in remote communities struggling to find ways of finding secure cash flows. As one man from the Alutiiq community of Old Harbour on Kodiak Island put it to me, "In fifty years there will be no subsistence or fishing. We have to think of alternative ways of making a living and tourism is one of them". Yet, Arctic tourism creates low-wage seasonal jobs, and much of the tourism industry does not benefit local communities, but the earnings go outside the state.[4]

LOCAL INVOLVEMENT IN ENVIRONMENTAL TOURISM

A currently fashionable argument in social science tourist literature is that, done well and with community participation (e.g. Murphy 1985), tourism can empower local communities by 'giving them a pride in their communities' development' (Whelan 1991: 4). As Rossell (1989: 5) has put it, 'socially responsible/environmentally viable tourism can't be fostered without dialogue constructed and controlled along indigenous needs and in indigenous terms'. Arctic tourism represents an interesting test case as to the effectiveness of this, as in many parts, such as Alaska, Canada and Greenland, indigenous communities are participating in environmental and cultural tourism projects at both planning and implementation stages, as well as benefiting from the outcome. Nickels *et al.* (1991: 166) have described how tourism development in Baffin Island in Canada's eastern Arctic is viewed by residents of Inuit communities as a potentially viable industry. While people remain ambiguous about the cultural and environmental impacts, their main fears 'revolve around the potential lack of community involvement in the industry and the possibility that tourists may break local rules'.

Capitalising on tradition as a resource and determined that communities should benefit directly from tourism, several Native-owned tour companies have also emerged in Alaska over the last few years. This development of a Native-owned tourism industry is linked both to the emergence of specialist adventure tourism and eco-tourism and to the politics of community empowerment. The tour companies are owned by village corporations which were established as profit-making enterprises by the Alaska Native Claims Settlement Act of 1971. Native communities see in tourism an opportunity for developing cash-earning enterprises based on the desire of other people to experience wilderness and visit non-Western societies, and at the same time gain control of an industry that outsiders have otherwise dominated. Linked to indigenous political movements that emphasises the importance of indigenous knowledge for sustainable development, locally-controlled tourism also represents an opportunity for Arctic communities to educate visitors about indigenous ways of life and about human-environment relationships. Alaskan Native leaders see the local control of tourism as an industry that can form part of diversified local economies and at the same time regulate the numbers of visitors to Native lands.

But is local participation in, and control of, the tourism industry also one way for the indigenous peoples of the Arctic to mitigate stereotypes of themselves and of the environment? In his discussion of the touristic construction of the Native image, Cohen (1993: 49) posed an interesting question. How do Native people represent themselves as objects of the tourist gaze? Do they reproduce the idealised images imposed upon them by outsiders, or do they represent themselves in a way which runs counter to such stereotyping and which, from an indigenous perspective, is more 'accurate' and 'authentic'? Cohen's own study of the images of three groups of indigenous peoples provided different answers. I argue here that in the Arctic, self-representation for touristic consumption remains simplified and idealised because Arctic tourism will continue to depend on images of wilderness, untouched frontiers and timelessly traditional cultures, as these images are, from a marketing point of view, necessary to nourish the spirit of a restless age. In the rest of this chapter, therefore, I show how Native-owned tour companies play on the idea of the Arctic as a wilderness and last frontier to attract tourists seeking to experience both landscape and traditional Native culture. In the process, they construct indigenous views of the Arctic environment and represent indigenous culture for touristic consumption, which only serves to confirm the tourist's beliefs and expectations. After all, if the tourist's hosts and guides are locals, then what they see and experience must be authentic rather than staged. However, much of what local communities reveal to tourists is staged, rather than authentic. Local rituals and events, which are often private, become public cultural performances. But, by marketing themselves as a tourist attraction, indigenous communities attempt to empower themselves and constantly reconstruct and renegotiate cultural identity.

As a promotional leaflet of the Alaska Native Tourism Council puts it, the Native peoples of Alaska 'welcome visitors with a smile' and the tourist to Alaska is invited to visit Alaska's Native peoples 'for a few hours or for a few days'. [5] Native-owned tour companies produce leaflets and brochures that emphasise the environmentally-friendly and educational nature of the tours they offer, in contrast to the mass tourism in other parts of Alaska close to urban centres and linked to the state highway system.

The casual visitor to Alaska, with money enough to spare, can choose from a number of 'cultural experiences' that range from one-day visits to Inupiaq Eskimo villages such as Barrow (marketed as the 'Top of the World') and Kotzebue, where they are greeted by traditional dancers and can learn about whaling and the local subsistence culture, to journeys of several days along the Koyukon River, in the company of Athabascan hunters and fishermen. None of these tours are cheap, and on top of the cost of reaching Alaska in the first place tourists can expect to pay over $500 for a one-day tour to Barrow from Anchorage. Tourists making an excursion from Anchorage to

Nome or Kotzebue would pay almost $500 and once there have a choice of extending their itinerary (and parting with a further $300 or so) to include sightseeing in surrounding villages only accessible by air, but where they will 'learn about the subsistence lifestyle' of their 'friendly hosts'.

Visitors with little time and money can also attempt to gain insight into Native culture by visiting villages close to Anchorage (such as the Dena'ina Athabascan Eklutna Village Historical Park), Fairbanks (which is connected to several Athabascan villages by road and which also has a Native village in Alaskaland, the local theme park), and other villages in south and southeast Alaska accessible by road or coastal ferry. Most Native communities are able to provide regular guided tours. For example, half-hour tours of Eklutna Village Historical Park begin every thirty minutes, and in Sitka in southeast Alaska, the Sitka Tribe of Alaska operate bus tours that give visitors the history of Sitka from the perspective of the indigenous Tlingit tribes. Yet, tourists can only hope to glimpse a little of what their tour companies have selected to show them. Yukon River Tours, for example, which is owned by the Athabascan people of Stevens Village, take tourists on a one and a half hour-long trip on the Yukon River to visit not the village itself (which is out of bounds to tourists), but a fishcamp and the Stevens Village Cultural Centre, a considerable distance downriver.

Yukon River Tours describes itself in its brochures as 'dedicated to offering environmentally responsible and educational tours for all to enjoy and appreciate' and the emphasis of its tours is on hardship, survival and tradition in a remote region 'where the air is clean and the land is blessed with an abundance of wildlife and natural beauty'. Tourists are told that they are to 'embark on a journey that others have only read about' and that they will be 'encouraged to peek inside the smokehouse' and will be able to 'participate in the traditional ritual of Salmon harvesting or just relax and enjoy the peaceful majestic beauty of this truly unique last frontier'. They are lectured on Athabascan culture and customs, and the exhibitions at the Stevens Village Cultural Centre focus on life on the Yukon River in the 1930s and 1940s.

Another Athabascan tour company is Arctic Village Tours, owned by the Gwich'in people of Arctic Village in northeast Alaska. Residents of Arctic Village already require visitors to have a permit to visit the community and Arctic Village Tours offers one day cultural tours from Fairbanks, as well as overnight 'wilderness' excursions. In this way, Arctic Village residents can control how many people visit their community, how they get there, and ensure that they spend money. As of 1995, a one-day tour from Fairbanks cost $250, while an overnight wilderness excursion cost $150 per person per day, plus a return air fare of $260. The Arctic Village Tours brochure describes the Gwich'in as 'a people anxious to share their village and the simple pleasures of life in this far-north locale with visitors from southern climes'. A visitor to Arctic Village will have already read promotional tour leaflets produced by Arctic Village Tours from which they will learn that the village is the Northern-most Indian community in the world, that the Gwich'in are 'a people dependent physically, culturally, and spiritually on a way of life that includes a large measure of hunting, fishing, berry gathering and other subsistence skills. A people deeply committed to the care of the land that sustains and nourishes them'. Furthermore, the residents of Arctic Village are marketing themselves as 'the Last Indians on the Last Frontier', and Arctic Village Tours informs its potential clients that

> you will set foot on the Last Frontier where you will experience the traditional Native culture. This is not a commercialized attraction, but a chance to experience life on the VERY LAST FRONTIER as it exists today. It is one of the very last areas in North America to be touched by Western Culture which has had both negative and positive impact. CULTURAL PRESERVATION through CULTURAL PRE-SENTATION, while educating the public about our traditional way of life is the aim of our tourism program.

A one-day visit to Arctic Village from Fairbanks (from 9 a.m. to 4 p.m.) includes a guided tour of the village by local residents (contrast this turn of events with Smith (*ibid*.) who noted that guides in the past were non-Natives with little experience or knowledge of the Arctic), a lunch consisting of traditional food, and presentations of songs and dances. Overnight journeys have wildife watching focus, sports fishing, and hiking. In a similar vein, Athabasca Cultural Journeys offers a wilderness experience of several days duration on the Koyukuk River. As their brochure enticingly puts it

> Come, share our culture with us. Let us teach you to read animal signs, set a fish net, and learn traditional Athabascan crafts. Or listen as we share ancient myths and folklore of our ancestors. Our Native culture is alive and well, not something to experience in a museum. We invite you to become part of our culture and experience the spirit of this great land called Alaska.

Such indigenous representation plays on the image of Alaska as the last frontier and a remote wilderness and contributes to the perpetuation of the myth of the Arctic environment as hostile, wild, untamed, and pristine. In the imagination of the tourist, primitive Native culture still survives in remote Alaska, and Native-owned tour companies try their best not to disappoint. This is in stark contrast to political reaction by indigenous leaders to the Arctic being labelled a 'frontier' or 'wilderness' and who have called instead for international recognition of Arctic lands as *homelands* (Nuttall 1992). For the Gwich'in, who are faced with the possibility of oil development in the Arctic National Wildlife Refuge threatening the migratory routes and calving grounds of the Porcupine caribou herd, the representation of their lands as wilderness serves to enlist the support of environmentalist groups, politicians and members of the public opposed to drilling. As other chapters in this book have shown, in both regional and international contexts the Arctic's indigenous peoples construct for themselves an identity as custodians of the Arctic environment, but one consequence of the politicisation of Arctic peoples has been the emergence of an indigenous environmentalism that appeals to and emphasises enduring spiritual values and traditional culture. That this should underpin indigenous representation for tourists is entirely consistent with current indigenous discourse.

Alaskan Native communities are beset by severe social and economic problems But tourists visiting Alaska are looking to experience authentic and traditional Native culture, and do not want to be presented with lectures on social problems and how Alaskan villages are ravaged by unemployment, alcoholism and substance abuse. Some things are worthy of the attention of the tourist, while there are other things that they cannot see, such as, 'hidden behind the ceremonies and the masks, the poverty and the suffering that would dismay them' (Zurick *ibid.*: 158). Similarly evidence of modernity and change is either hidden or played down. Locals dress in traditional clothing to meet tourists and to perform for them, men hold demonstrations of how to make hunting and fishing equipment, and banquets of traditional foods are laid on by women, who also sell their homemade crafts while visitors munch on dried salmon.

Following Greenwood's (*ibid.*) influential anthropological perspective on tourism as cultural commoditisation, Alaskan Native culture is appropriated as a commodity by tour companies who then package it and sell it. Greenwood's argument, based on his own work in a Basque village, is that the cultural meanings of local rituals and events that have religious significance and importance for community identity become commoditised, depriving local people of the meanings of vital societal events. Local rituals and events, which are often private, become public cultural performances subject to the agendas and demands of tourists, tour companies and tourist boards. This perspective sees local 'colourful' and 'ethnic' rituals as being exploited by the tourism industry for profit, and for consumption by tourists. And the sense that cultural events become colourful displays is heightened by the fact that tourists themselves are also deprived of understanding cultural meanings. For example, organised tours to Barrow include a display of Inupiaq Eskimo dancing and a blanket toss on the beach, where a person, usually a child, is thown in the air by a group of people holding a large bearded sealskin or walrus skin. Tourists are invited to participate, by holding the skin and helping to throw the child in the air. On the occasions I witnessed this, the tour guide did not explain the significance of the blanket toss: that it was practised traditionally so that a person might glimpse bowhead whales beyond the pack ice and thus herald the beginning of the spring whaling season.

In a sense tourists induce tradition and their appearance provokes a search by the host community for those aspects of culture that visitors value as traditional (cf Jedrej and Nuttall *ibid.*), with the particularities of local history, subsistence lifestyles and indigenous environmental knowledge underpinning the cultural production of authenticity. In this way, tourism contributes to an indigenous representation of Alaskan Native culture, such as dancing, singing, storytelling, mask making, the sewing of skins, basketry and ivory carving, as forever traditional. Above all, the people themselves are portrayed as remaining in harmony with their environment, in complete contrast to those for whom they are performing.

Whatever labels Native tour companies use for their tourism (sustainable, environmentally responsible, etc.), and while an aim may be cultural preservation or cultural conservation, they are still involved in commercial ventures that need to make a profit, and which may not be entirely compatible with traditional values (e.g. see Hinch 1995). Anders and Anders (1987), for example, have written on the conflict between individualism and the profit motivations of Alaskan Native corporate organisational culture established by the Alaska Native Claims Settlement Act, and the communal, kinship-based values of Alaskan Native villages. More research on specific case studies is needed before it is clear whether tourism development is generating Native prosperity at the cost of further erosion of local culture.

When aspects of culture become commodities and enter systems of exchange, splits within communities become possible as indigenous entrepreneurs run the risk of being accused of trivialising aspects of traditional culture. There is also, in many communities, lack of awareness of what tourism is. Nickels *et al.* (1991: 166) make this specific point in their discussion of tourism development in the Baffin Island community of Clyde River, where tourism 'is just a perception in the minds of the community' and most people do not have direct experience of the industry. Similarly in Greenland, some regions of the country have been singled out for tourism development by Greenland Tourism. Many communities are either not ready for tourists, or do not have the ability to cope with tourist demands. Some regions will also benefit from tourism, while others will lose out, with tourism contributing to the development of uneven development in some parts of the country.

Alaskan Native communities, through the activities and marketing skills of both outsiders and Native peoples themselves have become tourism market places where visitors can consume images of aboriginal people and the wilderness in which they live, purchase traditional handicrafts, and view staged culture. In controlling the level and extent of tourism development Native communities are seemingly enjoying a degree of empowerment consistent with other aspects of political and economic development made possible by land claims settlements. But host communities may not necessarily be able to exercise total control over what their guests can and cannot do. As environmental, cultural and other forms of alternative tourism continue to grow in popularity and expand into more peripheral regions of the world, local communities may not be able to withstand entirely tourist demands for services, a situation evident in many parts of the world.

As research carried out on the impact of tourism on remote communities in other parts of the world shows, tourism development injects a new group of resource users into the social and economic landscape (Johnston 1990). For example, the considerable pressure from tourists to the Western Isles of Scotland for facilities to be available on Sundays, exemplifies this. Sunday is a day of strict religious observance in the Western Isles, yet tourist demands now mean that shops, public houses and petrol stations are opening on Sundays. This is not only considered by many residents of the Western Isles to be a threat to local ways of life and to cultural identity, it is seen to encourage activities alien to local culture and has divided community opinion over the maintenance of tradition vis a vis the perceived benefits of change (Jedrej and Nuttall *ibid*.). Tourism thus contributes to the straining of cultural values and to the redefiniton of the identity and role of the host society.

In Alaska and elsewhere in the Arctic, Native communities face demands from tourists who expect to see authentic, traditional culture. Ironically, these demands threaten the cultural integrity of the communities tourists are so eager to discover and experience. It may be idealistic, for example, to expect tourists to accept marine mammal hunting. As I have observed on a number of occasions in Greenland, while tourists often describe Greenlandic culture as 'fascinating', they are less enthusiastic to see Greenlanders cutting up whales and seals down at the 'colourful' harbour. On Baffin Island, Wenzel (1995) has pointed our that local people fear losing out on valuable tourist dollars if visitors happen to witness subsistence hunting activities. Local discussion of the benefits of tourism centres on the real costs involved to the subsistence-based economy by protecting tourists from seeing seals shot, or by abandoning hunting altogether in certain areas during tourist visits. Such local anxieties are precisely what conservationists and animal welfare groups are keen to provoke in the hope that local attitudes towards marine mammals will change. For instance, campaign groups such as the Whale and Dolphin Conservation Society and the World Wide Fund for Nature hope that local people in Norway, Iceland and Greenland will become more involved in whale watching tourism and less interested in whale hunting.

By way of response to the attitudes of outsiders, members of indigenous communities construct an identity as a people living in areas largely untouched by modernity and change and represent indigenous culture for touristic consumption. Both hosts and guests, therefore, conspire together in the production of authenticity. In the words of Lanfant (1995a: 36), 'tourists and the receiving society are thus engaged in a process of reciprocal misconstruction'. The guests get what they pay their money to see (while not having their sensitivities offended)—the hosts sustain their local economy and empower themselves by renegotiating their perceived cultural identities and restricting access to Native lands and communities. For the most part, and because of resolved land claims issues, Arctic communities can benefit from tourism in economic and cultural ways. They can earn money in a way which can be incorporated into an existing local mode of production and, as this chapter has discussed, can attempt to use tourism as a way of preserving local culture.

As more remote communities in Siberia, Greenland and Canada experience growing numbers of tourists, local involvement in tourism in Alaska has lessons for other parts of the Arctic. Tourism can contribute to small-scale local economies and, if properly managed, can stimulate the development of other sectors such as cottage industries. In this way, indigenous peoples' organisations such as the ICC see tourism as a natural resource but warn that it should be subject to management policies and express local concern that, compared with other industrial activities, the tourism industry 'is seldom required to present any environmental, social, or cultural assessments of its impact on local communities' (Inuit Circumpolar Conference 1993: 74). If tourism is to provide opportuities for economic diversification and environmental protection, the ICC argues that local people and locally-based businesses and tourism ventures control both the number of tourists to the Arctic and the nature and character of tourism projects. The first steps have been taken towards implementing a code of practice for Arctic tourism. In January 1996 the World Wide Fund for Nature and the Norwegian Polar Institute held a workshop in Longyearbyen on Svalbard on how to develop guidelines for Arctic tourism within the framework of the work initiated by the Arctic Environmental Protection Strategy. Appropriate nods were made in the direction of indigenous peoples' organisations and among the various recommendations was one that stressed the need of tour operators to recognise local knowledge and skills.[6]

Protection of both the Arctic environment and the diversity of indigenous cultures needs to go hand in hand. Instead of seeing tourism as a form of sustainable development, it should be recognised that the industry has to be managed sustainably. Just as co-management aims for sustainable renewable resource exploitation, so partnerships between local communities, tour operators and regional and national governments must strive to ensure that tourism development and environmental conservation are mutually beneficial (although, ironically, travel to and within the Arctic makes use of non-renewable resources). But if tourism does present opportunities for small-scale sustainable development, there are serious questions which need to be addressed. Will resource management decisions meet the needs of the tourism industry first, and the needs of local people second? Can tourism be limited to meeting specific niche markets rather than mass markets? Will tourism in peripheral and vulnerable regions create dependency relationships? How sustainable can tourism really be? How possible is it to balance social and environmental needs with economic profit and the survival of the tourism industry? How far will tourism transform, revitalise, or redefine indigenous culture? How far will community members be consulted and be made aware of tourism development plans? As local communities, tourism boards and tour operators work to adopt policies and guidelines to ensure sustainable tourism development these are hard questions requiring realistic answers.

1   As oil production in Alaska is now declining there are doubts as to whether any other single industry or combination of industries can provide a viable alternative. Yet, while politicians, economists and industrialists debate what natural resources will underpin the state economy, tourism is considered important for the future.

2   Greenland Tourism has reported that a survey carried out in 1995 on the Greenlandic population's attitude to tourism has revealed a generally positive attitude and support for the development of tourism on a large scale. *Greenland Tourism Travel News* No. 1, February 1996.

3   'Dalton Breaks in the Tourists' *Fairbanks Daily News-Miner* June 27, 1995

4   By far the largest numbers of tourists to the state come in the summer months on cruise ships to southeast Alaska. The cruise companies are based outwith Alaska and the short stops that each ship makes in southeast communities are usually only long enough for passengers to buy souvenirs. Similarly, backpackers and other budget travellers spend relatively little on accommodation.

5   Alaska Native Tourism Council 1994, *Alaska Native Journeys* 4

6   A study prepared for Unaaq Inc., an Inuit company operating in Canada's Baffin Island and Nunavik regions identified poor levels of knowledge among travel agents of the Northwest Territories and recommended that greater cooperation between local and outside tour operators would result in more successful marketing strategies (Robert J. Higgins Consulting 1995).

Chapter 7

CONSTRUCTING INDIGENOUS ENVIRONMENTALISM

Without denying the significance and value of indigenous knowledge and indigenous perspectives on human-environment relationships, in this chapter I put forward some critical reflections on knowledge gathering and consider whether, in advocating indigenous environmental knowledge, we run the risk of idealising it and perpetuating the myth of primitive ecological wisdom. The ability of indigenous peoples to present themselves as being in a position to protect the Arctic environment rests on how far they are able to construct an identity as nature conservationists and represent themselves as having environmentalist cultures, or at least cultures that can accommodate environmentalist ideas in order to take a protectionist stance. I also consider, therefore, what happens when indigenous knowledge is gathered, decontextualised, reified, packaged and used in a political sense by indigenous representatives to inform and underpin an indigenous environmentalism.

ORIGINAL ECOLOGISTS?

It has become a cliche in the anthropological literature, and also a central theme of indigenous texts, documents and reports on environmental issues, that non-industrial peoples continue to live in harmony with their surroundings, and that they offer lessons to industrial societies separated from the rhythms of the earth by modernity. Thus, indigenous subsistence whale hunts in the Arctic differ from commercial whaling, Malaysian and Amazonian tribal peoples have a negligible impact on tropical forests compared to the activities of timber companies and cattle ranchers, and so on. As we have seen for the AEPS and Arctic Council this aspect of indigenous knowledge is now widely recognised in policy arenas.

But the application of indigenous knowledge in resource management not only serves the political and cultural interests of indigenous peoples fighting for self-determination and control over lands and resources. The idea that indigenous peoples have a conservation ethic that underpins alternative yet viable resource management systems also has immediate appeal for environmental groups campaigning to protect the environment from unsustainable human activities. The success (and continued appeal) of environmentalism depends on its ability to present realistic forms of alternative, sustainable societies living in harmony with the environment. In seeking to define the kinds of values and institutions of a sustainable, post-industrial society,

Euro-American environmental groups have looked to indigenous peoples and non-Western societies in India, China and Japan as role models for providing environmental paradigms that differ from Judaeo-Christian perspectives on nature (Paehlke 1989).

The spiritual reverence Native North Americans have for the environment, for instance, is often contrasted with the consumer-driven, environmentally-destructive nature of modern American society. Native North Americans are considered original ecologists who have a profound spirituality that guides them in their interactions with the natural world (Booth and Jacobs 1990, Udall 1972). The point of reference taken by environmentalists inspired by Native American philosophy is the destruction of the North American environment during the westward expansion of an ecologically-unsound white society. It is the actions and practices of colonists, not the aboriginal inhabitants of the land, which has resulted in the damage to, and loss of wildlife and landscape.

O'Riordan (1981) sees the development of an ecocentric form of modern environmentalism in the ideas and philosophies of American romantic transcendentalists such as Emerson and Thoreau, who emphasised the intrinsic value and beauty of nature beyond a rational and pragmatic use. They were in a position to assess the history of European settlement and the subsequent development of North America. European settlers had encountered vast forests which, in time, were cut down to create a humanised landscape. To the Europeans, brought up to see forests as enchanted and places to fear, the various species of trees were considered resources. Great oaks were felled to provide timber for the construction of ships for the English navy as well (along with other species) as providing building material and fuel for the North American colonies. The destruction of the North American forests came to symbolise the domination of nature by humans. But environmental degradation was not confined to deforestation. As Petulla (1980: 25) observes,

> Fifty years or more of strip mining for coal left the lands of Appalachia in ruins by the middle of this century. Oil was important for lamps during the last century, but millions of barrels of it were wasted. The oil drained into rivers and streams, caught fire, or evaporated in open containers and dams mainly because, like everything else in the country, there seemed to be plenty of it. Natural gas was used to push oil to the surface—the market did not justify its containment—so every day for decades billions of cubic feet were lost.

With westward and northward expansion of the American frontier, wildlife such as buffalo, sea otters, beavers, whales and seals also constituted a source of quick and easy profit. In contrast to the environmentally-destructive colonists, the Native peoples of North America (including Arctic hunters) have been represented by anthropologists, popular writers and spokespersons for indigenous communities and organisations as peoples who 'speak with courtesy and respect of the land, of animals, of the objects which made up the territory in which they lived' (McLuhan 1971: 1), who are guided in how to act in their everyday lives by the sacred power of animals and the environment (Brown 1992, Nelson 1983), and who live in societies that have traditionally rejected individualism and private property, but celebrate group relationships and communal solidarity and egalitarianism. Their social organisation and relationships with nature are also expressed symbolically through rituals, taboos, myths and the sharing of food, which it has been claimed act as adaptive mechanisms to overcome environmental problems (e.g. for the Inuit see Sabo and Sabo 1985). Similarly, Asian perceptions of nature have been idealised by Western environmentalists who point to the Japanese, Chinese and Indian love and reverence of nature as signifying protection (Kalland and Asquith 1997, Callicott and Ames 1989).

Primitive ecological wisdom is used to full effect in environmentalist critiques of industrialism (Milton 1996), and by selectively drawing on aspects of indigenous worldviews the appropriation of indigenous cosmology for use in national and international political arenas goes some way to endorse a Western ecocentric myth of non-Western peoples as ecologically aware. Kalland and Asquith (1997) point out in their discussion of Japanese and Chinese perceptions of nature that love and reverence is only one dimension of human-environment relationships in Eastern societies. At best, Japanese and Chinese attitudes towards nature can be described as ambivalent rather than explicitly protectionist.[1] Kalland and Asquith urge caution before claiming that a religious or spiritual relationship with nature, or seeing nature as divine, results in a conservation ethic and protectionist stance. As they argue, 'spirits can be removed through ritual means and spirits of killed animals can be placated through memorial rites. A divine nature is no guarantor against environmental degradation…on the contrary such a world view can prevent the development of a true concern for nature as such' (Kalland and Asquith 1997: 30–31). The ambivalent attitudes towards nature demonstrated by China and Japan are evidence that Eastern societies do not offer appropriate models for environmental stewardship. Even though Eastern cultures have produced poetic and artistic expressions of nature, there is considerable evidence that these societies have their own records of environmental destruction (Huddle et al. 1975). Writing of Japan, Kalland and Asquith (ibid.) argue that the close relationship that exists between people and the spirits believed to inhabit the landscape can be exploited for another purpose—to entice the spirits to leave their abodes so that ground can be used for construction or so that forests can be cut down.

Similarly, controversy surrounds the idea that indigenous peoples in the Arctic and elsewhere are natural or even original conservationists. While writers such as Usher (1987), Freeman (1979), and Berkes (1988) advocate that they are (for example, Berkes writes that Cree have environmental values based on morality towards nature), others counter this view and argue that it is necessary to make a distinction between environmentally-sound ideologies or practices and societies that are inherently environmentally-protective. From this perspective, conservationist ideologies or reverential attitudes to nature should not be mistaken for resource management regimes. Shiva (1988: 241) suggests that resource management and environmental conservation can only be possible 'in a society in which checks and controls on the utilization of resources are built into the organizing principle of the society'. Hames (1987), for instance, argues that while indigenous peoples develop effective strategies of resource exploitation and possess intricate and detailed knowledge of the ecology and availability of the resources they rely on, this does not mean that they are regulating their subsistence activities and being good conservationists. In a celebrated study of the Mbuti of Zaire, for example, Turnbull (1961) shows that although the Mbuti perceive the forest as a parent (and thus, following Bird-David, a giving environment) they nonetheless burn down trees to flush out animals. More recently, for the Arctic, Wallin Wiehe (1997) reports on a study which concludes that overgrazing and trampling by domesticated reindeer owned by Saami herders in Finnmark in northern Norway threatens vegetation and damages lichen and that the number of reindeer greatly exceeds Finnmark's carrying capacity. Other claims are made that Arctic hunters are not aware of the extent to which they have depleted marine mammal, bird and fish populations (e.g. Mikkelsen 1996).

Even if agreement could be reached that indigenous peoples did once have conservationist strategies, some argue that this changed with extensive contact with outsiders and with population growth. Martin (1978) has argued that human-environment and human-animal relationships in the Arctic and sub-Arctic have been irretrievably altered over a two hundred year period by the fur trade, resettlement and a wage economy. The corresponding economic and social changes in Native societies as a result of the fur trade increased the impact of Native hunters on animal populations (e.g. see Slezkine 1994 for an account of this in Siberia, and White 1994 on Native peoples in North America). Brightman (1987), however, questions whether indigenous peoples actually have, or indeed ever had, a concept of conservation and suggests that Cree killed animals indiscriminately in both pre-contact and post-contact times, while Duerden (1992: 219) argues that the 'assertion that indigenous peoples are role models for sustainable development is a logical extension of the view that North American indigenous communities are environmentally conscious/friendly'.

Hames (*ibid.*) likewise puts forward the view that indigenous peoples and their particular views of the world have been romanticised. Rather than putting indigenous conservation strategies into practice in a conscious way, small-scale societies more likely owe their 'sustainable' way of life to the availability and abundance of resources over a considerable period of time, or to an inability to overexploit local resources irrespective of their particular views of the world and their relationships to nature. Sustainability, from this perspective, is due to people practising optimal efficiency rather that having a conservation ethic. In some cases, resources may be conserved simply because people do not have the means, ability or technology to reach them or exploit them. Ellen (1986) warns that, while some societies do express a cultural ideal of living in harmony with the environment, human-environment relations are kept in fine balance for reasons other than (or in addition to) religious belief or spiritual ideology, such as maintaining a small population, or being geographically isolated and uninvolved in market economies which would otherwise require them to produce more from the environment for sale and exchange.

To elaborate Bird-David's discussion of the 'giving environment', people would probably take from the environment if they could. Smith (1991) concludes from both data gathered during his own fieldwork in Arctic Quebec and from a survey of the literature on Inuit hunting that there is little evidence to endorse the idea that the Inuit had indigenous resource management practices. Rather, 'the co-existence of Inuit and their prey over long periods of time suggests that foraging strategies have the *effect* of avoiding prey extinction in most cases' (Smith *ibid.*: 256). Following this argument, the conservation of resources has been a consequence of successful and efficient hunting strategies, rather than a strategically-planned intention. As long as Arctic hunting bands remained small, utilised simple technology and hunted and fished in a large territory, then their success 'need not be attributed to their aboriginal regard for conservation. In fact, now colonised and considerably acculturated but still comparatively small in numbers, these peoples, equipped with…high-powered rifles, snowmobiles, nylon nets, and motorboats, often demonstrate a blatant disregard for conserving important stocks' (McGoodwin 1990: 60). It is precisely this particular argument that animal welfare groups use in their anti-whaling and anti-sealing campaigns.

It is easy to see how such practices can be attributed to the loss of a traditional culture entailing a belief system that regulated human-environment relationships. Reflecting on my own fieldwork in small Greenlandic settlements, I have over several years and in many parts of the country participated in subsistence activities and lived with hunters and fishers and their families, experiences that lead me to conclude (like many other anthropologists who work with hunting and gathering peoples) that hunting involves an interction with the natural world and entails an ideological and ritual responsibility towards animals and the environment (see Nuttall 1992, for a fuller discussion of this in one community). Nonetheless, is this conservation? Although I argue that hunting is an expression of the intimacy between the human and natural worlds, and even though I personally know people who respect animals and will not hunt more than they or their families need, I also know hunters who occasionally harvest seals for their skins and who have no use for the meat. I have witnessed hunters shoot seals, take the skin and leave the carcass in the water. I have been with these same hunters on different occasions when they have hunted seals for food, uttered a quiet word of thanks when hauling their catch out of the water, taken the seals home to be cut up by their wives who, acting as spiritual facilitators in the hunt and distribution of the meat, have been careful to observe the correct rituals (such as throwing away the kidneys, or thanking the spirit of the seal so that it may return to the sea, find a new body and return to be hunted once more). But it would be difficult for me to generalise and argue that when all Greenlandic hunters go out hunting, and even though they may be extremely knowledgeable about sea mammals and possess the necessary skills and techniques to hunt them, then they are practising conservation. They are, however, and regardless of what way they may use the animals they catch, hunting to survive.

In a highly significant study that adds a complicated twist to the debate over indigenous conservation practices, Brightman (1987) suggests that a belief among northern hunters that animal spirits are recycled might actually be a contributing factor in the overexploitation of animals. If animals are, as Brightman says, an infinately renewable resource, then as long as the correct rituals are observed, the souls of animals will be reincarnated in new bodies and return to give themselves to hunters. Thus, animal species can never become extinct, only temporarily displaced if rituals are not observed or people offend animals spirits. One historian remarks that Native North Americans interpreted diminishing game in terms of disrespect and disregard to animals and animal spirits, rather than overhunting. Speaking of the Sioux dependence on the buffalo White (1994: 245) observes that when the buffalo finally disappeared from the plains, the Sioux did not view their demise as permanent nor the cause as biological. The buffalo had, they believed, gone underground because whites had killed the animals with disrespect. The buffalo would return when Indians could ensure that the animals would receive proper treatment.

Lending support to Brightman's argument, White claims that 'Indians could thus, in good conscience, hunt animals even as those animals grew less and less numerous' (*ibid.*). Such an argument, which suggests that it is misguided to believe overhunting is not possible if ethical beliefs about animals and the proper ritual treatment of animals remain constant, could potentially defuse attempts by indigenous peoples to claim that they are conserving the animals they hunt, especially when indigenous representatives emphasise that hunters believe that animals have souls that are respected and recycled. Ironically, then, and contrary to what anthropologists and indigenous peoples' organisations like the ICC are saying in defence of indigenous hunters, a religious or spiritual perception of nature does not necessarily provide the foundation for an environmentally-protective attitude. Rather, it may be the Western separation of culture from nature (which is blamed for the environmental crisis) which may nurture conservationist values: by objectifying nature it can be appreciated and looked at in an entirely different way and encourage a protectionist outlook.

The debate over whether indigenous peoples are original or natural conservationists arises because 'scientists and laymen alike have searched for new inspiration' to deal with the problems of the modern world (Kalland 1994: 152). Indigenous peoples who appear to live in harmony with the environment are contrasted with a social paradigm that sets human behaviour apart from nature and creates the conditions for human activity which is at the very root of the global environmental crisis. For this reason, the cultures and environmental ideologies of indigenous peoples have been appropriated by environmentalists, New Agers, complementary medical practitioners and others seduced by the notion of a primitive ecological wisdom.

Part of the problem lies with the tendency to reify indigenous peoples and their knowledge as traditional, timeless and unchanging and to romanticise the paradigm of communalism as providing an alternative way of knowing and acting in the world. By inventing the category of primitive society (Kuper 1988) we are comforted by the existence of 'Noble Savages', be they Inuit, South Sea Islanders or Amazonian Indians because of the antidote they seem to offer to the feelings of individual rootlessness, alienation and social and environmental problems caused by modernity; but we are disappointed when we discover that they no longer conform to our images of tradition or do not meet our expectations of how they should live and behave towards nature and animals.

If human behaviour in the modern world leads to environmental change and if materialist values have made consumers of us and separated us from nature and our true selves, then how unsettling it must be to find that 'traditional' peoples are now the same as us. As the author of a travel guide to Greenland, while extolling the beauty and ruggedness of the country along with the isolation and traditional nature of the people, feels compelled to put it in order to prepare the adventurous tourist,

> Today it's a country of far-flung towns and villages, virtually none connected by road. Even so, people visit their neighbours by Mercedes in the summer and dog-sled in the winter. In the supermarkets they buy pineapples from Hawaii, tomatoes from Mexico and frozen seal steaks from the nearest fjord. They live in 100-unit blocks of flats or in brightly painted Scandinavian bungalows, and for a living, they practise anything from law or word processing to fishing or seal hunting. [2]

It is not an easy task to identify true indigenous models of human-environment relations (or for that mattter, to identify true forms of 'traditional' society) when other globalised forms of knowledge interact with and come to inform indigenous knowledge, and when indigenous peoples have long been involved in the global economic system. But then again, would we even find such 'true' indigenous models if we looked hard enough? Whether all pre-modern cultures had effective resource management systems and found long-term solutions to local problems is also debatable. Yet it would also be incorrect to suggest that the indigenous peoples of the Arctic have no environmentally-benign beliefs or practices, or that they show no respect to animals, the environment and the spiritual forces inherent in nature. As I have shown in Chapter 4, anthropologists have documented in detail the environmental knowledge of Inuit, Athabascan, Cree and other peoples for whom animals and elements of nature have consciousness and personhood, and belong with humans to a single moral community. The point made in this chapter is that we need to exercise caution before seeing these relationships towards nature as signifying environmentalist cultures. However this chapter also shows later that the case for indigenous peoples being in a position to protect the Arctic depends on them demonstrating that they do indeed belong to environmentalist cultures.

Avoiding for the moment the question of whether Inuit, Cree, Saami or other Arctic peoples are environmentally-friendly, what needs to be stressed is that these peoples have interpreted, understood and responded to environmental hazards and crises in local terms. Of crucial importance is that localised worldviews, regardless of the level of technological development, are vital for resource management. Throughout the Arctic, resource use takes place mainly in a specific, bounded localised area, what I have termed a memoryscape (Nuttall 1991, 1992, 1993), which links persons, community and landscape and the contemporary, historical and mythical activities, events and stories that invest the environment with meaning. Hunters, herders and fishers experience this area and the resources they exploit on a daily basis and in different seasons. They are uniquely placed to observe resource fluctuations, and their knowledge of resources is extensive and detailed whether they are natural conservationists or not.

The environmental knowledge of Arctic peoples such as the Inuit has been dynamic, rather than static. It is also context-specific, holistic, processual and localised, rather than reductionist and generalisable. By examining and understanding adaptive strategies of local peoples, how they cope with changing environments, and the decisions they make, we can understand not only long-term processes of environmental change in the Arctic, but draw on indigenous knowledge to define and implement appropriate resource management systems. As we shall see later in this chapter, however, indigenous peoples cultivate and perpetuate an image of themselves as environmentally-protective societies for political reasons to gain control over the use and management of lands and resources, and to achieve a degree of self-determination.

THE ELUSIVE NATURE OF INDIGENOUS ENVIRONMENTAL KNOWLEDGE

Given the importance of indigenous environmental knowledge and the increasingly global recognition of its role in conserving biodiversity and sustainable development, how easily can it be accessed and collected? Because of methodological, epistemological, political and cultural barriers to gaining access to a community and to individual informants much of the environmental knowledge of indigenous peoples must necessarily remain elusive to the knowledge gatherer. Furthermore, a researcher who gathers whatever information they can on indigenous views of the environment is still a long way from an epistemological understanding of what that knowledge actually means in its social context of lived and shared environmental relations. Thus, while I may have accompanied Greenlandic hunters on hundreds of seal hunts and can claim to have some 'knowledge' as an anthropologist of seal hunting, I can never hope to experience and know what a Greenlandic hunter experiences and knows when he goes seal hunting. Knowledge also differs in quantity and quality between members of any given community and knowledge of a specific resource or environment may be 'shallow' or 'deep' depending on individual experience (Rasmussen 1997).

Chapter 5 discussed co-management and participatory approachs to resource use, and used the example of whaling as a relatively successful example of this. But even when a participatory approach involving local people claims success, only a few local representatives may have been consulted and given responsibility for making decisions on behalf of the community as a whole. As Mosse (1993: 18) argues, in a participatory approach to development a particular context is established 'which gives privilege to certain types of knowledge and representation and suppresses others'. The level of local involvement also varies, from advisers and policy makers merely acknowledging the fact that local people exist, and can therefore be used as informants, to developing relations of trust and actually involving them as true participants in the control of projects and management of resources.

All local interests may not be recognised by those who have their own agendas. For example, gender and generational differences are often muted and ignored, thereby obviating recognition of the different perspectives, levels of decision-making, self-interests, rights and obligations, and the different kinds of knowledge men and women have even though they are members of the same family, household and community. While these differences may be apparent within households and communities, they are not always recognised by researchers and environmental managers who neatly sidestep epistemological concerns, are uncritical of indigenous knowledge and often take it at face value, without questioning how it is constituted or what underpins it, and fail to understand the diversity of experiences and environmental knowledge that people have. There is also an ever present danger that a partial understanding of a community's environmental knowledge, based on the information of only a few individuals, can be mistaken for, and come to represent, a shared system of knowledge. In this way the focus is on systems of knowledge, an abstracted totality, not people and personal beliefs, experiences and diverse ways of knowing.

Knowledge does not simply exist as something which is immediately identifiable, something waiting to be gathered or collected—it is constructed, created, changed and modified in specific social contexts (Mosse *ibid.*: 3). Any research project on indigenous knowledge will present both the informants and subjects of the research with the difficulty of externalising intensely personal beliefs and experiences, and the researcher with the problem of representing what their informants tell them. This exposes the representation of local people's knowledge by outsiders to criticism of it being decontextualised and filtered through the intellectual tradition of another cultural context.

Given these difficulties, even when a researcher reaches a reasonable level of understanding of the environmental knowledge of an individual or community, is it possible for an outsider to represent what is ordinarily hidden and implicit in everyday life? Mark Badger, an Alaskan ethnographic filmaker, has said of his award-winning work portraying Koyukon Athabascan spiritual beliefs that any attempt by an outsider to describe the indigenous spiritual relationship with the natural world would not make sense to the Koyukon themselves because they do not see and articulate their everday lives and their interactions with the environment in terms of it being a spiritual relationship (Mark Badger 1995, personal communication).

As ethnographers understand only too well, gaining insight into the status and content of local knowledge in a lived, everyday context is often (if not always) elusive. People do not usually live their lives conscious that their environmental knowledge underpins a theoretical formulation of reality, or that it structures, informs and guides social relationships. As Descola (1996: 86) puts it, 'most members of any given community will find themselves unable to state explicitly the elementary principles of their cultural conventions'. Ethnographic texts on human-environment relations are the result of in-depth, intensive field research, whereby the ethnographer patches together observations, snippets from conversations, the occasional word, statement or action from everyday life. It is in the process of reflection and writing, of piecing together the bits and pieces from fieldwork, that human-environment relationships are systematised and common-sense knowledge is represented as indigenous or local systems, concepts and ideas.

Despite an increasing number of projects on indigenous knowledge in the Arctic, people are often reluctant to talk about the knowledge they have of their local environments. As well as personal difficulties in externalising inner beliefs and cultural experiences, this may be because of a complexity of taboos that guide people in their relationships with nature, as illustrated by two episodes from my own fieldwork. During the summer of 1995 I was visiting an Inupiaq Eskimo fishing camp on Alaska's Seward Peninsula. One woman told me of her fear of encountering bears and that she had recurring dreams about bears entering the camp and killing her children. When I asked her further about the dreams, she replied "I can't tell you about what I dream about bears. If I did that would be an affront to the bear's spirit". For some people, then, to talk about such things is often to transgress cultural taboos and to offend spiritual forces inherent in nature. Reluctance to reveal knowledge to the ethnographer, or to the knowledge-gatherer, may also stem from an unwillingness to talk of traditional spiritual beliefs that are still held because such beliefs may be inconsistent with other introduced and dominant religions, such as Christianity. Once, sitting in a tent on the sea ice in northern Greenland, a hunter in his late fifties told me, "You know, we still believe in spirits. Listening to the ice move at night, I start to think a lot about the spirits of the bears I've hunted. Outside my house in the village, I tie part of the bear's skin or its bones to my meat drying rack. I leave these parts of the bear to blow in the wind. Because we don't talk about our beliefs doesn't mean we don't believe".

There is also often local opposition to the appropriation of local knowledge, to 'extracting it from the social context of its expression' (Fairhead 1993: 99), and to it being made accessible to an audience beyond the immediate community. Such exposure is often seen as a betrayal of personal and cultural beliefs. Given this, there is a strong case to be made that problems of documentation, translation and representation make it essential that local people themselves gather and document their own indigenous knowledge and have control over its uses and application. Yet this kind of methodology does not necessarily solve the problem of translation. Doing anthropology at home, or being a researcher in one's own community does not always give privileged access to informants or special insight into one's own cultural milieu. As Johnson (1992: 14) has pointed out

> even younger members of an aboriginal community may not know the proper way to approach an elder to discuss certain subjects. Likewise, they may be unfamiliar with all of the subtleties and sophisticated terms of their aboriginal language.

Furthermore, the local documentation of knowledge may not reduce local anxiety about betrayal, as illustrated by a case in Alaska in 1993, when a book written by Velma Wallis, a Gwich'in Athabascan woman, was published in the United States. This book, *Two Old Women: an Alaskan legend of betrayal, courage and survival* tells the tale of two Gwich'in elders abandoned by their tribe during a harsh winter, in the hope that the tribe as a whole would be saved from starvation. Wallis describes how, by drawing on hidden strengths, the two women were able to survive the winter and return to their tribe. Yet, in the Gwich'in villages of northern Alaska the book received a negative reaction, as the following extract from a local newspaper article illustrates,

> "It's kind of revealing and people don't like to be revealed," says Wallis. When she gave an anxious first reading in the village this spring, she found most people receptive. But she perceived some villagers as dumbstruck by the material and later heard tremors of dissent. She heard at least one person complained anonymously to a newspaper that Wallis had no right to portray Gwichin people the way she had....The book was nearly scrapped when one Native leader said it made Athabascan people look bad.[3]

The controversy was generated by the fact that the two women had been abandoned by their kin. Local people and Native leaders alike responded to what they saw as the contemporary representation of a barbaric act (albeit an effective social and environmental management strategy), and their feelings of unease over unsavoury aspects of their own history must be seen in the context of their self-representation as indigenous people in the modern world. In the same article, the president of the Tanana Chiefs Conference, a non-profit organisation representing the Indians of Alaska's interior, said that the book depicted a "very unsavory situation, and I'm not sure the Gwichin people would appreciate that depiction....It either supports or rejects your preconceived notions of what aboriginal people are like."

The gathering of indigenous knowledge may be made much more difficult because residents of Arctic communities are increasingly aware of the ethical conduct of research and of intellectual property rights. In parts of the Arctic, knowledge is often seen as a marketable commodity to be traded, quite often for cash, especially if the price is right. In some parts of the world, especially the Amazon, indigenous knowledge is readily gathered and exploited like any other resource for profit. Traditional medical knowledge is used by the pharmaceutical industry, and journalists, travellers and anthropologists make money or build careers from books and articles. Several years ago, Posey (1990: 14) wrote that there

> are no provisions anywhere for the protection of knowledge rights of native peoples. Despite repeated pleas from indigenous leaders that their traditional culture and knowledge systems are being exploited without just compensation, little action has been taken.[4]

In the contemporary Arctic serious questions are thus raised for both knowledge-gatherers and those whose knowledge is being gathered, such as who 'owns' knowledge?, how can people be protected from the exploitation of their knowledge?, how should it be stored and who should have access to it?, and should people be compensated? These and other questions are very much at the forefront of anthropological debate. As Posey (*ibid.*: 15) suggested, anthropologists are likely to oppose compensation for indigenous knowledge on the grounds that

> Incomes from published dissertations and other books, slides, magazine articles, gramophone records, films and videos—all will have to include a percentage of the profits to the native subjects. It will probably become normal that such 'rights' be negotiated with native peoples prior to the undertaking of initial fieldwork. This kind of behaviour has never been considered as part of the 'professional ethic' of scientific research, but certainly will become so in the near future.

This is already the case in many parts of the Arctic, especially in those communities in Alaska and Canada which have been inundated with anthropologists and other researchers. The Alaska Federation of Natives (AFN) require researchers to have their proposals for research vetted and approved by local research committees, which in some cases would have to be paid for out of the project's research funds. The International Arctic Social Sciences Association has formulated guiding principles of ethics for the conduct of research. Among the principles which researchers are responsible for implementing, some such as respect for local cultural traditions and acknowledging the principle of cultural property, consultation with and involvement of local people, and making research results available to local communities, are already responsibilites that anthropologists take upon themselves. Many anthropologists would not even be welcome in communities if they did not know how to behave. The imposition of these kinds of principles as mandatory implies that indigenous communities are unable to look after themselves and that anthropologists do not know how to relate to their hosts. The discussion of intellectual property rights and the formulation of principles such as 'efforts should be made to provide meaningful experience, training and economic opportunities for local people'[5] are bound to continue to influence debate about not only the gathering of indigenous knowledge, but about the nature of social science research in the Arctic.

WOMEN'S KNOWLEDGE AS MUTED KNOWLEDGE

Social differentiation and specialisation in spheres of social and economic activity means that indigenous knowledge systems are gendered. Although this is not in itself a startlingly new anthropological observation, environmental managers, however, often assume otherwise and do not recognise gender differentiation in the generation and transmission of knowledge. Because of this 'participation' in development and environmental management is, among other things, limited from a gender perspective. As Jackson (1994: 120) puts it, participatory approaches to development

> assume that communication is unproblematic and ungendered beyond the need to make sure that women and men are represented in the decision-making or consultative bodies involved....there is no recognition of the degree to which views expressed by participants reflect dominant/dominated models and knowledges, "false consciousness" or mutedness.

Historically and across cultures men and women have had distinct roles to play in economic production and as a consequence they have different experiences and understandings of the natural world. For example, Fernandez (1992) has shown how, in parts of the Andes, women have more knowledge of livestock management practices than do men. Men, in turn, know more about soil classification than women. This is recognised and acknowledged within local communities: women are consulted about grazing and breeding strategies, men are consulted when decisions need to be made about the use of fields and the planting of crops. Yet evaluations of women's roles in production by outsiders, as well as by different groups based on gender, generation and occupation within local communities, has resulted in biases against women's knowledge and against the technology and needs of women. As Chambers (1983: 80) points out,

> Ploughing, mainly carried out by men, has received more attention than weeding or transplanting, mainly carried out by women. Cash crops, from which male heads of household benefit disproportionately, have received more research attention than subsistence crops, which are more the concern of women.

Women are often seen to be peripheral contributors to the economic viablity of a community and understandings of human-environment relations are often based on men's practical knowledge, their direct engagement with resources and their experiences of the environment. The practical knowledge and strategic interests of women are seldom considered. This is a point taken up by Merchant (1990), who argues that conceptual frameworks for understanding human-environment relationships are incomplete unless they include consideration and analysis of different gender roles in a culture's mode of production as well as the different impacts men and women have on the environment. This is not merely in terms of production and socio-economic relations, but in a cognitive and conceptual sense and Merchant calls for a greater awareness of how women's roles in spiritual and cosmological ideas can enrich environmental history.

Women's knowledge may be muted or ignored for a variety of reasons. There may be institutionalised discrimination in a society, or many anthropologists may be male. As Mosse (*ibid*.: 24) points out, knowledge gathered in development projects 'is likely to be problematic because it is produced in a social context where the influence of power and authority and gender inequality are likely to be great'. Local knowledge is only made accessible to outsiders in a fragmentary and partial form. In the Arctic, because of the dependence of many small communities on renewable resources (and also because of the scientific interest in ecological adaptations), policy makers, environmental managers and anthropologists have taken more of an interest in subsistence practices such as hunting large land and marine animals. These are productive activities which often carry much prestige within communities. In Greenland, for example, hunting is an exclusively male activity. The word *anguvoq*, which means 'to kill a seal' is derived from the masculine root *angu-* (*angut* meaning 'man'). Within local contexts the involvement of women in subsistence activities tends to be regarded as low in prestige and anthropologists and other researchers, with the exception of those who have documented indigenous plant classification, only tend to take an interest in women's subsistence activities when women hunt. In the small villages of south, north and east Greenland hunting is differentiated from women's work (*suliaq*), which belongs to the domestic sphere, as opposed to hunting which takes place in an environment that both gives meaning to and derives meaning from hunting (Nuttall 1992).

Few researchers anywhere in the Arctic have documented in detail the daily routines of women and the vital contributions they make to the social and economic vitality of their communities, nor do we understand fully women's roles as resource managers (e.g. in the way they distribute resources within communities) and their roles in childrearing and the generational transmission of knowledge, social values and cultural traditions. When hunting and fishing activities and local knowledge of natural resources are mapped, for instance, women are often excluded and the representation of certain types of knowledge marks it out 'as the province of men' (Mosse *ibid*.: 16). As a Yup'ik woman from southwest Alaska commenting on indigenous knowledge projects told me, "What a woman understands and knows is never considered".

In Arctic hunting societies, women fish, gather plants, hunt small animals, collect bird's eggs, process meat, and sew skin clothing, while the different types of knowledge women possess relating to fertility, marriage, birth and death, social organisation and cultural values are also embedded within cultural understandings of the environment. Women play vital roles in the spiritual, economic and social aspects of hunting, observing taboos before men go in search of game, ensuring that the souls and spirits of hunted animals are respected, preparing meat and skins, and sharing meat within families and between households. Women exchange information and discuss personal experiences when they are involved in these tasks. Similarly, men gather by harbours and markets and other meeting places and discuss the day's hunting, fishing, or reindeer round-ups. They exchange information on the habits and activities of animals, and on the weather and advise each other on subsistence activities. Tasks within households and communities, then, are specialised. But gender differences are evident in different channels of communication about local resource management systems. In Arctic hunting communities, boys accompany their fathers on hunting and fishing trips, girls stay in the village to learn productive and reproductive roles. Information is exchanged in informal ways, or through more formal channels as hunter's and trapper's associations, or women's cooperatives, which again are gender-based

Cultural understandings of the environment can only be enhanced once emphasis is also placed on women's knowledge. Former ICC President Caleb Pungowiyi said in his presentation to the Arctic Leaders Summit in Tromsø, Norway in early 1995 that

> Much of the fabric of our communities and our economies is due to the strength and talents of our women. This is something that we men do not openly acknowledge....I believe we should once again bring elder women with us to meetings of the International Whaling Commission, to the meetings of the Convention on International Trade of Endangered Species and to the IUCN. We should let them speak more loudly to the United States hearings of the U.S. Marine Mammal Protection Act. In particular we should let our elder women once again tell the story of what life was like, what life can be like and what it still continues to be like in many of our communities.[6]

While for the most part, women's voices are still muted in Arctic anthropological research, there is an emerging literature about women's views of landscape and environmental knowledge in the Arctic (e.g. Cruikshank 1990), women's life stories that reveal their perspectives on changing social, economic and political situations affecting their communities (e.g. Blackman 1989), women's perspectives on health (O'Neil and Kaufert 1990), and their contributions to economic life and subsistence activities (e.g. Bodenhorn 1990, Briggs 1974, Turner 1990). But there is urgent need for more research on how far men and women have different environmental knowledge, how far decisions that relate to the use of resources and particular geographical locations lie with women, whether women are more environmentally protective than men, how women and men experience environmental change, seasonality and family size, how women organise, preserve and transmit environmental knowledge, the kinds of experiences women associate with local landscapes, and the way greater gender awareness in the social differentiation of local knowledge is used in a strategic way to further women's interests. In short, the documentation of indigenous knowledge systems and research on environmental change and human-environment relationships should aim to consult both men and women.

But just as communities are considered homogenous and undifferentiated, knowledge-gatherers must also be cautious about seeing men and women as similarly undifferentiated gendered groups. Knowledge is not evenly distributed throughout any given population. Men have different knowledge about similar things than other men, as do women. As well as different gender roles in productive and reproductive activity, there are individual and generational differences in economic activities and subsistence techniques. Hunters think, believe, know and have experiences of animals and the landscape in different ways from other hunters in the same community or household. People have different opportunities to gain access to resources, they experience the environment differently, and they participate in different and diverse ways in productive and reproductive activities. This knowledge and these experiences differ in both quantity and quality. The use of indigenous knowledge for environmental management can only be strengthened if heterogenous sets of knowledge are recognised, valued and incorporated.

THE POLITICAL USE OF INDIGENOUS KNOWLEDGE

While the idealised and simplified image of community can prevent resource managers from understanding the diversity and wealth of knowledge within localities, this image of community can nonetheless be used to vital effect by indigenous peoples as a rhetorical device in political contexts. In policy arenas advocates of co-management, participatory approaches to development, and community-based development have represented communities as well-ordered sites of consensus, harmony, tradition and stability (Li 1996). Li (*ibid.*: 502) argues that such representations, 'though idealized, are capable of producing strategic gains, as they counter prevailing development orthodoxies, open up opportunities, and provide a legitimating vocabulary for alternative approaches'. Anthropologists have shown that rural communities are not homogenous entities (e.g. Cohen 1982, 1985), and have drawn attention to competing representations and to the difficulty of both defining community and identifying its specific features (Jedrej and Nuttall 1996). Yet despite the diversity of worldviews and multifarious meanings and interests within localities, images and representations of traditional communities are deployed within political, economic and discursive contexts to defend interests and gain a degree of control over resources. This is what Li (*ibid.*) refers to when she suggests that the representation of an idealised form of community has political potential and is often embraced strategically to achieve positive results.

Land claims are easier to advance and argue for if competing and heterogenous ideas about what different groups within a region should get are not apparent. Similarly, the claim of indigenous knowledge is stronger if politicians and representatives of indigenous peoples' organisations construct simplified images of a community or people in harmony with the environment, possessing undifferentiated sets of knowledge relating to appropriate environmental conservation. Although the idea of harmonious, stable, traditional communities in contrast to modern, fragmented, urban societies has been critiqued as romantic or invented, it is nonetheless a seductive idea for many that continues to hold the promise and possibility of alternative strategies to resource management and development. To assert practical knowledge of resources, to demonstrate that one has the necessary know-how and skills to manage wildlife, for example, is to use indigenous environmental knowledge as a strategy to gain more influence and involvement in decision-making processes that determine who has access to key resources.

Arctic hunters, fishers and herders often feel that state regulations, game management and international environmental groups place pressure on their ways of life and restrict their activities. They also complain that biologists, wildlife managers and environmentalists ignore their perspectives on resource use and their systems of environmental management, and that the hegemony of science marginalises traditional systems of knowledge. State regulation and management of resources, scientific knowledge and the activities of environmentalists and animal-welfare organisations not only pose a threat to the cultural and economic survival of indigenous communities, they also have political implications. The response to state intervention, science and special interest groups and the assertion of indigenous paradigms for environmental management is essentially, then, a political struggle. Assessing the validity of various representations and idealised images of community becomes less of an issue in this respect. Rather, it is 'the political-economic contexts in which particular representations are deployed, and the effects that they bring about' (Li *ibid.*: 502) which assume significance and are worthy of attention.

Indigenous peoples see state management and top down development as threats to cultural and political autonomy. As in other areas of social, economic and political life, loss of knowledge or being unable to use that knowledge is also perceived as a loss of competence (Nuttall 1998). To reiterate the well known phrase, knowledge is power. To regain knowledge, to use it and therefore to regain a sense of competence is to become empowered and to feel that one can become responsible for one's self and actions. In this way, indigenous knowledge is used increasingly as a political resource by indigenous leaders and indigenous communities. Power for indigenous peoples' organisations includes the power to determine the trajectory of development and to manage resource use on their own terms.

Breyman (1993: 127) argues that the success of social movements concerned with the environment (be they indigenous peoples, grass-roots activists or environmental organisations) 'depends on the effective mobilization of resources'. In asking exactly what kinds of resources are available to them, Breyman points to knowledge as a crucial resource which 'best reflects both the promise and the problems of the globalization of environmental issues and the groups that champion them' (*ibid*.: 128). In the Arctic indigenous peoples' organisations use knowledge to define their interests and to pursue various claims. They also use it as a political lever to influence policymakers and to empower themselves so that communities can take decisive action on the future of natural resource use and environmental protection, as well as claiming the right to determine the course of economic development. As Breyman (*ibid*: 126) points out, in order to obtain this power groups must demonstrate that they

> possess knowledge of the workings of the biophysical world, of the characteristics of natural resources, and of the nexus between resources, environment, and humanity. When individual activists and movement organizations act upon such knowledge as they attempt to control their environments and their own lives as well, we can then speak of knowledge-as-power.

The globalisation of environmental issues has provided the means by which local groups can express and publicise their concerns. Just as environmental organisations, such as Greenpeace, Friends of the Earth, and the World Wide Fund for Nature, fall back on scientific knowledge to support and validate their claims for environmental conservation (Yearley 1991, 1994), in similar ways, indigenous peoples' organisations base their own claims to power on local knowledge. One way to do this is to reconstitute indigenous knowledge as a form of indigenous scientific knowledge, something which exists 'out there', is empirically-verifiable, waiting to be gathered, decontextualised, and ready to be put in databases and archives. Increasingly indigenous peoples also feel compelled to show how local environmental knowledge can inform and enhance scientific knowledge.

Traditional systems of knowledge may not by themselves provide the solutions to environmental problems, but advocates of indigenous peoples' knowledge argue that we need to creatively reassess scientific systems of knowledge and knowledge construction and integrate indigenous perspectives on resources. As Chapters 2 and 3 discussed, indigenous environmental knowledge has been institutionalised by the AEPS process and by the initial work of the Arctic Council. This emphasis on the importance of indigenous knowledge in international discussion on Arctic environmental protection and sustainable development enhances the status of indigenous peoples as experts, professionals, 'keepers of the treasures' and so on.

The rights of indigenous peoples to continue hunting whales and other sea mammals, for example, has depended on their ability to argue and demonstrate that, not only is hunting essential for cultural and economic survival, it is also a sustainable activity and that, more importantly, that they *know* it is a sustainable activity. In this way their defensive language becomes proactive,

as they argue that they have long-established patterns of sustainable and equitable resource use, and that they are also traditional communities living in harmony with the environment. Rational-minded scientists attending the annual meetings of the International Whaling Commission may find it hard to accept the Alaskan Inupiaq Eskimo whaling captain who talks eloquently about the bowhead whale coming to him, shedding its outer parka of blubber, giving itself up to his people who then return its soul to the sea. But the whaling captain has to ensure that those scientists must nonetheless recognise and respect the traditional dependence of his community on bowhead whales and other marine mammals and acknowledge that Inupiaq Eskimo hunting practises and cultural and economic needs do not necessarily threaten whales to the point of extinction.

For scientists, whales may be an endangered species; for the Inuit they are a renewable resource, although the elders may not have thought about them in this way. The problem is how to get this message across in international fora. Post-Brundtland Report and Rio Earth Summit, they do this best by speaking the language that everyone else uses. Cultural survival and the threat of international moratoria on traditional harvesting activities has made the ICC and many individual indigenous people adept and fervent preachers of the gospel of sustainability. As the Inuit Circumpolar Conference puts it,

> Inuit and other indigenous leaders agree that the essence of sustainable development to most Arctic indigenous peoples is related to subsistence harvesting, including recognition of their nutritional needs and the rights of renewable resource harvesters, while protecting the resource base and its use for present and future generations.

> ...as experience with heavily industrialized regions in the Russian Arctic has shown, non-renewable-resource-based cultures and economies can destroy the biological productivity of the Arctic ecosystem. The renewable resource economy is and will remain central to sustainability in the Arctic.

> (Inuit Circumpolar Conference 1994: 2–3)

However, the ICC has been careful to emphasise that it has not simply jumped on the sustainable development bandwagon:

> Inuit, as an indigenous people living in a sensitive and vulnerable environment and without direct sovereignty over there homelands, are in the midst of any discussion on the Arctic environment. The concept of sustainable development is not for them merely a fashionable trend to be embraced on a temporary basis. It rather represents an urgent need to sustain their traditional life-styles, economy, and culture, while at the same time managing outside influences that are encroaching into the Arctic.

> (Inuit Circumpolar Conference 1993: 4)

By advancing the argument that Inuit practise sustainable resource use, yet live in a fragile environment threatened by industrial society, the ICC produces representations of the indigenous peoples of the Arctic as nature conservationists and constructs an identity for the Inuit in particular that it claims derives from having an environmentalist culture. Already environmentally-protective, Inuit accommodate environmentalist ideas and meet head on the arguments advanced by environmentalist organisations that potentially threaten Inuit culture. As we have seen in Chapter 5, Finn Lynge (1992) provides an excellent example of this by saying that Inuit environmental philosophy is consistent with the ideas of environmentalist groups.

In Chapter 4, I made reference to how Arctic peoples have perceived their environments to be environments of risk, in that climatic changes, changes in the behaviour of animals, and human actions all influence hunting and fishing activities. These factors have made life uncertain and unpredictable and Arctic peoples have responded with appropriate adaptive strategies which have been the object of study for a number of anthropologists. Today, indigenous peoples perceive the environment to be at risk from pollution and industrial development. Such threats continue to influence the climate, animal movements and animal habitats, and also have an impact on human health. However, such threats are no longer simply attributed to localised human actions, but are the result of a multiplicity of linkages and interconnections between the states, societies and economies making up the modern world system. Because indigenous peoples see themselves as living in a giving environment or a reciprocating environment where human action, attitudes and behaviour can influence the environment (either positively, in the sense that the environment will give and reciprocate; or negatively causing the environment to withhold and refuse to reciprocate), they are in a position to be able to take a protective role towards it.

DECONTEXTUALISING KNOWLEDGE

The political aspect of indigenous knowledge is noticeable in the preferred terminology. The use of 'indigenous' tells us more about its ideological relevance than the actual construction, content and nature of the kinds of knowledge it is meant to denote. It draws attention to the fact that this is the knowledge of *indigenous* peoples, peoples situated within colonial relationships, or peoples who are marginalised, oppressed and powerless in the face of dominant states or structures. There is a danger is assuming that non-indigenous peoples do not have valid knowledge about the environment and therefore to conclude that their experience and insight cannot be used in

policy making. As Palsson (1991, 1994) has shown for Icelandic fishermen, for instance, non-indigenous user groups do have vital environmental knowledge about how resource use should be organised and managed.

The Declaration of the Arctic Council states that the Council is a forum for involving 'Arctic indigenous communities and other Arctic inhabitants' in cooperation on 'common Arctic issues, in particular issues of sustainable development and environmental protection in the Arctic'. The Declaration also states that the Arctic Council is established 'to provide a means for promoting cooperative activities to address Arctic issues requiring circumpolar cooperation, and to ensure full consultation with and the full involvement of indigenous people and their communities and other inhabitants of the Arctic in such activities'. At face value, this should be taken to mean that the Arctic Council is a forum for promoting cooperation between the Arctic states, indigenous peoples and other Arctic residents, including user groups such as Icelandic fishermen, Norwegian whalers, Canadian loggers, or Russian trappers. Yet there is no further mention of 'other Arctic inhabitants' in the Declaration, nor is there mention of the importance of the environmental knowledge of these 'other Arctic inhabitants'. There are however several references to 'including recognition of the special relationship and unique contributions to the Arctic of indigenous people and their communities', and the importance of recognising 'the traditional knowledge of the indigenous people of the Arctic and their communities'. [7] Perhaps the emphasis on indigenous peoples is due to their visibility as marginalised groups within the Arctic states, whereas non-indigenous peoples are seen as having constitutionally-protected rights and are already suitably represented by government institutions (which some may feel is often not the case at all). Indigenous peoples exploit this official acknowledgement of their traditional knowledge. Knowledge becomes the way indigenous peoples can become involved in policy-making, especially as the Arctic Council Declaration makes it clear that the use of the term 'peoples' does not mean that the Arctic states are recognising 'the rights which may attach to the term under international law'. [8]

There is a danger that the politicisation of environmental knowledge as traditional or indigenous knowledge may divert attention from an awareness of its processual nature, and seeing it as embedded within changing and complex cultural and environmental contexts. In international fora, and in indigenous texts, leaders and spokespersons for Native communities lean towards a reification of knowledge as 'traditional' and unchanging, seemingly wary that an acknowledgement of its changing nature would invalidate the claims they advance for it. The image of a successful resource-based society, however, is vital if indigenous peoples are to win the argument for a greater shift in power from the state towards local communities, creating the conditions for community-based sustainable development. But practical knowledge is not easy to document. It is a difficult and long enough process to explain and teach in local contexts, where it is vital and real, so how can it be gathered and stored in databases without decontextualising it and depriving it of meaning? Palsson (1996: 75) also questions the use of 'traditional' and 'indigenous', arguing that reference to these terms 'tends to reproduce and reinforce the boundaries of the colonial world', and asks where skills, expertise, and knowledge have to be located (and indeed how old they must be) before they can be classified as 'indigenous' or 'traditional'. In this way, the categorisation of knowledge as traditional and indigenous does nothing to address underlying inequalities of power and control (Agrawal 1995).

To decontextualise knowledge, to gather it through interviews and brief conversations with local people, and then claim that this is authoritative and has universal applicability, is to 'alter the relationship between person and world by subordinating or eclipsing the non-objectifiable, local specificities which render meanings everywhere so implicit and inextricable' (Hornborg 1996: 53). Hornborg is objecting to the tendency of western rationality to systematise, generalise and codify local knowledge by simplifying the complexity of close and long-term experience of local practitioners. He advocates a contextualist position as a 'sober recognition of the limitations of totalising institutions and knowledge systems. It is an argument not for regression but for a *recontextualisation* of the production of knowledge' (Hornborg *ibid.*: 54, emphasis in original). Hornborg's position on a contextualist approach to the use of knowledge is that traditional, non-industrial societies do have something to tell us about how to live sustainably if practical knowledge, based on experience of local conditions, is put to use within those local spheres rather than abstracted. So that the claim that 'the Inuit know how to live sustainably', or a generalisable ethnographic observation that 'the Inuit believe that marine mammals have souls', tells us nothing of the socio-cultural contexts within which such environmental knowledge is produced and which enable it to persist. If knowledge is to be re-located within local spheres its legitimacy and value for resource management can only be recognised if is gathered, not as a resource to be tapped mainly through interviews with local practitioners, but through long-term ethnographic research.

Local knowledge is forever changing, always being lost through death and always being modified through observation. Chambers (1983: 91) emphasises that 'perhaps the least recognised aspect of rural people's knowledge is its experimental nature' (as I have observed many times in various parts of

Greenland, hunters constantly test each other's stories of hunting, knowledge of animals and their habitats, the ice, currents and so on). And as Johnson points out, 'with its roots firmly in the past, traditional environmental knowledge is both cumulative and dynamic, building upon the experience of earlier generations and adapting to the new technological and socioeconomic changes of the present' (Johnson 1992: 4). Fairhead (1993: 193) claims that 'local knowledge is better envisaged as empirical and hypothetical', while Chambers has also drawn attention to how 'rural people's knowledge is also added to, influenced by, and destroyed by knowledge from outside the area' (*ibid.*: 83).

Although Arctic peoples have elaborate and complex knowledge of wildlife, many of the terrestrial and marine species they hunt are migratory. For a good deal of the year many animals, such as harp seals, bowhead whales and caribou, exist outside and beyond the physical and conceptual worlds of the hunters. There is a fundamental difference between the knowledge people possess of, say domesticated and wild reindeer herds in Siberia. And whale biologists often argue that indigenous knowledge of whales can only be localised and therefore partial and incomplete. Effective management plans for a species become problematic and indigenous peoples cannot reasonably claim to know everything about a particular species of animal they may see and harvest during a few months of the year. For example, hunters in northeast Greenland harvest barnacle geese which nest and breed in Iceland during the summer months, and overwinter in southwest Scotland and the west of Ireland, but go to Greenland to moult from their summer nesting sites. Presumably, a comprehensive and effective management plan for barnacle geese would have to incorporate the local knowledge about barnacle geese to be found in four different countries. Acknowledging Chambers, who says that 'rural people's knowledge is at its strongest with what is observable and its local *what, where,* and *when.*' (*ibid.*: 95), effective resource management can only proceed from a recontextualisation of knowledge, to re-locate knowledge within local spheres and not abstract it.

To decontextualise knowledge is to raise questions about how empowering indigenous environmental knowledge actually is for local communities. The ironic consequence is that, once stored in archives and databases, access to this knowledge is denied to the very people who have shared it in the first place and who are the ones who should benefit most from its application. The extent to which researchers and leaders of indigenous groups decontextualise knowledge, appropriate it, seek to apply it, and construct indigenous views of the environment which seem universal for the group or society in question invites extensive investigation. The strength of indigenous environmental knowledge lies in its localised nature. Knowledge is tacit. The case for its integration into scientific environmental management regimes is weakened if it is taken out of the context of its immediate engagement with the everyday lives of local people. As Palsson argues, by reifying practical, everyday knowledge 'we fall into the trap of Cartesian dualism that we may be trying to avoid, separating body and mind (*ibid.*: 76).

Idealised images of community and an emphasis on indigenous knowledge as traditional knowledge informs a rhetorical vocabulary and provides indigenous peoples with the epistemological tools necessary to advance and legitimise indigenous concerns over environmental damage and environmental management in the Arctic. The challenge is how these concerns can continue to be expressed and articulated by recontextualising knowledge, and through this recontextualisation, how to build prescriptive models for resource management and sustainable development.

1   As Kalland and Asquith (1997: 29) put it
    The Taoist, Buddhist and Shintoist and other bases for defining the human-nature relationship have not been concerned with understanding and preserving nature as a healthy ecosystem. They have, instead, been used to define humanness, morality, aesthetic appreciation and to explain noumenal and metaphysical phenomena
2   Deanna Swaney (1997: 354) *Iceland, Greenland and the Faroe Islands* Hawthorn: Lonely Planet Publications
3   *Fairbanks Daily News-Miner* September 26, 1993.
4   Things may be changing, however. At the annual meeting of the International Bar Association (BAR) in Berlin in October 1996, an International Convention on the Human Genome was drafted. This hinted 'that tribal peoples should receive a share of the rewards if studies of their unusual genetics leads to lucrative commercial products' (Coghlan 1996: 8)
5   IASSA Newsletter, Fall 1995, p. 5.
6   Caleb Pungowiyi 1995, 'Trade and knowledge: strength of the Inuk woman', Presentation to the Arctic Leaders Summit, Tromsø, Norway, January.
7   *Declaration on the Establishment of the Arctic Council* 19th September 1996.
8   *Declaration on the Establishment of the Arctic Council*

Afterword

CULTURAL SURVIVAL AND CULTURAL DIVERSITY

Throughout this book I have discussed the increasing attention given to indigenous perspectives on resource use, environmental management and development, and have illustrated some of the ways indigenous peoples have responded to the social, economic and environmental problems faced by the remote communities of the circumpolar north. As we reassess human-environment relationships in the light of global environmental crises, and as we become more critical of industrialism, the global economic system and of the forms of society, values and institutions that characterise modernity, there is much to learn from how indigenous peoples in the Arctic and elsewhere look upon themselves, their cultures, their environments and their systems of knowledge as offering alternative views of how to live with nature.

Indigenous concerns over resource development and environmental change arise because of the close relationship between the cultural, economic and political situations of remote communities and their local environments. Incorporating indigenous knowledge into environmental management and sustainable development strategies is crucial and recent international co-operation on Arctic environmental matters has made great headway in acknowledging that indigenous peoples and their communities should be involved at local, regional and national levels in resource management, conservation strategies and sustainable development. Agenda 21 emphasises the importance of indigenous knowledge and recommends that national and international efforts to implement environmentally-sound sustainable development should recognise, promote and strengthen the role of indigenous peoples and their communities. Effective participation and local control over resource management and sustainable development strategies is, however, dependent on greater self-determination and it is one of the failures of Agenda 21 that it does not address issues of self determination and self-government for indigenous peoples.

Scientists and environmentalists stress how vitally important it is that global forms of management ensure biodiversity. The argument is that if we care about the planet, then we should care about the diversity to be found in the natural world. Anthropologists put forward similar arguments for cultural diversity. Fears that globalisation results in cultural homogeneity are not necessarily expressed by anthropologists because they have idealised and romantic views of traditional societies. Rather, most are concerned that rapid social change and globalising forces threaten to extinguish different ways of knowing, thinking and acting in relation to the environment. If we care about human survival, then we must ensure the survival of cultural diversity. Although I have pointed out that we need to be careful in assuming that traditional peoples are, or ever were, natural conservationists, the distinctiveness of indigenous peoples, their cultures and their unique relationships with their environments should be recognised. As the survival of indigenous peoples is the best guarantee of environmental protection, cultural diversity becomes a prerequisite for biodiversity. In the Arctic today, indigenous peoples are achieving degrees of empowerment through land claims and types of self-government, involvement in resource management and sustainable development. These measures go some way to ensuring cultural survival and cultural diversity.

Bibliography

Agrawal, A. 1995. 'Dismantling the divide between indigenous and scientific knowledge' *Development and Change* 26 (3): 413–439.

Alaska Division of Economic Development, 1994. *Alaska: Economy Performance Report 1994* Juneau: Department of Commerce and Economic Development.

Alaska Division of Tourism, 1995. *Good News Travels* Spring Issue, Juneau: Department of Commerce and Economic Development.

Alaska Native Tourism Council, 1994. *Alaska Native Journeys* 4.

Alaska Native Tourism Council, 1995. *Alaska Native Journeys* 5.

Alvares, C. 1988. 'Science, Colonialism and Violence: a Luddite view' in Nandy, A. (ed.) *Science, Hegemony and Violence: A requiem for modernity* Delhi: Oxford University Press.

Anders, G. and Anders, K. 1987. 'Incompatible goals in unconventional organizations: the politics of Alaska Native corporations' in T. Lane (ed.) *Developing America's Northern Frontier* Lanham: University Press of America.

Anderson, D. 1995. *Belonging in Arctic Siberia* Unpublished PhD dissertation , University of Cambridge.

Archer, C. and Scrivener, D. in press. 'International co-operation in the Arctic Environment' in Nuttall, M. and Callaghan, T.V. (eds) *The Arctic: environment, people, policy* Harwood Academic Publishers.

Arctic Council. 1996. Joint Communiqué of the Governments of the Arctic Countries on the Establishment of the Arctic Council, Ottawa, September 19th, Arctic Council: Ottawa.

Armstrong, T.E. 1988. 'Soviet proposals for the Arctic: a policy declaration by Mr Gorbachov' *Polar Record* 24(148): 68.

Armstrong, T.E., Rogers, G. and Rowley, G. 1977. *The Circumpolar North* London: Methuen.

Bauman, Z. 1992. *Intimations of Postmodernity*. London: Routledge.

Baudrillard, J. 1988 'Consumer society' in Poster, M. (ed.) *Jean Baudrillard: Selected Writings* Stanford: Stanford University Press.

Beach, H. 1994. 'The Saami of Lapland' in Minority Rights Group (ed.) *Polar Peoples: self-determination and development* London: Minority Rights Publications.

Beck, P. 1989 'Entering the age of the polar regions' *Ambio* xviii(1): 92–94.

Beck, U. 1992. *Risk Society: towards a new modernity*. London: Sage.

Benton, T. 1994. 'Biology and Social Theory in the Environmental Debate' in Redclift, M. and Benton, T. (eds.) *Social Theory and the Global Environment* London and New York: Routledge.

Berger, P. and Luckmann, T. 1984. *The Social Construction of Reality*. Harmondsworth: Penguin.

Berkes, F. 1982. 'Waterfowl management and northern native peoples with reference to Cree hunters of James Bay' *Musk-ox* 13: 187–208.

Berkes, F. 1988. 'Environmental knowledge of the Cuisasibi Cree people of James Bay' in Freeman, M.M.R. and Carbyn, L.N. (ed.) *Traditional Ecological Knowledge and Renewable Resource Management in Northern Regions* Edmonton: Boreal Institute for Northern Studies, pp. 7–21.

Berkes, F., George, P. and Preston, R. J. 1991. 'Co-management: the evolution in theory and practice of the joint administration of living resources' *Alternatives* 18(2): 12–18.

Berkes, F. 1992. *Traditional ecological knowledge in perspective*. Winnipeg: Natural Resources Institute.

Berman, M. 1986. *Strategies for economic self-reliance in rural northern economies* Institute of Social and Economic Research, University of Alaska, Anchorage.

Bernes, C. 1996. *The Nordic Arctic Environment: unspoilt, exploited, polluted?* Copenhagen: The Nordic Council of Ministers.

Bielawski, E. 1992. 'Inuit indigenous knowledge and science in the Arctic' *Northern Perspectives* 20 (1): 5–8.

Bird, E. A. R. 1987. 'The social construction of nature: theoretical approaches to the history of environmental problems' *Environmental Review* 11: 255–64.

Bird-David, N. 1990. 'The giving environment: another perspective on the economic system of hunter-gatherers' *Current Anthropology* 31 (2): 189–196.

Bird-David, N. 1992. 'Beyond the "original affluent society": a culturalist formulation' *Current Anthropology* 33(1): 25–47.

Blackman, M.B. 1989. *Sadie Brower Neakok: An Inupiaq Woman*. Seattle:University of Washington Press.

Bodenhorn, B. 1989. *The Animals Come to me; They Know I Share: Inupiaq Kinship, Changing Economic Relations and Enduring World Views on Alaska's North Slope* Unpublished PhD thesis, Cambridge University.

Bodenhorn, B. 1990. 'I'm not the great hunter; my wife is: Inupiat and Anthropological Models of Gender' *Etudes/Inuit/Studies* 14(1–2):55–74.

Bodenhorn, B. 1997. 'Person, Place and Parentage: Ecology, Identity and Social Relations on the North Slope of Alaska' in Mousalimas, S.A. *Arctic Ecology and Identity* Budapest and Los Angeles: Hungarian Academy of Sciences and ISTOR.

Booth, A. and Jacobs, H.M. 1990. 'Ties that bind: Native American beliefs as a foundation for environmental consciousness' *Environmental Ethics* 12: 27–43.

Boorstin, D.J. 1964. *The Image: a guide to pseudo-events in America* New York: Harper and Row.

Breyman, S. 1993. 'Knowledge as Power: Ecology Movements and Global Environmental Problems' in Lipschutz, R.D. and Conca, K. (eds) *The State and Social Power in Global Environmental Politics* New York: Columbia University Press.

Briggs, J. 1974. 'Eskimo women: makers of men' in Matthiasson, C.J. (ed.) *Many Sisters: Women in Cross Cultural Perspective*. New York: The Free Press, pp. 261–304.

Brightman, R.A. 1987. 'Conservation and resource depletion: the case of the Boreal Forest Algonquians' in McCay, B.M. and Acheson, J.M. (eds). *The Question of the Commons: the culture and economy of communal resources* Tucson: University of Arizona Press, pp. 121–141.

Brightman, R. A. 1993. *Grateful Prey: Rock Cree human-animal relationships*. Berkely: University of California Press.

Brody, H. 1975. *The People's Land* Harmondsworth: Penguin.

Brody, H. 1981. *Maps and Dreams: Indians and the British Columbia Frontier*. Toronto: Douglas and McIntyre.

Brokensha, D., Warren, D.M. and Werner, O. (eds). 1980. *Indigenous Knowledge Systems and Development* . Washington: University Press of America.

Brooke, L.F. 1993. *The participation of indigenous peoples and the application of their environmental and ecological knowledge in the Arctic Environment Protection Strategy*. Ottawa: Inuit Circumpolar Conference.

Brown, J.E. 1992. *Animals of the Soul: sacred animals of the Oglala Sioux* Massachusetts: Element, Inc.

Budowski, G. 1976. 'Tourism and environmental conservation: conflict, coexistence, or symbiosis'. *Environmental Conservation* 3: 27–31.

Butler, J.R. 1992. 'Tourism in the Canadian Arctic: problems of achieving sustainability' in Kempf, C. and Girard, L. (eds) *Tourism in Polar Regions* Proceedings of the First International Symposium, 21–23 April, Colmar, France.

Callicott, J.B. and Ames, R.T. (eds) 1989. *Nature in Asian Traditions of Thought: essays in environmental philosophy* New York: State University of New York Press.

Caulfield, R. 1991. *Qerqertarsuarmi Arfanniarneq: Greenlandic Inuit Whaling in Qerqertarsuaq Kommune, West Greenland*. University of Alaska Fairbanks: Department of Rural Development.

Caulfield, R. 1992. 'Alaska's subsistence management regimes' *Polar Record*.

Caulfield, R.1997. *Greenlanders, Whales, and Whaling: Sustainability and self-determination in the Arctic* . Hanover and London: Dartmouth College, University Press of New England.

Chambers, R. 1983. *Rural Development: putting the last first* Harlow: Longman Scientific and Technical.

Chance, N.A. 1990. *The Inupiat and Arctic Alaska: An Ethnography of Development*. Ft. Worth, Harcourt Brace.

Chatterjee, P. and Finger, M. 1994. *The Earth Brokers: power, politics and world development* London: Routledge.

Chaturvedi, S. 1996. *The Polar Regions: a political geography* Chichester: John Wiley.

Chokor, B.A. and F.O. Odemerho 1994. 'Land degradation assessment by small-scale traditional African farmers and implications for sustainable conservation management' *Geoforum* 25 (2): 145–154.

Coates, P. 1993. *The Trans-Alaska Pipeline Controversy* Fairbanks: University of Alaska Press.

Coates, K. 1994. 'The rediscovery of the North: towards a conceptual framework for the study of Northern /Remote regions' *The Northern Review* 12/13: 15–43.

Coghlan, A. 1996. 'Gene treaty promises rewards for unique peoples' *New Scientist* 2 November, p. 8.

Cohen, A.P. 1982. *Belonging: identity and social organisation in British rural cultures* Manchester: Manchester University Press.

Cohen, A.P. 1985. *The Symbolic Construction of Community* London: Tavistock.

Cohen, E. 1979. 'A phenomenology of tourist experiences' *Sociology* 13: 179–201.

Cohen, E. 1988. 'Authenticity and commoditization in tourism' *Annals of Tourism Research* 15(3): 371–86.

Cohen, E. 1993. 'The study of touristic images of native people: mitigating the stereotype of a stereotype' in Pearce, D.G. and Butler, R.W. (eds) *Tourism Research: critiques and challenges* London: Routledge.

Cuba, L. 1987. *Identity and Community on the Alaskan Frontier* Philadelphia: Temple University Press.

Creery, I. 1994. 'The Inuit of Canada' in Minority Rights Group (ed.) *Polar Peoples: self-determination and development* London: Minority Rights Publications.

Croll, E. and Parkin, D. 1992. *Bush Base: Forest Farm* London: Routledge.

Cruikshank, J. 1984. 'Oral traditions and scientific research: approaches to knowledge in the north' in *Social Science in the North: communicating northern values* Occasional Studies No 9. Ottawa: Association of Canadian Universities for Northern Studies.

Cruikshank, J. 1990. *Life Lived Like a Story* Lincoln and London: University of Nebraska Press.

Crumley, C.L. 1994. *Historical Ecology: Culture, Knowledge and Changing Landscapes.* Santa Fe: School of American Research.

Dahl, J. 1986. 'Greenland: political structure of self-government' Arctic Anthropology 23 (1 & 2): 315–324.

Dahl, J. 1989. 'The integrative and cultural role of hunting and subsistence in Greenland' *Etudes Inuit Studies* 13(1): 23–42.

Dahl, J. 1990. 'Beluga whaling in Saqqaq' *North Atlantic Studies* 2 (1 & 2): 166–169.

Dahl, J. 1993. 'Indigenous peoples of the Arctic' in *Arctic Challenges* Report from the Nordic Council's Parliamentary Conference in Reykjavik, 16–17 August 1993.

Derocher, A.E. and Stirling, I. 1991. 'Oil contamination of polar bears' *Polar Record* 27(160): 56–57.

Descola, P. 1994. *In the Society of Nature* Cambridge: Cambridge University Press.

Descola, P. 1996. 'Constructing natures: symbolic ecology and social practice' in Descola, P. and Palsson, G. (eds) *Nature and Society: anthropological perspectives* London: Rouledge.

Dewalt, B.R. 1994. 'Using indigenous knowledge to improve agriculture and natural resource management' *Human Organization* 53 (2): 123–131.

Dey-Nuttall, A. 1994. *Origins, Development and Organisation of National Antarctic Programmes* Unpublished PhD dissertation: Cambridge University.

Doiban, V.A., Pretes, M. and Sekarev, A.V. 1992. 'Economic development in the Kola region, USSR: an overview' *Polar Record* 28(164): 7–16.

Drijver, C. 1992. 'People's participation in environmental projects' in Croll, E. and Parkin, D. (eds) *Bush Base: Forest Farm: culture, environment and development.* London:Routledge.

Duerden, F. 1992. 'A critical look at sustainable development in the Canadian North' *Arctic* 45(3): 219–225.

Dybbroe, S. 1991. 'Local organisation and cultural identity in Greenland in a national perspective' *North Atlantic Studies* 3(1): 18–24.

Dyer, C.L., Gill, D.A. and Picou, J.S. 1992. 'Social disruption and the *Valdez* oil spill: Alaskan Natives in a natural resource community' *Sociological Spectrum* 12: 105–126.

Dyer, C.L. and McGoodwin, J.R. (eds). 1994. *Folk Management in the World's Fisheries: Lessons for modern fisheries management.* Colorado: University Press of Colorado.

Ellen, R. 1982. *Environment, subsistence and system* Cambridge: Cambridge University Press.

Ellen, R. 1986. 'What Black Elk left unsaid. On the illusory images of Green primitivism'. *Anthropology Today* 2(6): 8–12.

Ellen, R. 1988. 'Foraging, starch extraction and the sedentary lifestyle in the lowland rainforest of central Seram' in Ingold, T., Riches, D. and Woodburn, J. (eds) *Hunters and Gatherers: History, Evolution and Social Change* Oxford: Berg.

Elliot, L. 1992. *International Environmental Politics: protecting the Antarctic* New York: St Martin's Press.

Faegteborg, M. 1990. 'Inuit organisations and whaling policies' *North Atlantic Studies* 2(1&2): 124–129.

Fairhead, J. 1993. 'Representing knowledge: the new farmer in research fashions' in Pottier, J. (ed.) *Practising Development: social science perspectives* London: Routledge.

Fast, H., and Berkes, F. 1993. *Native land use, traditional knowledge and the subsistence economy in the Hudson Bay bioregion* Canadian Arctic Resources Committee report. Ottawa: CARC.

Fienup-Riordan, A. 1983. *The Nelson Island Eskimo* Anchorage: Alaska Pacific University Press'.

Fienup-Riordan, A. 1990. *Eskimo Essays* New Brunswick, NJ: Rutgers University Press'.

Fernandez, M.E. 1992. 'The social organization of production in community-based agro-pastoralism in the Andes' in C.M. McCorkle (ed.) *Plants, animals and people: agropastoral systems research*. Boulder: Westview'.

Fikkan, A., Osherenko, G. and Arikainen, A. 1993. 'Polar Bears: The Importance of Simplicity' in Young, O.R. and Osherenko, G. *Polar Politics: Creating International Environmental Regimes* Ithaca and London: Cornell University Press.

Foucault, M. 1976. *The Archaeology of knowledge* New York: Harper Colophon.

Freeman, M.M.R. (ed.) 1976. *Inuit Land Use and Occupancy Project*. Ottawa: Department of Indian and Northern Affairs'.

Freeman, M.M.R. 1979. 'Traditional land users as a legitimate source of environmental expertise' in J. Nelson *et al.* (eds) *Canadian National Parks Today and Tomorrow* . Studies in Land Use and History, no. 7. Waterloo.

Freeman, M.M.R. and Carbyn, L.N. (eds) 1988. *Traditional Knowledge and Renewable Resource Management in Northern Regions.*

Freeman, M.M.R. 1989a. 'The Alaska Eskimo Whaling Commission: successful co-management under extreme conditions' in E. Pinkerton (ed.) *Co-operative Management of Local Fisheries*. Vancouver: University of British Columbia Press.

Freeman, M.M.R. 1989b. 'Graphs & gaffs: a cautionary tale in the common-property resources debate' in F. Berkes (ed.) *Common Property Resources: ecology & community-based sustainable development*. London: Belhaven Press.

Freeman, M.M.R. 1990. 'A commentary on political issues with regard to contemporary whaling' *North Atlantic Studies* 2(1&2): 106–116.

Freeman, M.M.R., Wein, E., and Keith, D. 1992. *Recovering Rights: bowhead whales and Inuvialuit subsistence in the western Canadian Arctic* Edmonton: Canadian Circumpolar Institute.

Gilligan, J.H. 1987. 'Visitors, outsiders and tourists in a Cornish town'. in M. Bouquet and M. Winter (eds) *Who from their labours rest? conflict and practice in rural tourism* Aldershot: Avebury.

Graham, B. 1997. *Canada and the Circumpolar World: meeting the challenges of co-operation into the twenty-first century* Report of the House of Commons Standing Committee on Foreign Affairs and International Trade.

Greenland Home Rule Government. 1989. *Greenland Subsistence Hunting* Report prepared for the International Whaling Commission meeting 1989, San Diego.

Greenland Home Rule Government. 1995. *Greenland 1995–96*. Statistical Yearbook, Nuuk: Statistics Greenland.

Greenwood, D. 1989. 'Culture by the pound: an anthropological perspective on tourism as cultural commoditization'. in V.L. Smith (ed.) *Hosts and Guests: the anthropology of tourism* Philadelphia: University of Pennsylvania Press.

Griffiths, F. 1988. 'Introduction: the Arctic as an international political region' in K. Mottola (ed.) *The Arctic Challenge* Boulder and London: Westview Press.

Grove-White, R., Kapitza, S.P. and Shiva, V. 1992. 'Public awareness, science and the environment' in Dooge, J.C.I. *et al* (eds) *An Agenda of Science for the Environment and Development into the 21st Century* Cambridge: Cambridge University Press.

Gurvitch, G. 1971. *The Social Frameworks of Knowledge* Oxford: Basil Blackwell.

Hall, C.W. and Johnston, M.E. (eds) 1995. *Polar Tourism: tourism in the Arctic and Antarctic Regions* Chichester: John Wiley & Sons.

Hames, R. 1987. 'Game conservation or efficient hunting?' in McCay, B.J. and Acheson, J.M. *The Question of the Commons: the culture and ecology of communal resources* Tucson: University of Arizona Press.

Hansen, J. *et al* (eds) *The State of the European Arctic Environment* Luxembourg: European Environmental Agency.

Harrison, P. 1993. *The Third Revolution* Harmondsworth: Penguin.

Heide-Jørgensen, M. 1990. 'Small cetaceans in Greenland: hunting and biology' *North Atlantic Studies* 2(1&2): 55–58.

Hinch, T.D. 1995. 'Aboriginal people in the tourism economy of Canada's Northwest Territories' in C.H. Hall and M.E. Johnson (ed.) *Polar Tourism: tourism in the Arctic and Antarctic regions* Chichester: John Wiley and Sons.

Hornborg, A. 1996. 'Ecology as semiotics: outlines of a contextualist paradigm for human ecology' in Descolla, P. and Palsson, G. (eds) *Nature and Society: anthropological perspectives* London: Rouledge.

Huddle, N. Reich, M. and Stiskin, N. 1975. *Island of Dreams: environmental crises in Japan* New York: Autumn Press.

Huskey, L. and Morehouse, T.A. 1992. 'Development in remote regions: what do we know?' *Arctic* 45(2): 128–137.

Ingold, T. 1976. *The Skolt Lapps Today* Cambridge: Cambridge University Press.

Ingold, T. 1986. *The Appropriation of Nature* Manchester: Manchester University Press.

Ingold, T. 'Culture and the perception of the environment' in Croll, E. and Parkin, D. (eds) *Bush Base: Forest Farm: culture, environment and development* London: Routledge.

Ingold, T. 1996. 'Hunting and gathering as ways of perceiving the environment' in Ellen, R.E. and Katsuyoshi, F. (eds) *Redefining Nature: ecology, culture and domestication* Oxford: Berg.

Inuit Circumpolar Conference. 1992. *Principles and Elements for a Comprehensive Arctic Policy.* Montreal, Centre for Northern Studies and Research, McGill University.

Inuit Circumpolar Conference. 1993. *Analysis of Agenda 21 in the context of circumpolar sustainable development* (draft).

Inuit Circumpolar Conference. 1994. *Circumpolar Sustainable Development*, A report by the Inuit Circumpolar Conference.

IWC. 1981. *Report on Aboriginal Subsistence Whaling* IWC Document 33/14, Cambridge: IWC.

IWGIA. 1991. *Arctic Environment: Indigenous Perspectives* Document 69, Copenhagen: IWGIA.

Jackson, C. 1994. 'Gender Analysis and Environmentalisms' in Redclift, M. and Benton, T. (eds) *Social Theory and the Global Environment* London and New York: Routledge.

Jakobsen, A. 1994. 'In violation of human rights' *IWGIA Newsletter* 2: 52–55.

Jarvenpa, R. 1994. 'Commoditization versus cultural integration: tourism and image building in the Klondike'. *Arctic Anthropology* 31(1): 26–46.

Jedrej, C. & Nuttall, M. 1995. 'Incomers & locals: metaphors & reality in the repopulation of rural Scotland' *Scottish Affairs* 10: 115–129.

Jedrej, C. & Nuttall, M. 1996. *White Settlers: the impact of rural repopulation in Scotland.* Luxembourg: Harwood Academic Publishers.

Jenkins, R. 1996. *Social Identity.* London: Sage.

Jenkins, R. 1997. *Rethinking Ethnicity: Arguments and Explorations.* London, Thousand Oaks and New Delhi: Sage Publications.

Johnson, M. (ed.) 1992. *Lore: capturing traditional environmental knowledge* Ottawa: IDRC.

Johnston, B.R. 1990. 'Breaking out of the tourist trap' *Cultural Survival Quarterly* 14(1): 2–5.

Kalland, A. 1990. 'Whaling and whaling communities in Norway and Japan' *North Atlantic Studies* 2(1&2): 170–178.

Kalland, A. 1992. 'Aboriginal subsistence whaling: a concept in the service of imperialism' in *Bigger than the Whales* High North Alliance (publication prepared for the 44th Annual Meeting in International Whaling commission, Glasgow, Scotland, June 1992).

Kalland, A. 1994. 'Indigenous Knowledge—Local Knowledge: prospects and limitations' in Hansen, B. (ed.) *AEPS and Indigenous Peoples Knowledge* Reykjavik, Iceland: Arctic Environmental Protection Strategy, 20–23 September.

Kalland, A. and Asquith, P.J. 1997. 'Japanese perceptions of nature: ideals and illusions' in *Japanese Images of Nature: cultural perspectives*. London: Curzon Press.

Kawagley, A.O. 1995. *A Yupiaq World View: a pathway to ecology and spirit*. Waveland Press.

Kemp, D. 1990. *Global Environmental Issues: a climatological approach*. London: Routledge.

Kleivan, I. 1989. 'De grønlandske stednavnes vidnesbyrd om vandringer og forskellige aktiviteter' in *Vort Sprog, Vor Kultur*, Proceedings of a symposium held at the University of Greenland, Nuuk, 1981. Nuuk: Pilersuifik.

Korsmo, F. 1994. 'The Alaska Natives' in Minority Rights Group (eds) *Polar Peoples: self-determination & development*. London: Minority Rights Publications.

Krauss, M. 1994. 'Crossroads? A twentieth century history of contacts across the Bering Strait' in Fitzhugh, W. and Chaussonet, V. (eds) *Anthropology of the North Pacific Rim* Washington and London: Smithsonian Institution Press.

Kuper, A. 1988. *The Invention of Primitive Society: transformations of an illusion* London: Routledge.

Kuptana, R. 1995. 'The Recognition and Exercise of Inuit Rights and Responsibilities' in Martin, V.G. and Tyler, N. (eds) *Arctic Wilderness: The 5th World Wilderness Congress* Colorado: North American Press.

Kwon, H. 1993. *Maps and Actions: Nomadic and Sedentary Space in a Siberian Reindeer Farm* Unpublished PhD thesis: University of Cambridge.

Kwon, H. 1997. 'Movements and Transgressions: Human Landscape in Northeastern Sakhalin' in Mousalimas, S.A. (ed.). *Arctic Ecology and Identity* Budapest and Los Angeles: Hungarian Academy of Sciences and ISTOR.

Lanfant, M. 1995a. 'International tourism, internationalization and the challenge to identity' in M. Lanfant *et al.* (eds) *International Tourism: identity and change. London*: Sage.

Lanfant, M. 1995b. 'Introduction' in M. Lanfant *et al.* (eds) *International Tourism: identity and change* London: Sage.

Langdon, S. 1987. 'Commercial fisheries: implications for western Alaska development' in Lane, T. (ed.) *Developing America's Northern Frontier* Lanham: University Press of America.

Latta, M. 1995. 'Dene schoolchildren benefit from indigenous knowledge' *Alternatives* 21(2): 13.

Lee, M. 1991. 'Appropriating the primitive: turn of the century collection and display of Native Alaskan art'. *Arctic Anthropology* 28(1): 6–15.

Lewis, J. and Wood, E. 1996. 'A physical scientists' perspective of the human dimension of global change' in *Unity and Diversity in Arctic Societies* Rovaniemi: International Arctic Social Sciences Association.

Li, T.M. 1996. 'Images of community: discourse and strategy in property relations' *Development and Change* 27(3): 501–528.

Lipschutz, R. and Conca, K. (eds) 1993. *The State and Social Power in Global Environmental Politics*. New York: Columbia University Press.

List, M. and Rittberger, V. 1992. 'Regime Theory and International Environmental Management' in Hurrell, A. and Kingsbury, B. (eds) *The International Politics of the Environment: actors, interests and institutions* Oxford: Clarendon Press.

Litfin, K. 1993. 'Eco-regimes: Playing Tug of War with the Nation-State' in Lipschutz, R.D. and Conca, K. (eds) *The State and Social Power in Global Environmental Politics* New York: Columbia University Press.

Lopez, B. 1986. *Arctic Dreams: imagination and desire in a northern landscape* London: Macmillan.

Lynge, F. 1988. 'Conflict treatment old and new: From Singaajuk to EEC and Greenpeace' *Folk* 30: 5–22.

Lynge, F. 1992. *Arctic Wars, Animal Rights, Endangered Peoples* Hanover: University of New England Press.

Lyotard, J. 1979. *The Postmodern Condition: a report on knowledge* Minneapolis: University of Minnesotta Press.

MacDonald, G. *et al.* 1993. 'Rapid response of treeline vegetation and lakes to past climate warming' *Nature* 361: 243–246.

Marquadt, O. and Caulfield, R. 1996. 'Development of West Greenlandic markets for country foods since the 18th century' *Arctic* 49(2): 107–119.

Martin, C. 1978. *Keepers of the Game: Indian-Animal Relationships and the Fur Trade*. Berkeley: University of California Press.

Mason, P. 1995. 'Tourism codes for the Arctic' *WWF Arctic Bulletin* 3.95:10.

Mawes, C. 1990. *Green Rage: radical environmentalism and the unmaking of civilization* Boston: Little Brown & Co.

McBeath, G.A. and Morehouse, T.A. 1994. *Alaska Politics and Government*. Lincoln and London: University of Nebraska Press.

McCannell, D. 1976. *The Tourist: a new theory of the leisure class* London: Macmillan.

McGoodwin, J.R. 1990. *Crises in the World's Fisheries: People, Problems and Policies*. Stanford, California: Stanford University Press.

McLuhan, T.C. 1971. *Touch the Earth: A self-portrait of Indian existence* London: Abacus.

Merchant, C. 1990. 'Gender and environmental history' *The Journal of American History* 76 (4): 1117–21.

Michaud, J. 1995. 'Frontier minorities, tourism and the state in Indian Himalaya and northern Thailand' in Lanfant, M. *et al.* (eds) *International Tourism: identity and change* London: Sage.

Mikkelsen, A. 1996. 'A challenge for the future' *WWF Arctic Bulletin* 4.96: 15.

Milton, K. 1991. 'Interpreting environmental policy: a social scientific approach' *Journal of Law and Society* 18: 4–18.

Milton, K. 1996. *Environmentalism and Cultural Theory* London: Routledge.

Mirovitskaya, N.S., Clark, M. and Purver, R.G. 1993. 'North Pacific Fur Seals: Regime Formation as a Means of Resolving Conflict' in Young, O.R. and Osherenko, G. *Polar Politics: Creating International Environmental Regimes* Ithaca and London: Cornell University Press.

Mosse, D. 1993. 'Authority, gender and knowledge: theoretical reflections on the practice of participatory rural appraisal' *ODI Agricultural Administration Network Paper* 44.

Murphy, P. 1985. *Tourism: a community approach* London: Methuen.

Nakashima, D.J. 1990. *Application of Native Knowledge in EIA: Inuit, eiders and Hudson Bay oil*. Report prepared for the Canadian Environmental Assessment Research Council. Hull, Que.: The Secretariat, CEARC.

Nakashima, D.J. 1991. *The Ecological Knowledge of Belcher Island Inuit: a traditional basis for contemporary wildlife co-management*. PhD dissertation, Department of Geography, McGill University, Montreal.

Nash, D. 1989. 'Tourism as a form of imperialism' in V.L. Smith (ed.) *Hosts and Guests: the anthropology of tourism* Philadelphia: University of Pennsylvania Press.

Nash, R. 1982. *Wilderness and the American Mind* New Haven and London: Yale University Press.

Neff, J.M. 1988. 'Composition and fate of petroleum and spill-treating agents in the marine environment' in Geraci , J.R. and St. Aubin, D.J. (eds) *Synthesis of Effects of Oil on Marine Mammals* US Department of the Interior, Minerals Management Service: 1–40.

Nelson, R.K. 1983. *Make Prayers to Raven: A Koyukon View of the Northern Forest*. Chicago: University of Chicago Press.

Nickels, S. Milne, S. and Wenzel, G. 1991. 'Inuit perceptions of tourism development: the case of Clyde River, Baffin Island, NWT' *Etudes Inuit Studies* 15(1): 157–169.

Nikiforov, V. 1997. 'Gold mining threatens Koryaksky nature reserve' *WWF Arctic Bulletin* 2.97: 21.

Nuttall, M. 1991. 'Memoryscape: a sense of locality in Northwest Greenland' *North Atlantic Studies* 1(2): 39–50.

Nuttall, M. 1992. *Arctic Homeland: kinship, community & development in northwest Greenland*. London: Belhaven Press and Toronto: University of Toronto Press.

Nuttall, M. 1993a. 'Place, identity and landscape in northwest Greenland' in G. Flood (ed.) *Mapping Invisible Worlds* Edinburgh: Edinburgh University Press.

Nuttall, M. 1993b. 'Inuit subsistence whaling: indigenous resource management in the Arctic' *Anthropology in Action* 16: 9–11.

Nuttall, M. 1994. 'Greenland: emergence of an Inuit homeland' in Minority Rights Group (eds) *Polar Peoples: self-determination & development*. London: Minority Rights Publications.

Nuttall, M. 1996. *Aboriginal Subsistence Whaling: a case study from Greenland* Report submitted to the Whale and Dolphin Conservation Society.

Nuttall, M. 1997. 'Nation-building and local identity in Greenland: resources and the environment in a changing North' in Mousalimas, S.A. (ed.) *Arctic Ecology and Identity* Budapest & Los Angeles: Hungarian Academy of Sciences and ISTOR.

Nuttall, M. 1998. 'States and categories: indigenous models of personhood in northwest Greenland' in R. Jenkins (ed.) *Questions of Competence: culture, classification and intellectual disability* Cambridge: Cambridge University Press.

Odner, K. 1992. *The Varanger Saami: habitation and economy AD1200–1900* Oslo: Scandinavian University Press.

O'Neill, J. 1990. 'AIDS as a globalizing panic' in M. Featherstone (ed.) *Global Culture* London: Sage.

O'Neill, J. and Kaufert, P.A. 1990. 'The politics of obstetric care: the Inuit experience' in Penn Handwerker, W. (ed.). *Births and Power: Social Change and the Politics of Reproduction.* Boulder, San Francisco and London: Westview Press.

Oosten, J. G. 1997. 'Cosmological Cycles and the Constituents of the Person' in Mousalimas, S.A. (ed.) *Arctic Ecology and Identity* Budapest & Los Angeles: Hungarian Academy of Sciences and ISTOR.

O'Riordan, T. 1981. *Environmentalism* London: Pion.

Osherenko, G. and Young, O.R. 1989. *The Age of the Arctic: Hot conflicts and cold realities.* Cambridge: Cambridge University Press.

Østreng, W. and Simonsen, H. 1992. 'The Barents Region and the Northern Sea Route' *International Challenges* 12(4): 95–105.

Osunade, M.A.A. 1994a. 'Community environmental knowledge and land resource surveys in Swaziland' *Singapore Journal of Tropical Geography* 15 (2): 157–170.

Osunade, M.A.A. 1994b. 'Indigenous grass ecology and socio-economic values in Swaziland' *Journal of Environmental Management* 41 (4): 283–292.

Paehlke, R. 1989. *Environmentalism and the Future of Progressive Politics* New Haven and London: Yale University Press.

Paine, R. (ed.) 1977. *The White Arctic* ISER: St. John's.

Paldam, M. 1994. *Grønlands Økonomiske Udvikling: hvad skal der til for at lukke gabet?* Aarhus: Aarhus University Press.

Palsson, G. 1991. *Coastal Economies, Cultural Accounts* Manchester: Manchester University Press.

Palsson, G. 1994. 'Enskilment at Sea' *Man* 29(4): 901–928.

Palsson, G. 1996. 'Human-environmental relations: orientalism, paternalism and communalism' in Descolla, P. and Palsson, G. (eds) *Nature and Society: anthropological perspectives* London: Routledge.

Parnwell, M. 1993. 'Environmental issues and tourism in Thailand' in Hitchcock M., King V. and Parnwell M. (eds) *Tourism in South-East Asia* London and New York: Routledge.

Parry, J. and Bloch, M. (eds) 1989. *Money and the Morality of Exchange* Cambridge: Cambridge University Press.

Patrick, D. 1993. 'Aboriginal self-government and the Canadian constitutional process' *Anthropology in Action* 16: 12–13.

Peluso, N.L. 1993. 'Coercing Conservation: The Politics of State Resource Control' in Lipschutz, R.D. and Conca, K. (eds.) *The State and Social Power in Global Environmental Politics* New York: Columbia University Press.

Petersen, R. 1989. 'Traditional and present distribution channels in subsistence hunting in Greenland' in Greenland Home Rule Government, *Subsistence Hunting in Greenland.*

Petulla, J. 1980. *American Environmentalism: values, tactics, priorities* College Station and London: Texas A & M University Press.

Pika, A. and Prokhorov, B. 1989. 'Soviet Union: The big problems of small ethnic groups'. *IWGIA Newsletter* 57: 123–135.

Plant, R. 1994. *Land Rights and Minorities* London: Minority Rights Group.

Poole, G., Pretes, M. and Sinding, K. 1992. 'Managing Greenland's mineral revenues: a trust fund approach' *Resources Policy*, September, pp. 191–204.

Posey, D. 1990. 'Intellectual property rights and just compensation for indigenous knowledge' *Anthropology Today* 6(4): 13–15.

Pretes, M. 1995. 'Postmodern tourism: the Santa Claus industry' *Annals of Tourism Research* 22(1): 1–15.

Pryde, P. 1991. *Environmental Management in the Soviet Union.* Cambridge: Cambridge University Press.

Pungowiyi, C. 1995. 'Trade and knowledge: strength of the Inuk woman' Presentation to the Arctic Leaders Summit, Tromsø, Norway, January 1995.

Rasmussen, H. 1997. 'Who knows? cultural interpretations in the knowledge-gap in Greenlandic reindeer ranching and sheep farming' Paper presented at the symposium on Aboriginal Environmental Knowledge in the North: definitions and dimensions. Foret Montmorency, Quebec 18–21 September.

Redclift, M. 1984. *Development and the Environmental Crisis* London: Routledge.

Redclift, M. 1987. *Sustainable Development: exploring the contradictions* London and New York: Methuen.

Redclift, M. and Woodgate, G. 1994. 'Sociology and Environment: Discordant Discourse' in Redclift, M. and Benton, T. (eds) *Social Theory and the Global Environment* London and New York: Routledge.

Reimer, C. 1993. 'Moving towards co-operation: Inuit circumpolar policies and the Arctic Environmental Protection Strategy' *Northern Perspectives* 21(4) Winter 1993–94.

Riches, D. 1982. *Northern Nomadic Hunter Gatherers* London: Academic Press.

Robert J. Higgins Consulting. 1995. *Arctic Ecotourism Market Research Study* Report prepared for Unaaq Inc.

Roginko, A. 1992. 'Environmental issues in the Soviet Arctic and the fate of northern natives' in Massey Stewart, J. (ed.) *The Soviet Environment: problems, policies and politics* Cambridge: Cambridge University Press.

Rosenau, J. 1990. *Turbulence in World Politics* Princeton: Princeton University Press.

Rosenau, J. 1993. 'Environmental Challenges in a Turbulent World' in Lipschutz, R.D. and Conca, K. (eds) *The State and Social Power in Global Environmental Politics* New York: Columbia University Press.

Rosing, H. 1985. 'Towards an Arctic policy' *Etudes Inuit Studies* 9(2):15–19.

Ross, D. and Usher, P. 1986. *From the Roots Up: economic development as if it really mattered.* New York: The Bootstrap Press.

Rossell, P. 1989. (ed.) *Tourism: manufacturing the exotic* IWGIA Document 61, Copenhagen: IWGIA.

Roussopoulus, D.I. 1993. *Political Ecology* Montreal: Black Rose Books.

Sabo III, G. and Sabo, D.R. 1985. 'Belief systems and the ecology of sea mammal hunting among the Baffinland Eskimo' *Arctic Anthropology* 22(2), pp. 77–86.

Sabo III, G. 1991. *Long Term Adaptations among Arctic Hunter-Gatherers* New York and London: Garland Publishing, Inc.

Sallenave, J. 1994. 'Giving traditional ecological knowledge its rightful place in environmental impact assessment' *Northern Perspectives* 22 (1): 16–19.

Sambo, D. 1992. 'Indigenous human rights: the role of Inuit at the United Nations Working Group on Indigenous Peoples' *Etudes Inuit Studies* 16(1–2): 27–32.

Sanderson, K. 1990. 'Grindadrap: the discourse of drama' *North Atlantic Studies* 2(1&2): 196–204.

Selwyn, T. 1993. 'Peter Pan in South-East Asia: views from the brochures' in Hitchcock M., King V. and Parnwell M. (eds) *Tourism in South–East Asia* London and New York: Routledge.

Shaw, G.E. 1980. 'Arctic haze' *Weatherwise* 33: 219–221.

Shields, R. 1991. *Places on the Margin* London: Routledge.

Shiva, V. 1988. 'Reductionist Science as Epistemological Violence' in Nandy, A. (ed.) *Science, Hegemony and Violence: A requiem for modernity* Delhi: Oxford University Press.

Simon, M. 1992. 'Environment, sustainable development and self-government' *Etudes Inuit Studies* 16(1–2): 21–26.

Singh, E.C., Saguirian, A.A. 1993. 'The Svalbard Archipelago: The Role of Surrogate Negotiators' in Young, O.R. and Osherenko, G. *Polar Politics: Creating International Environmental Regimes* Ithaca and London: Cornell University Press.

Sizy, F. 1988. 'The price of Yamal'. *Ogonyok* 46(Nov): 20–21.

Sklair, L. 1991 *Global Sociology* London: Harvester Wheatsheaf.

Sklair, L. 1994. 'Global Sociology and Global Environmental Change' in Redclift, M. and Benton, T. (eds) *Social Theory and the Global Environment* London and New York: Routledge.

Slezkine, Y. 1994. *Arctic Mirrors: Russia and the Small Peoples of the North.* Ithaca and London: Cornell University Press.

Smith, E.A. 1991. *Inujjuamiut foraging strategies: evolutionary ecology of an Arctic hunting economy* New York: Aldine de Gruyter.

Smith, S. 1997. 'Strong environmental goals wanted' *WWF Arctic Bulletin* 2.97: 5.

Smith, V.L. 1989. 'Eskimo tourism: micro-models and marginal men' in V.L. Smith (ed.) *Hosts and Guests: the anthropology of tourism* Philadelphia: University of Pennsylvania Press.

Stabler, J. 1989. 'Dualism and development in the Northwest Territories' *Economic Development and Cultural Change* 37(4): 805–840.

Stabler, J. 1990. 'A utility analysis of activity patterns of Native males in the Northwest Territories' *Economic Development and Cultural Change* 39(1): 47–62.

Stenbaeck, M. 1985. 'Arctic policy: blueprint for an Inuit homeland' *Etudes Inuit Studies* 9(2): 5–14.

Stern, P. *et al.* 1992. *Global Environmental Change: understanding the human dimensions* Washington D.C.: National Academy Press.

Stirling, I. 1988. 'Attraction of polar bears *Ursus maritimus* to offshore drilling site in the eastern Beaufort Sea' *Polar Record* 24: 1–8.

Swift, J. 1979. 'Notes on traditional knowledge, modern knowledge and rural development' *IDS Bulletin* 10(2): 41–43.

Tanner, A. 1979. *Bringing Home Animals. Religious Ideology and Mode of Production of the Mistassini Cree Hunters.* St. John's: Memorial University, Institute of Social and Economic Research.

Telekova, E. 1995. 'The Concept of Wilderness among the Indigenous Peoples of the North' in Martin, V.G. and Tyler, N. (eds) *Arctic Wilderness: The 5th World Wilderness Congress* Colorado: North American Press.

Turnbull, C. 1961. *The Forest People.* London: Cape.

Turner. E. 1990. 'Ethnographer's shared consciousness on the ice' *Etudes Inuit Studies* (14)1–2: 39–54.

Turner, L. and Ash, J. 1975 *The Golden Hordes* London: Constable.

Udall, S. 1972. 'First Americans, first ecologists' in *Look to the Mountain Top* San Jose, CA: Gousha Publications.

Urry, J. 1990. *The Tourist Gaze* London: Sage.

Usher, P.J. 1987. 'Indigenous management systems and the conservation of wildlife in the Canadian North' *Alternatives* 14(1): 3–9.

Usher, P. J. 1995. 'Comanagement of natural resources: Some aspects of the Canadian experience' in Peterson, D.L. and Johnson, D.R. (eds) *Human Ecology and Climate Change: People and Resources in the Far North* USA: Taylor & Francis.

Vakhtin, N. 1994. 'Native Peoples of the Russian Far North' in Minority Rights Group (ed.) *Polar Peoples: self-determination and development* London: Minority Rights Publications.

Van Beck, W. and Banga, P. 1992. 'The Dogon and their trees' in Croll, E. and Parkin, D. (eds)*Bush Base: Forest Farm: culture, environment and development* . London: Routledge.

Villepontoux, E.J. 1981. *Tourism and Social Change in a French Alpine community* London: UMI.

Vitebsky, P. 1990. 'Gas, environmentalism and Native anxieties in the Soviet Arctic: the case of Yamal Peninsula' *Polar Record* 156: 19–26.

Wallin Weihe, H. 1997. 'Finnmark: overgrazing by reindeer may create Arctic desert' *WWF Arctic Bulletin* 2.97: 19.

Warren, D.M., Slikkerveer, L.J. and Brokensha, D. (eds). 1995. *The Cultural Dimension of Development: Indigenous Knowledge Systems.* London: Intermediate Technology Publications Ltd.

Waters, M. 1995. *Globalization.* London: Routledge.

Watt-Coultier, S. Kunuk, J. and Fenge, T. 1996 'The Arctic Council, sustainable development and Inuit' *WWF Arctic Bulletin* 3(4): 7–8.

Wenzel, G. 1991. *Animal Rights, Human Rights.* Toronto: University of Toronto Press.

Wenzel, G. 1992. 'Comment on Bird-David' *Current Anthropology* 33(1): 43.

Wenzel, G. 1995. 'Warming the Arctic: Environmentalism and Canadian Inuit' in Peterson, D.L. and Johnson, D.R. (eds) *Human Ecology and Climate Change: People and Resources in the Far North* USA: Taylor & Francis.

Whelan, T. (ed.) 1991. *Nature Tourism: managing for the environment* Washington D.C.: Island Press.

White, R. 1994. 'Animals and enterprise' in Milner, C.A., O'Connor, C.A. and Sandness, M.A. (eds) *The Oxford History of the American West* Oxford: Oxford University Press.

Wilmer, F. 1993. *The Indigenous Voice in World Politics* Newbury Park: Sage.

Wolfe, R. 1989. 'Myths: what have you heard?' *Alaska Fish and Game* November-December: pp.16–19.

Wolfe, R. n.d. 'The place of indigenous hunting systems in marine mammal management regimes: the case of harbor seals and Steller sea lions in Alaska' Unpublished manuscript.

Worster, D. (ed.) 1988. *The Ends of the Earth: perspectives on modern environmental history* Cambridge: Cambridge University Press.

Wynne, B. 1994. 'Scientific Knowledge and the Global Environment' in Redclift, M. and Benton, T. (eds) *Social Theory and the Global Environment* London and New York: Routledge.

Yearley, S. 1991. *The Green Case: a sociology of environmental issues, arguments and politics*. London: Harper Collins.

Yearley, S. 1994. 'Social Movements and Environmental Change' in Redclift, M. and Benton, T. (eds) *Social Theory and the Global Environment* London and New York: Routledge.

Young, E. 1995. *Third World in the First: development and indigenous peoples* London: Routledge.

Young, O.R. 1991. *Natural Resources and the State* Berkely: University of California Press.

Young, O.R. 1992. *Arctic Politics: conflict and cooperation in the circumpolar north*. Dartmouth: University of New England Press.

Young, O.R. 1996. 'The Arctic Council: making a new era' in *International Relations* New York: The Twentieth Century Fund.

Young, O.R. 1997. 'A sustainable development strategy for the Arctic Council' *WWF Arctic Bulletin* 1: 6–7.

Zurick, D. 1995. *Errant Journeys: adventure travel in the modern age* Austin: University of Texas Press.

Index

aboriginal subsistence whaling, 20,
  97, 122
  co-management of, 97
  contested nature of, 109
  and development, 109
  critique of , 119
  critique of IWC definition, 103
  IWC definition of, 103
  and sale of whale products, 113
Agenda 21, 77, 185
Agreement on the Conservation of
  Polar Bears (1973), 28
Alaska Eskimo Whaling Commission
  (AEWC), 98, 105
Alaska Federation of Natives
  (AFN), 162
Alaska Native Claims Settlement
  Act (1971), 15, 17, 18, 65–67,
  138, 140
animal-rights groups, 115
  and marine mammal
    hunting, 115
Arctic, 1,4
  and atmospheric pollution, 8
  definition of, 21
  and ethnic diversity, 6
  as a frontier, 4, 141
  and the global economy, 50
  and global environmental
    change, 1
  as homelands, 2, 15, 143
  as homeland, 87
  images of, 137
  indigenous peoples, 3
  and multilateral international
    agreements, 27

as a natural scientific
  laboratory, 8
politics and conflict, 67
as a storehouse of natural
  resources, 4
as a wilderness, 4, 15, 141
Arctic Council, 20, 23, 32, 33,
  47, 149, 168
  exclusion of non-indigenous
    peoples, 171
  as forum for states, 171
  and indigenous knowledge, 72
  and sustainable development, 44
Arctic Council Declaration, 32,
  47, 49
Arctic environmental politics,
  indigenous participation in, 48
Arctic Environmental Protection
  Strategy (AEPS), 20, 23, 31, 32,
  36, 37, 44, 47, 51, 149, 168
  and indigenous knowledge, 72
Arctic haze, 8,13
Arctic Monitoring and Assessment
  Programme (AMAP), 38
Arctic National Wildlife Refuge
  (ANWR), 36, 37, 57, 64, 144
Arctic regions, 5
  and nation-states, 5
Arctic Slope Regional Corporation
  (ASRC),43
Arctic tourism, 20
Association of Indigenous minorities
  of the North, Siberia and the Far
  East of the Russian Federation, 47
Association of Indigenous Peoples
  of the Russian North, 3